THE NO-BULLSHIT GUIDE
TO SUCCEEDING IN CULINARY SCHOOL

THE NO-BULLSHIT GUIDE TO SUCCEEDING IN CULINARY SCHOOL

Kim Brauer

No-Bullshit Career Guides
www.NoBSguides.com
Cover design by Ivan Popov
Cover image by Zinkevych/Bigstock.com
ISBN-13: 9781516866274
ISBN-10: 1516866274

Welcome

My fellow and future comrades in the food industry, if you're thinking about going to culinary school, or you've already taken the plunge and enrolled, this book is for you.

A career in cooking isn't like any other. So this guide – with its cussing, irreverence, name calling, honest observations, and direct, hard-won advice – isn't some sappy, generic succeed-in-school-and-life-by-building-your-personal-brand pile of crapola. It's a war journal, a lifehacker's field manual, a no-bullshit guide to sucking the marrow out of culinary school, avoiding the stupid shit that's hard to shake later, and building yourself a solid foundation for a career in an industry that may never be easy, but can be a fuckton of fun to work in.

If my language has already offended you – *Why, swearing is crass; a sure sign of a faltering intellect and poor vocabulary!* – then for the love of God, don't try to read the rest of this book. Back slowly away, buy that colorful parachute one instead, and get a respectable job as an accountant, an astronaut, an astronaut's nanny – whatever else you can possibly do with yourself that doesn't involve working in a kitchen. This biz isn't for the faint of heart or the fearful of tongue.

This is a quick and easy read, because if you believe the press we get (we being the service-level, boots-on-the-ground heroes of the food industry), we may be a creative bunch, but we're a little dum, and not inclined to read and write much. While you're reading the good news about our industry's fine reputation, you'll also hear that we're a pack of thieves (who regularly slip beef tenderloins into the flattering black-and-white-checked pants we wear), so please accept my heartfelt thank you for buying this guide, rather than stealing it from a friend. I hope to return the favor (ten times over) by sharing with you the very best advice I've come across for how to genuinely succeed in this quirky industry – some that I've learned through my own experience, and lots that I've gleaned from a pile of helpful interviews I've done with food industry professionals of all sorts.

So lace up, and let's get this shit rolling.

Table of Contents

Part 1
Getting Started

You have a story in your head about what kind of student you are, right now. You love school, you hate school. You're a good student, you suck at school. You're smart, you're dumb, you're too smart for this bullshit, you're bored, you're working hard but it doesn't seem to click for you...

I'd bet you a crisp hundo, if I had one, that you could tell me right away what kind of student you are, and that that story has a lot to do with what kind of student you end up being. That's good information, but that's all it is – information, a starting point. Because whatever kind of student you've been in school so far, cooking school can be quite different.

The rules are different in culinary school. You're on your feet, working your ass off, learning physical skills in potentially-dangerous kitchens. It's relentlessly vocational – no one's quizzing you on the names of the Roman Emperors, and no one gives one shit about what you learn if you can't also put that knowledge and those skills to good use. The relationships you'll be thrown into are also different in culinary school, and you'll need to interact with your instructors and your peers in ways that might feel intense to folks who are used to sitting around in desks a lot at school.

That's why I wrote this super-practical "how to" guide: To help you get the most out of your time and your work in culinary school, focus on what matters the most, and avoid really common mistakes that I saw people making (and that, alas, I made myself). It's a collection of some of the funny, fantastic, and fucked-up things I've seen, heard about, and experienced – in both culinary school and in restaurant jobs, since gaining solid experience as a line cook is the primary goal for most peeps who enroll in culinary school (whether or not it's their long-term career goal).

I wrote this guide to help very specific people. Are you one of them?

- The anxious student (or prospective student) who thinks that doing well in culinary school means knowing a bunch of French terms, reciting the growing season of morels,[1] or coming in the door with great knife skills. This is your field manual to what really matters the most.

---

1 Check it out – this here guide has a glossary. Any terms that are randomly underlined like this will be defined in Part 5, way at the end. If you haven't encountered industry terms like Front of House, mise en place, or douchekazoo before, flip back to see what they mean. If there are terms you wish I'd defined, or ones you feel I've left out, just email me through the website at www.NoBSguides.com and let me know. Or share your favorite kitchen language and swear words. I'd love to hear those, too.

- The dude in the kitchen who sweats confidence, but has a ton of questions about his cooking career that he's – let's be honest here – never actually going to actually his peers or his sous. It's okay, lambchop – we can talk about all your secret questions and concerns.
- Career changers (like me) who want to know what the fuck they're getting into. I'll help you walk into school feeling competent, even confident, despite being a total newbie again.
- Those of you who love to cook, but are smart to be curious about the big-ass difference between throwing a dinner party for a dozen friends and cooking on the line. Grab the cocktail shaker and let's talk.
- And peeps of all ages who want a more interesting job, and some killer life-hack-style advice about how to most efficiently bump up your badass quotient while making money doing work you really dig.

I'm assuming that you're either thinking about going to culinary school, or you've signed on already and gotten started. Looking at the bigger picture, I'm also assuming you're interested in becoming a cook, and that you're one curious mofo, ready to do a little research to be better prepared for the challenges ahead.

Cooks are the finest folks on Earth.

As the great and handsome and never-swearing and ever-elegant Chef Eric Ripert said, "A cook and a chef are different entities. 'Chef' is a title... but when you are a cook, it is who you are. It is your spine and your soul."[2] The cooks I've had the honor of meeting and working with have been funny and fierce, crass and caring, skilled and still always learning, freakishly fast and *sometimes* amazingly patient. They have great nights and shit services, successes and failures, they have meltdowns and injuries and come back from them – like successful folks in any intense and creative line of work.

Cooking is different than other lines of work in important ways, though, and it's crucial to know what you're getting into if you think this might be a career for you. I've been working as a big-hearted gal in tough-ass industries for a long time, so I'm the last one who's going to shit on your dreams. If you are chock-ass full of grit and

---

2 From A Return to Cooking, by Eric Ripert and Michael Ruhlman.

persistence, and you have work ethic coming out of your ears, you can make any career work, including this one.

But I'm also not here to blow powdered sugar up your ass. This is tough goddamn work, and it's really not for everyone. Anthony Bourdain wrote pretty much the seminal work on whether or not someone should go into cooking. And by seminal, I mean he wrote it with his own semen, which he can produce better and faster than any other man-chef alive. It's a chapter called "So You Wanna Be a Chef" in his book *Medium Raw*, and there's a link to it at www.NoBSguides.com, in the long and hopefully-super-helpful resources page.

Bourdain focuses on line cooking in high-end restaurants, which *definitely* isn't for everyone. There are lots of different ways to work in this big giant industry. Maybe your little secret dream has nothing to do with working the line, and what really blows your skirt up is the idea of food photography, food styling, private or personal cheffing, catering, bakery work, recipe testing and product development, etc. Newsflash, though: All these folks are busting their asses, too. None of these peeps are sitting down playing desk jockey for the day. They're not even sitting down to eat lunch – they're plating that shit up all gorgeous, and standing off camera eating the over-charred shit out of a ninth pan for lunch just like any line cook would. There's no such thing as an easy corner of the food business to tuck yourself into. It's all hard work.

Chefs are on television now. They act like rockstars. The top 1% of them make big money, and for that reason alone, mothers don't cry (quite as much) when their babies decide to go into cooking. But being a cook still means working your ass off for years, building your foundational knowledge, your skills, your techniques, your palate, your speed, your muscle memory – learning step by step, with no shortcuts. If that doesn't appeal to you, you're heading for big trouble, because this is a career of hard work and then more hard work.

I'm getting ahead of myself, though. This isn't the part of the book where I'm supposed to scare the shit out of you. I'm still supposed to be charming you. So let's look ahead briefly. The menu for this big adventure will be roughly as follows:

Part 1: The Appetizers
Just the nuts & bolts kind of shit you need to know to get started. Do you need to go to culinary school, and what will you learn there? What's the best way to

make a good first impression with your new Chef Instructor? What knives and supplies will you need to drop some cash on in the first week or two?

Part 2: Getting into the Meaty Bits
Who teaches in culinary schools? How are these programs structured and organized? What do you need to do to kick ass in the kitchen *and* the classroom? This is the fundamental but very important information you'll need to start off on the right foot, so that you don't have to spend the second half of your program explaining to everyone that you're not actually a douchenozzle, you were just nervous.

Part 3: The Main Course
You don't just want to survive culinary school, you want to thrive in it, and leave there strong and ready to explode into a cooking career. Read the basics, okay? But this is where we'll roll up our sleeves and start talking strategy. This is where you make the power moves that will set you up well for the cooking career that follows.

I'll be your guide in this adventure. My name is Kim, and I'm a couple years into what I hope is a long and successful cooking career.

The *No-Bullshit Guides* operate on a two-steps-ahead philosophy. You're not getting culinary school advice here from someone who learned to poach an egg from Escoffier himself. You're not even getting culinary school advice from some executive chef who went to the Culinary Institute of America in the 1980's and has built a profitable empire in the decades since. Those books may exist, but this ain't one of them.

I went to cooking school three years ago, and for me it was a gift – both a luxury and a challenge. Like many students, I went to culinary school to build my confidence and professional-level skills and techniques. Plenty of people start long and successful cooking careers without any culinary schooling – certificate, degree, or otherwise – but I didn't have the nuts to roll into a professional kitchen, talk my way into a job (much less pull off the tryout-style interview to land that job), and adopt a fake-it-'til-I-make-it attitude while I quickly learned the ropes. I've nabbed jobs I was blatantly under-qualified to tackle in the past, but I knew I wasn't going to take that route into professional kitchen work. I got a lot more out of it than I expected, and I'm really thankful for the knowledge, skills, habits, and community that I built in school.

I've had three jobs in the culinary field so far: Recipe development and retail for a specialty foods company; prep cooking; and line cooking. Culinary school prepared me for all of these jobs very well, and for me was worth every penny – and, more importantly, all the time I invested in it.

But I'm also interested in dissecting the experience – talking about how to get the most out of what can be a significant investment of both time and money, looking at the things that will probably annoy and frustrate the shit out of you in school, and evaluating how closely school lines up with entry-level cooking jobs, and where it falls short in preparing you for real food industry work.

I also talked to a whole pile of culinary school instructors, cooks, chefs, and students while writing this book. They come from a tribe of skilled and generous folks that I love being a part of, and I'm thrilled to share their voices and thoughts with you, too. The experiences and insights they've shared with me inform this whole book, and are also featured in quotes and stand-alone interviews throughout the sections that follow.

On The Rail:

- If being a cook is part of "your spine and your soul," you might want to get that looked at.
- This is a career that's going to require a huge amount of hard work and persistence.
- It's also a fuckton of fun, though.

*   *   *

AN ALTERNATIVE APPRENTICESHIP

For centuries, most skilled trades were taught through an apprenticeship system. There were guilds for painters and masons and cooks, for butchers and bakers and candlestick makers. When you were new to a trade, you went and worked in the studio of a master. You did all the shit work – the sweeping and the latrine cleaning and whatever the fuck they told you to do, for however long they told you to do it. The master was hardly aware of your presence, and the folks who were one or two steps ahead of you delighted in crapping upon you. But you persisted and showed grit, and eventually you got to paint the blue sky, and then the mountains, and then the angels, and eventually *you* were the dude painting the fat, naked Baby Jesus. Jackpot!

That's pretty much how kitchens still work, centuries later. Maybe you get your foot in the door by offering to work for free, as a <u>*stage*</u>, and you settle in to small dice onions for the rest of your life, but then the <u>prep</u> cook flames out and they stick you in that role. Or you start by washing dishes, and you peel a <u>metric fuckton</u> of fava beans all spring. Maybe you make it onto the line, on <u>pantry</u> or <u>garde manger,</u> and you make salads until your hands smell like vinaigrette all the time. And then you move up to fry station, or to sauté or grill, and then eventually you're the <u>sous chef</u> and then the <u>chef de cuisine</u>, running the whole kitchen.[3]

Working your way up from the bottom is not only a viable option in the restaurant industry, it's a well-respected path. Tough-nut chefs who started at the bottom just *love* telling people about how they started at the bottom. I'm not knocking this. They should be proud. It's hard fucking work, and they stuck with it. That brings them serious cred in an industry that requires and therefore values an incredible amount of hard work.

This is all to say, you don't need to go to culinary school in order to kick off a cooking career. You can just show up in a kitchen, talk your way into a job, and work your way up from there.

Becky Selengut, Private Chef:

If there was someone in a restaurant willing to give you an intensive apprenticeship, and you knew you wanted to be a restaurant chef, I would take the apprenticeship. Say you already know this is the life for you, and you've been studying the lives of restaurant chefs, and through connections

---

3 We'll talk about the whole kitchen brigade system and its hierarchy in the "Kitchen Rules" section in Part 2.

you've been able to get someone to commit to putting you through an intensive three-month apprenticeship, and if you do well they'll hire you on staff. And it's the type of restaurant and the chef you want to learn from. Okay, don't say no to that in order to go to culinary school. That seems like a special opportunity you may never get again, and you could always go back to culinary school after that kind of apprenticeship, if you felt you still needed the schooling. If you already know what you want to do, I think you can learn the same amount in school or in a good apprenticeship.

But if you don't know what you want to do, or you don't have that offer on the table, culinary school is a great way to figure out where you might want to go in this career. And it's a very nurturing way to introduce you to the concepts in a supportive environment.

I absolutely agree with Becky, but look at the number of ifs that she takes the time to insert into this hypothetical situation:

1. IF someone's willing to take you on as an apprentice, and
2. IF they're a chef and the type of restaurant you want to work with, and
3. IF you already know this is *exactly* what you want to do, and
4. IF they'll take the time to really structure a learning experience for you, and
5. IF they'll then commit to hiring you—

THEN go ahead and jump on that opportunity, you gorgeous unicorn-fucker, because you've won the apprenticeship lottery. I've made most of my big life decisions pretty capriciously, and even I prefer my if/then equations to come with fewer than five ifs.

But say you do find a great fit in a learning kitchen – go thrive there. Learn the shit out of everything they can teach you, and if you decide down the road that you'll still benefit from culinary school, you can always tackle that next. Students with solid previous work experience often get the most out of culinary school, which is why some schools require applicants to work in the industry before they can even apply.

Work vs. culinary school is not an either/or question. You can choose to do both, in whatever sequence works best for you.

If School's Not Required, Why Go?

Culinary school is absolutely not a requirement for becoming a cook – but it's another great path into the industry. In fact, you can think of it as another form of apprenticeship. The chefs who work in culinary schools are not only willing to take you on as an apprentice, they're *paid* to do so. They're working full time to teach you the skills you'll need in the field. They will take the time to structure a solid learning experience for you, and if you do well, many of them will reach out to work their personal connections in the industry to help you land a job during or after your time in school (more on this in the section *Yep, It's Still Who You Know* in Part 3).

Culinary school will help you develop such broad foundational skills that you'll be able to work in all kinds of different roles within the food industry, not just as a line cook in a specific type of restaurant.

> *Michael Jordan, Chef Instructor:*
>
> People ask "Do you need cooking school?" and I think that's a ridiculous question. Are you willing to go to school and take it seriously enough to become better than the other people in the room?
>
> Just going to cooking school isn't enough. This argument happens because so many people who go to culinary school just get put through. That's one thing I like about our school: We'll fail you. A lot of schools don't fail students, so mediocre people are walking out with these degrees.
>
> But the people who go to school and take it seriously, and hand over two years of their life to that education, are at a distinct advantage over the guy who's been standing in the same restaurant cooking the same food for five years. Yes, he's technically proficient, and any chef would be happy to train him, but is that a guy you're willing to turn into a well-rounded sous chef in another two years? Probably not. The guy coming out of school who took it seriously is the one who will be moving ahead.

If you do it the right way, cooking school is one of the smartest things you can do. But if you are not ready for it, then go work for a while. And then when you're ready to make those defining moves that put you in a better position, and really grab that education, then get your ass to school – the best one you can afford, and suck the life out of it and move forward.

Kären Jurgensen, Chef Instructor:

Here's the big reveal: I didn't go to culinary school. But I'll tell you that I had to learn backwards. I was very organized and could manage things, so I'd get promoted really fast, but I didn't necessarily have the technical skills to be in my position. I had to rely on other people's talent. I could create, but I had to learn the nuts and bolts of it and the basics on my own. I learned a lot of things on the job from other people, and that's absolutely valuable.

You don't have to go to culinary school, but I think it gets you somewhere faster. One of the biggest things is confidence. It also gets you connections, and helps you build a community, compared to just applying at a restaurant and wondering how to get your application to the top of a pile. Again, we throw a lot of things at you, so you have very broad exposure, you see a variety of ingredients, and you learn some professionalism. All of those are valuable things that you don't necessarily get on your own. I think you succeed more quickly if you've been to culinary school. Your path to the top is faster, and the pay that you can get is better.

I think Thomas Keller was the one who asked, "Why would you advocate for a less educated workforce?" If you have a degree, then you can add things to that. You open up your opportunities. And it often helps to get loans, if you want to go out on your own. If you have a degree, people see that you've completed something. And it's good for your brain. And it's fun.

There are lots of considerations that go into choosing a culinary school that will be a good fit for you. If you're still mulling this over, and wondering whether culinary school will be right for you, there's a shorter and free-er mini guide called *The No-Bullshit mini-Guide to Considering Culinary School* on the www.NoBSguides.com website that you might find helpful. In it, I'll walk you through the key factors that go into making a well-considered decision – the money, the time you'll be investing, how to suss out the instructional approach, whether to go for a degree vs. a certificate, and so on.

For now, let's slip beneath the pros and cons and tackle the underlying question: What will you learn in culinary school?

On The Rail:

- Culinary school is not a requirement for working in this industry. Many cooks and chefs learn on the job.
- Culinary school is like an apprenticeship that's structured to give you a well-rounded foundation.
- "Just going to school isn't enough." Be ready to throw yourself in and take it seriously if you want to benefit.

*   *   *

GREAT EXPECTATIONS

You're not going to culinary school to learn how to be a chef.

If you have a mom, she's probably telling the neighbors right now that you're in culinary school to learn how to be a chef. Tell her to shut the hell up. Unless she's paying your tuition.

Folks who don't know shit about the industry throw the term chef around like crazy. A dude cooks a rabbit at home once, and his wife's telling all her friends he's *quite a chef*. Cut them a break. They have no idea how restaurants actually work, or what kind of effort goes into making memorable meals day in and day out, perfect every time. If they knew all the details, they'd probably feel too guilty to eat out, and then we'd all lose our jobs. So just smile and congratulate the husband on his bunny dinner.

You become a chef by working, typically for years and years, mastering every station in a restaurant, or enough of them that your skills well exceed those of the cooks you manage, so that at any moment during any clusterfuck of a dinner rush, you can step onto their station, blow their minds with your technique and speed, and save the day. Being a chef means you've developed the creativity, palate, math skills, and discipline to plan a menu that's cost effective and can be executed by your cooks, keep a thumb on costs, repair the equipment that's always breaking, take care of the ordering, the HR bullshit, the endless hiring and firing, and create the paperwork and maintain the processes that everyone from the city health inspector on up to the IRS demands. Maybe it also means you train a crew to cover things perfectly while you're smiling for the cameras, teaching a talk show host how to flip an egg, or selling some secret sauce at state fairs.

If you're considering culinary school, you're years away from being a chef. It doesn't matter if you're a child prodigy, a career changer who's gotten used to being on one fast track or another, a gifted home cook, or James Beard's long lost grand-daughter. There's a long road right now between you and the title of chef. That's a good thing. It means there's plenty of time to learn all the things you'll need to know to earn a "yes, Chef" of your own, and your work ethic and your persistence can get you there.

But for now, you're in culinary school to learn how to be a cook. That's a very different thing. You don't *have* to fuck with the paperwork, fire anyone, crawl under the broken stove, come in four hours early to let the plumber in. You'll be in the enviable position – as a student and then as a cook – of being able to constantly learn and improve your skills, to put your head down and work, to think hard and dream big – and yes, you can still occasionally save the day. Becoming a good cook is a solid and kickass goal, and culinary school can help you get there if you really focus on getting your knife skills together, building your foundational skills, and bulking up the mental muscles of persistence, work ethic, and discipline.

If that doesn't sound sexy to you, please pause for a moment before you sign that tuition check.

It's good to be ambitious, and to have the long game firmly in your mind if you want to be a chef someday. Don't confuse ambition with impatience, though – that's murder on your chances to succeed in this field. If folks in the industry think poorly of culinary school students, it's almost always because either (1) a *stage* gave them crabs, or (2) graduates think going to culinary school gives them an express ticket up the ladder, and they want promotions, recognition, and status before they've put in the time to really develop and demonstrate the skills they'll need to take on more advanced positions.

Wanting to surge directly into the lofty heights of chefitude isn't just delusional, it will also set you up to have a shitty attitude. Every once in a while I'll have beers with friends from culinary school and one of us will talk about That Guy in one of our kitchens – the bitter and burned-out dude, who has big stories about his mad skills, complaints about how the menu could be so much better, big opinions about how a classic dish is so stupid or boring. Why has he been on the pantry station for six years? Why is he still talking about his powdered foie dessert idea when he just broke another emulsification? Dude, we just need a workable vinaigrette, not your big vision. This is probably the guy who complained that his instructors in culinary school were old-fashioned, who looked down on his peers and was a dickhole in group projects, who cut off the chef with a curt "I know" instead of asking for advice when a dish failed.

Ambitious people work hard to master even the simplest skills. Impatient people want to skip over the simplest skills to get to the "real stuff" – and of course, miss the real stuff by doing so. This is the kind of impatience that will comprehensively fuck you down the line. So, just for a while, table that "becoming a chef" stuff and put your head down and work hard. You're in culinary school to learn to be a cook. To train for the kitchen, not <u>Kitchen Stadium</u>.

> *Kären Jurgensen, Chef Instructor:*
> You really have to have an open mind. You're paying for your education. Why come in with a chip on your shoulder? Keep your ego out of it. Come in and listen, and absorb just as much as you possibly can. And show up on time, in a clean uniform.

On The Rail:

- You're training to become a cook, not a chef (yet) – and that's a really good thing.
- Culinary school will not give you an express ticket into job titles well above your skill level.
- Ambitious people want to master the basics; impatient people want to skip over them.

*   *   *

THE FUNDAMENTALS

Kristina Glinoga, Line Cook:
There were things that I messed up in culinary school, and when I got out into kitchens I thought, "Shit, I'm sure glad I fucked that up during school so that I don't have to do it here."

So what are the fundamentals?

Often when people are talking about fundamentals, they're talking about the body of information that a chef will expect you to know when you roll into a restaurant and start unpacking your knives onto a new station. As with any industry, we could pass around a bottle of <u>Old Overholt</u> and squabble all night about which pieces of information do and don't qualify as "fundamentals," but there are some generally-agreed-upon basics that you will learn in culinary school. As we dive into what these are, I'll defer to one of my own Chef Instructors first, and then I'll chime in with some additional ideas:

Michael Jordan, Chef Instructor:
Students often want to get to the advanced levels of cooking too quickly. We need to slow down and focus on really basic methodology. Things as simple as properly blanching a green vegetable. Knife skills: Can you do a <u>brunoise</u>, or a simple <u>julienne</u>? A <u>chiffonade</u>? I still see these as big problems. Understanding the difference between sauté and pan fry and deep fry, and the temperature levels of the oil. Understanding the building blocks of flavor.

We all want to go work in <u>modernist</u> restaurants, but those guys all started off with really solid fundamentals and then moved on from there. If you really look at fancy food, it's a whole lot of perfectly-blanched vegetables that maybe get finished in a pan and then just put on the plate. It's about preparing the vegetable really well and then making it look really cool, and that involves really fundamental techniques.

You need to understand grilling and sauté. Those are your two big ones. If you can walk into any kitchen and understand good grilling and sautéing, you'll always find work.

Sauces. You have to have a solid understanding of your repertoire, and these days that's more about the <u>coulis</u> and the vegetable purees. <u>Beurre blanc</u> is still pretty powerful, but we see a lot less of the classic sauces. Modern sauces are more puree-driven, with less cream. Using cream and butter is like a sin now, which is just pathetic.

Seasoning is also a big issue for young cooks. It's always either, "I tend to oversalt" or "I don't like salt." Let's understand the *purpose* of salt, which is just to make things taste better than they are. Your opinion doesn't matter. I just want you to season it so that the carrot tastes more like a carrot.

I'd also add that in culinary school, you will:

- Start to build the good, solid, general knife skills you'll need in this business.
- Understand your knives, learn when to use each of them, and how to sharpen and maintain them.
- Learn how and when to *use* all those fancy knife cuts, and why they matter in terms of how food looks, the rate at which it cooks, the texture and flavor it develops, etc.
- Get a feel for basic dough work. You'll be able to knock out a good pasta on request, and develop some basic baking skills, which are becoming increasingly important among chefs.
- Learn the sets of techniques that collectively form each station within a restaurant kitchen, whether that's pantry, garde manger, fry, grilling and sauté, <u>saucier</u>, etc.
- Learn proper seasoning, and the purpose of salt.
- Learn how to use acid to elevate and balance flavor.

- Get a lot of your dumb mistakes out of the way, and will never get mocked in a restaurant for grabbing zucchini instead of cucumbers, unless you're really fucking hungover, and that's no way to work, son.
- Learn to love bacon. Even more.

And, perhaps most importantly:

- You'll learn the *why* behind classic cooking methods that most people just do robotically.
  - Why do you sear meat before braising it?
  - Why do you let meat rest?
  - Why don't you want to bring stocks to a boil? Why do so many recipes use simmering?
  - Why would you want to use whole grains, even if you're not a granola hippie?
  - Etc. etc. etc.
- You'll learn the *how*, and the science behind cooking processes.
  - How does searing meat affect its flavor and texture? (And no, it doesn't "seal in juices.")
  - How does resting affect meat? (And no, it's not about letting the juices "redistribute.")
  - How do you clarify soups, and what does protein coagulation have to do with it?
  - How are grains and flours processed, and how does it affect their cooking properties?
  - Etc. etc. etc.

In addition to this foundational knowledge and techniques, you'll also learn some of the important habits and mental approaches that are crucial to being a successful cook.

In every interview I did for this book, I asked, "What were the most valuable things you learned in culinary school?" Here are some of the other great answers I heard:

Rebecca Cooley, Farm Apprentice:

Organization. How to be prepared and organized in the kitchen was the number one thing I took from the experience. I learned the skills and had the tools to go into any kitchen and figure out how to best succeed – of course, knowing that you're going to get your ass handed to you from time to time; it's going to get munched on. But you learn from that, too, and the next day you go back. So perseverance and organization. And being humble, because there's so much you don't know in a kitchen, and being open to that is important.

Rachel Duboff, Personal Chef:

Something I learned in culinary school that has served me well is that we don't cook for ourselves, we cook for the people who are eating our food. So you need to check your ego at the door. The customer needs to be the first thought in your mind. When I have a client who comes to me and says, "Snacks are difficult for my children," and I find out that they like cut up carrots, I cut up carrots for their children. It's not glamorous, but it's what my clients need. It's not the only thing they need or the only reason they hire me, but I'm not above cutting carrots and throwing them into Ziploc bags to make their lives easier. They hired me because their lives are complicated and I'm there to simplify things.

Michelle Nguyen, Chef:

Learning how work really effectively and efficiently.

I think that's one thing I've seen from people coming out of culinary school – they may be really good cooks, or have a good sense of taste, or lots of creativity, but none of that matters in a busy kitchen if you're too slow or you don't get certain things done.

Culinary school is good at putting a fire under your ass. Some teachers are better at that than others, but I really appreciated learning that you just can't stand there and talk about the food all day, you have to actually do something about it. The people who succeed are self-starters. They don't need a teacher to tell them every little thing, or their hand held throughout every process.

You have to think critically, too. If I hit a speed bump, I always tried to solve it myself, and if I really couldn't figure it out, *then* I would go to an instructor and ask questions. But learning that critical thinking and problem solving is important. When you're working in restaurants, you're constantly solving some kind of problem.

Kären Jurgensen, Chef Instructor:
What are the most essential skills students can and should learn in culinary school?

The biggest thing is to work clean.

Knife skills. That's pretty tangible.

You need to understand what things cost, and you have to have respect for that. The plastic wrap costs money, the water running down the drain costs money, the trim on your vegetables – and all of this is a piece of sustainability as well. How you can be resourceful and frugal is something an employer is looking for, and is a key to long-term success.

You should learn not to be heavy-handed. So often, we don't just put a little chile in, we put a lot. If it's going to be tarragon, we put too much tarragon. You want to build an intensity of flavor, but you don't want to mask the food with something else. Let the ingredients speak for themselves. Lighten up, have a delicate touch.

You need to know what's in season, because it gives you an understanding of flavor, which will improve your palate.

There are also a bunch of life skills – how to bathe, how to be nice to somebody. It's not all about you. How to look at yourself in the mirror – am I clean? Is my uniform blue instead of white? Are my fingernails clean? Do I have a big zit? What is it that I have to polish up about myself? Am I going to organize myself to be on time? We don't have any control of those kinds of things before students come here. People can only experience what they've experienced and only know what they know.

So I'd sneak listening in there. You need to know how to listen.

What you say to somebody will be an exact reflection of what you get back for the day. So being kind is important – firm, but kind. Stand up for yourself, but don't derail the train.

What skills do you think culinary students need to focus on more?
Culinary students need to learn to turn the heat down a little bit. There's a temptation to squash things and stir things and burn things. Treat things a little more gently, and let the ingredient remain juicy and not overcooked and overcharred and oversmoked. It happens a lot on the line – you've got a lot of BTUs, so you can go fast, and there's something exciting about that. But resisting that urge, and thinking about what's in the pan and how you can make it better is important. Have a delicate touch.

This is a long list, and we're leaving off loads of important information, ideas, techniques, and habits. If your head is spinning a bit right now, relax. You'll learn all this shit step-by-step if you're in a culinary program that's designed to get you there. For better or worse (according to some chefs), culinary school is not sink-or-swim to the extent that walking into a line cooking job with little experience can be. You'll learn from your instructors and your peers, and pretty soon you'll catch yourself make smart decisions gracefully, problem solving effectively, managing time like a ninja, or recovering from a big old fuck-up and getting back on track like exactly the kind of humble hard worker that does well in this business. Patience, grasshopper.

On The Rail:
- Don't be a big diva – this biz is all about getting the basics right, every time.
- We can sit and argue over our shifties about what exactly "The Fundamentals" do and don't include, but quit yammering – get in there and learn them.

* * *

READY AT THE STARTING GATE

Day one. Are you in?

You look around – these are the people who will be your partners, friends, and arch-antagonists for the rest of your time here in school. The day I started culinary school, we all filed in quietly – a super diverse group with a pretty nice balance of age and gender – and sat down, and we never moved again, the rest of the quarter. They were not assigned seats, but the die had been cast. I sat next to the women who seemed right around my same age, and that was that.

In my program, we had three or four days of marathon classroom sessions before we even got to step into the kitchen we could see right behind our Chef Instructor – smaller than I expected, super clean and sterile, so alluring back there.

In those first few days, my To Do list got longer and longer. Each requirement added a new errand, and I wasn't sure how I'd fit it all in. My binder grew and grew, stuffed with reams of new paper every day. I hole-punched late into the night, trying to keep all this shit organized.

The first couple weeks can seem pretty damn overwhelming, but it's important to start strong and make a good impression. Not as a brown-noser, mind you. No one gives one shit what you know about tapioca maltodextrin or what Michelin-starred restaurants you've eaten at. Start strong by being a hard worker. At this point – in the first weeks of culinary school – work ethic matters so infinitely much more than knowledge. So show your instructor from day one that you're going to work hard and come prepared, and the whole quarter will go so much more smoothly for you.

Gregg Shiosaki, Chef Instructor:
Day one, you look out at a batch of brand-new students each quarter. What do you typically notice?

A combination of controlled excitement, a certain amount of confusion, a lot of deer in headlights: *What's going on? What did I get myself into?*

We throw out so much information the first three or four days. It can be confusing, not having a point of understanding when we're talking in theory about how to run around the kitchen, how to go to these stations, here's the dish room, here's the main kitchen, here are the walk-ins.

That's why I stress: Get comfortable. The sooner you can get comfortable – with each other, with your environment, with the faculty and staff – the sooner you'll start learning.

What are brand-new students typically the most worried about at the start?

Financial aid. A lot of financial issues. On top of that, fear – not having confidence, not having knife skills and cooking skills. Obviously they're coming here to learn new things, but some students don't have confidence that they can do it.

Are there things that students should worry less about?

In general, they probably shouldn't worry about the program itself, in the sense that everything will be presented to them in a scope and sequence that the well-trained faculty knows. They have no idea what's coming up, but if they go with the flow and make the most of every opportunity to learn and grow, then they'll naturally do well in the program.

Early in the first week or two I can see the students who are going to jump in, no matter what, and aren't afraid to make a mistake. That's a huge thing, too – don't be afraid to make mistakes.

What are your primary goals as the first quarter instructor?

I want students to become confident and comfortable in a kitchen.

I think it's very, very important that they learn to work well with each other – these will be your partners for the next two years.

I want to implement a solid work ethic. That's probably one of the most important things. There are slackers – the students who are dead weight, hard on the class, not by any means reaching their potential. If someone can instead show a good work ethic, they'll just get so much more out of their time here, by approaching it head first, being serious, doing their homework, doing everything that's asked of them.

What are things that students do that totally annoy you?

Coming to school unprepared. You knew what you were supposed to do, but you didn't put in the effort. That's frustrating because it makes it harder on your teammates. It also tells me that you just don't have it all together to make the best of this.

I can easily overlook mistakes – cooking mistakes, technical mistakes – but if you're making mistakes because you didn't prepare, then that's huge. It's all about preparation and mise en place, and that's spelled out in the first week. I'll correct a student once, maybe twice, but then it's just like: Well, you're not going to be putting in the effort. It's hard as an instructor to keep trying to pull someone up if they're not willing to put in the effort. You want to treat everyone fairly, but if this person's putting in 110% and that person's putting in 70%, who do you want to give more time?

Any advice for students just starting culinary school?

Make sure you can dedicate the time that it takes to do this and do it well, which includes the time here in class and the time studying. Make sure you have a good financial plan – we still lose people halfway through the program because their finances run out. And just give it your all every day.

This is an opportunity, not a requirement, and you're spending a lot of money being here. Absolutely make the most of it – ask questions, do research, read, grow as much as you can.

On The Rail:

- In the first week of culinary school, work ethic matters so much more than knowledge.
- Trust in the program, and make sure your finances are in order.
- "The sooner you can get comfortable – with each other, with your environment, with the faculty and staff – the sooner you'll start learning."

*   *   *

BUILDING YOUR KIT

Once you decide on a specific culinary school program, they'll spell out exactly what you'll need to buy in the way of uniforms and tools, and those requirements obviously trump any advice in this section. But in my experience, getting set up for school can be dauntingly expensive, and some of those costs can be spread out over time in a way that isn't immediately obvious.

So while your first aim should be complying with your school's requirements, check out this section for nitty-gritty tips and strategies for where to spend (and save) resources, and how to take great care of the uniforms and tools you're investing in.

What if Your Kit is Supplied / Required by the School?

Some schools will provide you with a kit at the start of your program. When I say "provide," I mean that they make you buy it from them. If this is the case, hope and pray that they haven't cut a kickback deal with some mediocre-ass brand like Mercer. And then use those knives. Bring them to class, have them ready when you need them, take good care of them, and nurse your tiny dreams of buying a hand-forged Japanese knife on your own time. Some individual instructors won't care if you supplement the kit with your own tools. Others might not want that, and will tell you to leave your knives at home. Either way? Yes, Chef.

The Culinary Institute of America (or CIA) is one of those schools that "provides" a kit to every student at the start of the program, so let's use them as a case study. We'll look at what they provide, and what their students have recommended adding to the kit – in a sanctioned, authorized way on the school website. So no, they're not going to say a box of whippits, a dozen Five Hour Energies, and <u>finger condoms</u> to tease your friends with. I hate to disappoint you.

CIA Culinary Tool Kit [4]

Backpack (including travel roll)
6" Boning knife
9" Serrated bread knife

---

4   The Culinary Institute of America. https://secure.ciachef.edu/purl/culinarytoolkit.html. Downloaded August 2015, and subject to change.

8" Chef's knife

7" Flexible fillet knife

3-1/2" Paring knife

10" Slicing knife

Fork

Sharpening steel

4" Offset metal spatula

12" Balloon whisk

Kitchen shears

Waiter's corkscrew

Melon baller

Measuring spoon set

Peeler

Large head spatula

14" Wood spoon

12" Tongs

Bi-Metal instant read thermometer

10" Straight spatula

CIA students have recommended[5] ditching the peeler for a lighter and better Y-peeler immediately, and then adding:

- A bench scraper.
- A fish spatula.
- Needle nose tweezers (I disagree, and would recommend flat-nosed fish tweezers).
- A mini sifter (I was surprised by this one, but it might be handy).
- A <u>tournet</u> knife (A dying dark art of potato masters, I never would've used this in my program, but my bestie says it's one of her favorite $5 secret weapons).
- A squirt bottle (which my community college provided by the dozens – maybe you CIA kids aren't paying enough tuition over there?).

---

5   Morgan (Student Blogger), Culinary Institute of America, http://ciastudentsdish.blogspot.com/2013/08/packing-for-culinary-school.html?utm_content=18270987&utm_medium=social&utm_source=facebook. Downloaded August 2015.

- I'd add a microplane, though Student Blogger Morgan didn't mention it. Maybe the school has so many of these lying around that they ran out of money for squeeze bottles.

CIA Baking & Pastry Tool Kit [6]

Backpack (including travel roll)
9" Serrated bread knife
8" Chef's knife
3-1/2" Paring knife
13" Cake slicing knife
Sharpening steel
Bench scraper
Round cutter set
Fluted cutter set
1-1/2" Pastry brush
Pizza wheel
4" Offset metal spatula
10" Straight metal spatula
10" Offset metal spatula
Digital probe thermometer
Six-piece measuring spoon set
Peeler
Large head spatula
12" Balloon whisk
14" Wooden spoon
12" Tongs
Kitchen shears
Melon baller
Apple corer
Rubber scraper
Four-sided decorating comb

---

6   Culinary Institute of America. https://secure.ciachef.edu/purl/bakingpastrytoolkit.html. Downloaded August 2015, and subject to change.

Decorating set (19 pieces)
Ruler

Student Blogger Morgan recommends[7] adding:

- A microplane or zester (since the culinary kids evidently stole all the baking ones?).
- An infrared thermometer.
- A cheap pastry brush (she says the bristles all fall out of the one they're given in their kit. I didn't realize that Mercer made pastry brushes).
- A medium offset spatula for frosting cakes.
- A bowl scraper with a squared-off edge.
- A wooden spoon or dowel with the end sharpened (to poke holes in eclairs, she says, which sounds delightful and weird to me. I want to try it right now).
- A practice turntable (the cake-frosting kind, not the DJ kind) to practice in your dorm room.

Set a Budget and Get the Best Knives You Can Afford

Your school may not offer a kit – which I prefer, since that seems like a shake-down, and anyway I'd like to have some choice over what tools I'm investing in. If this is the case, you have some errands to run – which can seem stressful when you're trying to start school and get your head around all the rest of it, but can also be pretty fun. So let's talk strategy first, then specifics.

When people say they hate to cook, the first thing I look for is whether they have dull knives and shitty pots. They usually have both. You'll have some shitty pots in school, guaranteed, but you have some leeway on the knives.

When I started school, the advice I heard most often was to start out with service-able, basic knives. In other words: *Buy the cheapest ones you can get away with*. This type of sensible advice is based on reasoning like this:

- Learn on basic knives and give yourself time to figure out what kind of knives you really want before investing in better ones.

---

7 Morgan (Student Blogger), see previous citation.

- Plenty of folks wash out of school or out of this career after a short time, so hold off on making a big investment in your kit until you know this work is for you.
- If you learn on a basic knife, a better one will feel so much better.

Greg Shiosaki, Chef Instructor:

I've had a change of thought in the last year or two on this. Save your money, buy your thousand-dollar knives when you've gotten into your career a little bit. Just get good, solid knife kits. A lot of schools do that; you buy their knife kit, and then when Christmas or your birthday comes, you can upgrade to a Shun or a Global or the big-name knives out there that are more expensive. By then, you have the skill to utilize that knife properly. Nothing worse than a very expensive knife and no skill. Find something to get by and learn the skills, and then upgrade.

Knives are so personal. The knives I like aren't going to be the knives you like; my hand's a different shape, my technique might be slightly different. At this point in my career, I've got the knives that are totally dialed in to me. They're definitely not the knives I would have bought in culinary school.

So don't put too big an emphasis on it, and don't put out too much money.

The opposite school of thought is: *Buy the most expensive ones you can get away with.* These folks are using the reasoning:

- You don't learn to drive a racecar by getting behind the wheel of a Ford Fiesta. If you're committed to learning high-end knife skills, get a knife that will help get you there, not get in the way.
- If you decide to buy different knives (or hang up your knife bag for good), it's not a total loss, since you can always sell these. Just put up a sign in the locker room at school.

My advice is somewhere in the middle.

First, set a budget – a realistic one, that won't leave you screwed for all the other expenses you'll have when you first start school (like tuition, registration fees, food cost fees, uniforms, good shoes, books, bus or parking passes, etc.) – and then be strategic.

Buy the most expensive knives you can afford only when it's crucial – like your chef's knife, and maybe your santoku. I have a friend who went all out on a spendy utility knife because he uses it all the time. I don't even own a utility knife because I suspect they're so all-purpose that they do nothing well. Two different opinions, and we're both happy. As an easy rule of thumb, though, spend the most on the knives that will be in your hand the most, and the ones you'll need to use with the most precision.

For the knives you'll use the most, it's not just about price point – you want these (eventually) to feel like extensions of your own hands. Which one will work best for you? And what length is ideal?

Broadly speaking, the European knives are a bit heavier and bring a little more muscle. When you're breaking down chickens and going at a case of cruciferous veg, that can be very welcome. These are the Hummers and the Land Rovers – long-haul utility vehicles, good for a rough trip without breaking down. The Japanese knives are lighter, and often feel a bit sharper and more nimble because you sharpen them at a slightly different angle – typically around 15 degrees, rather than 20. That makes speed a bit easier, at the sacrifice of some stability and muscle. You'll find more varied and innovative handle designs and blade shapes to evaluate, which may or may not work for you. These are the Ferraris and Teslas that get you there quick, and a bit more stylishly, but require a little more maintenance and effort on your part.

From what I've seen in the business, young male line cooks are all about the short, fast Japanese knives. They need to work fast, and stations in restaurant kitchens are typically small. Prep cooks and line cooks in restaurants that do bigger volume often prefer the Euros – they make breaking down cases of product so much easier on your hands and arms.

I use my 7-inch Global santoku for way more than I should, partly because I bought too long a chef's knife. Which brings me to length, which matters, but not in the pervy way you're thinking. You need a size that you'll grow into relatively quickly (new knives will often feel too long at the start, so don't worry about that) and that will also work for you over the long term. My first quarter chef strongly recommended we buy 10-inch chef's knives. He warned us that they'd feel enormous and dangerous in the beginning, but that we'd grow into them in a couple weeks of constant use, which was absolutely true. And a knife that long can be nice for bigger product – like cutting melons, or smoothly slicing large steaks when a boning knife's not necessary. But when I started working as a line cook, it was in a kitchen so small that my knife didn't fit on my station unless I carefully angled it, which is a waste of mental energy. Let me repeat: My knife was too big *for my whole station*. So I defaulted to the 7-inch santoku in my kit. I've gotten used to using it for most things, but I actually wish I had an 8-inch chef's knife instead. When I was interviewing my friend Vanessa for the second book, she disagreed. She got used to her 10" chef's knife in school and still loves using it now, and the length gives her versatility that a shorter knife wouldn't.

I'm giving you conflicting information because it comes down to personal preference. And you won't know which knives feel great in your hand until you hold 'em. What style of handle will work for the structure and size of your hand? What length will feel ambitious, but manageable and practical?

Give a few of them a test drive. You can often try out knives at private knife and cutlery stores, at high-end cookware chains like Sur La Table and Williams Sonoma, or at some restaurant supply stores. I rolled into a Sur La Table and cut up a couple carrots without buying anything. Then I came back with my own carrots and really tried to get a better sense of four or five different knives. For me, it came down to a nine-inch Wustof or a 10-inch Shun, and I went with the Shun. Surprisingly, with a temporary markdown plus a culinary student discount, it was cheaper there than online, and I figured if anything happened I could bring it back more easily. One caveat I should mention, though – many of these high-end cooking stores offer their own store-branded knives. I've heard that these tend to be the lower-range offerings of established companies like Henckels, Wustof, or Miyabi, for example. They'd be great for a skilled home cook, but based on what I've heard through rumor and gossip alone, I wouldn't recommend them for your professional kits.

So shoot most of your wad on the one or two knives you'll use most, and then, as a tradeoff, go cheaper on your other knives – your serrated, boning, and even paring knives. I didn't even own a serrated knife during school – I borrowed one on occasions when I needed to – and only bought a $17 Kuhn Rikon when I started working at a place where I sawed through industrial-strength baguettes all day. It works just fine, and it's so cheap that I don't mind occasionally opening boxes and cutting cardboard with it, too. Don't tell anyone that.

I've had a solid but cheap Victorinox boning knife for a couple years now, and I've been really happy with it, but I'm really itching to upgrade now, since a good boning knife makes banging through a case of chickens a lot more fun. If and when I do spring for one, it'll be from want, though, not need.

I went without a fillet knife for longer than I should have. My instructor got impatient with me during a fish fabrication workshop, but when he realized I was struggling with a crummy borrowed knife, he said "here, use mine" and handed me a super-flexible Wustof that went directly onto my Christmas list. Ever since Santa got it for me, I've sworn off blowing elves. Did I say that out loud? I *meant* to say, ever since Santa got it for me, it's made what can seem like a smelly, messy task totally fun. I like this goddamn knife so much I use it for weird shit, too, like hand-cutting pappardelle, which it does like a dream.[8]

In general, I'd much rather feel like I need to focus carefully and ensure my skills are keeping up with my knife than to have that frustrating feeling that I'm better than the raggedy-ass work I'm putting out because I have a shitty knife. But I had to space out my purchases to make that happen – so I bought a gorgeous chef's knife at the start of school, waited a year for a comparable fillet knife, and am still holding out for a better boning knife, pending the discovery of a generous trust find in my name (I get promising emails from Nigerian bank managers all the time).

Last advice: Don't ever buy a set of knives. My kit is the United Nations of knife manufacturing – a Shun chef's, a Global santoku, a Wustof flexy fillet, a Victorinox stiff boning.[9] If I went out and bought, say, a Wustof knife set, three of these four knives would work less well for me, and then I'd have to carry that 8-pound wood knife block

---

8   All these recommendations are on the website (www.NoBSguides.com), with handy links so that you can check them out yourself. I don't get any kickback for recommending these products, because I'm too un-famous and too lazy to try to shake anyone down. If you use my links to buy this shit online, though, I'll get an infinitesimally small percentage that would otherwise go to a much more worthy charity. I'm more appreciative than they'd be, though. You can think of this as the world's slowest-growing Fund A Line Cook drive.

9   I got yer stiff boning right here. Sorry: couldn't resist.

around school all day, too. Cherry pick the best from any line and pull them together in one badass mish-mash. Because you can.

Unless you can't. Again, some schools make you buy an entire kit directly from them. Hopefully they'll deliver some quality tools for you to learn on and still be able to grow into. Or they're just nickel-and-diming you, and you might end up outfitted top-to-tail with some shit brand. In which case, learn diligently with it, take good care of your kit, and sell it to a newer student on their way in, once you outgrow it.

What Do You Actually Need Right Away?

Unless your school requires you to buy a specific kit or provides a supply list that you must comply with, here's a general sense of what you'll need right away, a bit later on, and then way down the road, when the trust fund comes through:

Right Away:

- Chef's knife.
- Paring knife.
- A honing steel 2" longer than your longest knife.
- A good peeler (I prefer the Y-shaped type).
- Bench scraper.
- Digital thermometer.
- Sharpies, about 57 of them.
- A pocket notebook, ideally *Write In The Rain*, and a pen.

You'll need these, but you might be able to hold off a while to spread out the spend-fest:

- Santoku.
- Boning knife – buy one before your first butchery rotation.
- Fillet knife – buy one before trout week.
- Cake tester (also used for the purpose of looking cool).
- Plating tweezers (usually much later, in more fancypants rotations / quarters).

These are great to have eventually, so that you don't have to fight for kitchen resources:

- Flat-head fish tweezers.
- Fish spatula.
- Measuring spoons.
- Measuring cups.
- Microplane.

Try to avoid buying these as long as possible and borrow them from friends, unless your instructor specifically requires them, or you end up needing them for an internship or job:

- Serrated / Bread knife.
- Scimitar / Cimeter, or any specialized butchery tools, unless specifically required.

Becky Selengut, Private Chef:
What are the best items in your kit? The tools you can't live without.

A steel. Your arms get tired if your knife isn't sharp. It mentally frustrates you, and you don't even notice it. Your knives are your hands – working dirty and working dull makes you a very bad cook!

A big level down in importance are things that are hard to replace – pin boners, oyster shuckers. Maybe you could use keys or a screwdriver, but really? In a client's home, you're going to ask them for a screwdriver to open oysters? You'd be bummed. Everything else you could probably figure out. A good peeler is essential. Relying on a client's shitty old-fashioned swivel peeler sucks.

Bandaids. It sounds dumb to say that, but nothing will slow you down, embarrass you more, be more unsanitary, and be grosser for the customer than bleeding into their food. You need to be able to quickly and easily take care of that, so having fingercots, bandaids, and gloves in your kit, so that you can administer first aid to yourself and keep going is crucial.

Keeping Your Stuff Safe(ish)

Knife Rolls

First, you want to keep your equipment safe from wear and tear.

In the resources section of the No-Bullshit Guides website, there's a whole section of links to knife bags, kits, rolls, straight-up toolboxes – all different styles, quality levels, and prices.

You'll have to choose right away between a roll-style and a bag- or toolbox-style. Most people opt for knife rolls, which I did as well. Getting in and out of them isn't all that easy, though, since you have to unroll the whole thing (in most cases) in order to lift that flat inner panel and get at your knives. When I left my knife roll in my locker every night it wasn't a big deal, but when I started working at the smallest restaurant in the world, I wanted something that was lighter to carry back and forth with me, and easier to open on my tiny station. I've posted links online to some of the unconventional options I tried.

Whatever kit you choose to use will probably change over time, as you accumulate more knives, pare down to just the ones you use the most, start cooking on the road, or end up working in big huge kitchens or tiny kitchens. Even from quarter to quarter in school, you may need to adjust how you carry your knives based on the storage and working space available in each of the kitchens you move into. For this reason, I recommend you start sturdy and functional but cheap, so that you can swap when you need to down the road, and not feel like you're out a bunch of scratch.

Edge Guards

Inside whichever kit, roll, or bag you use, each of your knives has to be stored in its own correctly-sized edge guard. Without an edge-guard, your knives will dull and ding way too quickly, or they'll eventually poke their way through your knife roll (however thick and sturdy it is) and injure you or someone else.

Most edge guards are pretty much the same, and every once in a while your knife will start to bust through the closed edge of one of them and you'll have to replace it. The one exception is probably the magnetized Victorinox edge guards (links on the website) that are a little pricier, but hold your knife more firmly because the whole edge of the guard magnetizes to your knife blade.

When you're using edge guards of any type, dry your knives off well before you stick them in there. Obviously wash your knives after use – any bits of foods and schmutz that gets trapped inside an edge guard will get gross over time, and they're hard to wash thoroughly because their whole job is to stay pinched tightly closed. But make sure you also dry each blade completely. Slip a wet knife into an edge guard, and even a high quality blade can get pocked with dozens of tiny rust marks when it sits without any air flow inside the edge guard, inside a knife roll, inside your locker. Treat your shit well, and it will serve you well.

Security

In culinary school you sometimes have to keep your equipment safe from others as well.

Yes, theft can happen, but it's also pretty safe to assume that shit just gets mixed up in busy and disorganized school kitchens. Our first quarter chef spoke very highly of the Global santoku when he gave us our required supplies lists. By the following week, about 14 of us owned this same knife, and it wasn't a cheap one, either.

There are three ways to help people not to walk off with your things.

The first one's free: Mind your shit.

Don't leave stuff lying around. Always do a quick mental inventory of what you pull out of your kit and place on your station, and get in the habit of putting things in the same places every time. This will help you get faster over time, but it will also help you run a quick inventory of your stuff in seconds. Clean up is usually the most disorganized time of the day in school, so take care of your things first, and inventory them again as you put them away. Anything missing? Find it or deal with it right away, not later on.

If a classmate borrows something from you during the day, which happens all the time, make sure it comes back. If you're absentminded, take the two seconds to write a quick note on your <u>mise</u> list or <u>prep sheet</u> if you have one, or in the little *Write in the Rain* notebook that fits in your pocket, so that you remember who to talk to at the end of the day. If you have to track them down or if they return your item dirty or messed up in any way, call them on it. Right then. Don't stew on it and hate them in private. That's not how good kitchens work. Say, "Really, man? You're gonna borrow this and then return it all [dirty / fucked up]?" or "I really had to chase you down to get my shit back?" You're doing them the favor of making your expectations known, and it clears the air. They can do better next time because they know what you want. Or, if you pussed out and didn't say anything, it's still fair when they come to you the next time to borrow something to say, "Hey, last time I had to chase you down. You can use this if you'll bring it back in 20 minutes." Or, "Sorry, but you returned it dirty last time. Borrow from someone else." It's possible to be direct and honest without being angry. If you're getting all emo it's because you weren't honest soon enough, and then you come off like the dick in the whole situation. So be honest as soon as situations arise, say what you mean with calm clarity, and let them work out their own shit however they want.

Second, you can engrave your knives with your name directly on the blade, but this can get pricey fast. The only option I found locally when I was first starting culinary school was way too pricey to use for all my knives, so I just got my name put on my most expensive knife.

Third, you can make genius use of nail polish. Before I started school, a culinary grad told me to use nail polish to mark my knives. I'm a little anal, so I put masking tape around the base of all my knives, about 1/4" from the end of each handle. Then I painted three or four layers of bright orange nail polish on the end of the knife, and pulled off the tape to leave a nice clean line. I used the masking tape method to put orange stripes on my Y-peeler and my microplane, even.

I was assuming that if someone walked off with my knife it was probably because they were being absentminded or thought it was theirs, not that they were nefarious thieves (who could peel off the nail polish anyway if they really wanted to). I just wanted a visible marker to remind people what stuff was mine, and this method worked really well. It can get washed a million times, and go through the dish machine. I had to touch it up once a quarter or so on some of the knives, but nothing time consuming.

On The Rail:
- Don't buy knives in sets, unless your school requires it.
- Set a realistic budget that won't leave you hosed, and then spend most of your dough on the knives that will be in your hand the most.
- Give a few knives a test drive at higher-end cookware shops.
- Keep your kit safe with edge guards and the cunning use of nail polish.

* * *

YOUR UNIFORM, AND KEEPING IT SQUEAKY CLEAN

You'll be required to show up each day in culinary school wearing a clean and tidy uniform. So let's talk about the various purchases and decisions this involves.

Get Good Shoes

Good shoes are one of the best investments you can make at the start of school.

You're going to be on your feet for hours in culinary school, and even longer once you're working in restaurants (or for caterers, or for private chefs – everyone in this field's on their feet for half of forever). Footwear is not where you want to save money. So spend the scratch for shoes that:

1. Are designed for work, and provide dreamy arch support for your feet (which may still feel terrible after 14 hours of kitchen work, but will hopefully delay fatigue and injuries like plantar fasciitis better than a cheap-ass shoe would),
2. are sturdy enough to protect your feet if you drop knives or equipment, and
3. have oil-resistant treading. This is a step above plain old non-skid, and it's well worth paying for. Slipping and falling can fuck your shit up, especially if you're carrying a <u>hotel pan</u> full of hot anything. I didn't think it was a big deal until I forgot my shoes once, and was slipping and sliding all over floors that looked clean and dry to the eye.

It pains me to say this, but you'll probably need to spend at least 100 bucks for shoes that meet all three of these needs. They should last at least a year, even at the pace of kitchen work, and will help keep you a little safer and a little healthier.

Our first quarter chef also told us to wear 100% cotton socks. He had a student who tipped a steam jacket kettle too fast and filled his shoes with boiling hot stock, which would have sucked anyway, but sucked even worse when his poly-blend socks melted *into* his boiling skin. So fucking gross.

Our sanitation teacher also spent a lot of time talking about our feet. I had no idea why until I started working more physically-demanding hours in hot and sweaty kitchens. It turns out that the kitchen <u>brigade system</u> borrowed from the military isn't the only thing line cooks share in common with WWI soldiers – we also get trench foot! So be diligent about your foot care, and try lots of different things – foot baths, Epsom salt soaks, creams or sprays if the skin on your feet starts peeling off or you start getting Athlete's Foot (which really could be called Linecook Foot). You're on your feet all day long, so do everything you can to keep them healthy.

Laundry: Necessary Evil or Readiness Ritual?

Some schools will issue you a set number of uniforms once or twice during their program, which you've paid for in your tuition. If you need replacements or extras, they'll cost more. Other schools provide an order sheet and fitting times before or during the first week of school, and you can choose how many of each item you buy.

If this is the case, make sure you've bought all of the required items. If they specify four-way aprons and bistro aprons, for example, those are different (the first is for your <u>Back of House</u> / cooking uniform, and the second is for your <u>Front of House</u> / serving uniform), and you need to buy both.

Second, buy a reasonable number of each item, balancing out cost and convenience. I bought three jackets and three hats to start with (most folks stuck with just two). I eventually bought enough jackets and hats to last me a whole week, so that I didn't have to worry about mid-week laundry. I could soak my used jackets at home during the week, and only had to head to the Laundromat on weekends. If you have a more pimpin' and convenient laundry setup, you may not need that many. Just between you and me, I could usually get more than a single use out of my checkered pants and four-way aprons, so I needed fewer of those.

Third, replace them when you need to. I made it though mole week – the Mexican sauce, not the small animal (I didn't go to Roadkill Cookin' Academy, thanks very much) – without destroying anything, but during Creole seasoning week, I lost a jacket and a 4-way apron in one fell swoop. Devastating. I lost one more jacket to a click-type Sharpie pen that I slid into my arm pocket still open, which slowly bled a big black circle of ink across my arm until I noticed it. If you end up with stains that no laundry method can vanquish, replace the jacket rather than showing up to class looking like a spaghetti killer.

Finally, take great care of your uniforms, so that you don't have to replace them a bunch. It's very important that your uniform be clean every day. You'll have instructors who will be sticklers about it, and who will kick your ass out of class if you look like Dumpy the Grey Turd. And even if your instructor at any given moment isn't a stickler, you should be. You're serving food to people who are going to put it inside of their bodies. If you can't look clean, are they going to assume you're being clean?

There was a guy in my culinary school who was a dreadlocked, funky-looking pothead who lived in a bus, and still came to school every day in a notably clean uniform. So I asked him, "What's your secret, man?"

J.D.'s Laundry Magic Recipe
Mix together:

- Powdered Tide
- One scant capful of bleach
- Dawn dish detergent

Use whatever amounts will yield you a nice medium-consistency paste. Rub it in wherever you got shit on your jacket, pants, apron (just the white ones, although you can use this on those ugly-ass checked pants, too), and leave it on there for at least a few hours, preferably overnight. Wash as usual, later or the next day.

This paste method works well because it directs the bleach just where it's needed. Adding too much bleach to your whole load of laundry will ruin any logo that's on your coats, and will eventually give your pants a gross dingy grey look.

I also had good luck with soaking my coats overnight in Borax or in Oxyclean before washing them with regular detergent + more Oxyclean. And my bestie swears by Cascade dish soap – soaking her whites in that before washing with regular detergents kept them so squeaky clean that she made a little extra money on the side washing stained coats for her peers while she was in school.

Since we're on the topic, let's also talk about the *when*, not just the *how*.

Please, I beg of you in the name of all that's holy, don't wear your pants forever. Those black-and-white checkered cook pants can go half of *forever* without showing all the little stains and spills of your everyday work. That does NOT mean they should.

Kitchens are hot and we're running around all day. Pants are sweaty places. Your col-leagues and guests want to smell the delicious aromas of slow-braising food, not the funk of the personal tofu ranch you've got going down there. Wash 'em once a week, at least. Jesus wept, do I need to be your mother here?

Signs you're overdue for some laundry love:

- That special smell. If you can smell it, the rest of us have been, for at least two days already.
- For me, it was always the big grease and dirt circle on my right knee, where I'd go down to a knee to get into my <u>low boy</u> three thousand times a workday.
- There's a two-inch border of greasy gray around your pockets.
- You can't distinguish the black checks from the white checks anymore.

If laundry and ironing and all this general upkeep feel like a shitty chore to you, try shifting your mindset a little. A woman farther along in culinary school than me was ironing her coat in the women's locker room, and someone pointed out that you could get away with avoiding the iron completely if you just don't leave your coat in a lump at the bottom of your locker. She kept on calmly, and said, "Ironing just sets me right. It's like, okay, the week's starting."

Think of laundry and ironing your readiness ritual, part of the centering routine that gets you ready to go in there and kick ass, week after week.

One of our chefs started his career in a super-high-end corporate kitchen, and they wore white leather shoes as part of their uniforms – yep, even in the kitchen. He said they'd all come in early on the first day of every week and, before they clocked in, they'd sit to-gether and polish their white shoes. When he told us the story, it was clear he was nostalgic about a ritual that reinforced his sense of being part of a team that was doing serious and high quality work. This was a welcome way for them to enact a ritual of control and care that readied them to go in there and dominate the work in the coming week.

The Checked Pants Secret Handshake

I do my laundry at a Laundromat, which will be the first thing that changes when this little book makes me filthy stinking rich. But I've got to say, those ugly-ass checkered pants? They're the best ice breaker ever. I meet so many people in Laundromats who smile and nod at the pants and say, "You a cook?" And then I get to say yes, and we have a conversation about where they're a cook or a dishwasher, or where their cousin or brother or wife works.

This is true on buses when I'm riding home after work, too. There are millions of people working their asses off in this industry. We don't have a secret handshake because fuck it, that's just unsanitary. But we can spot all the little signs of membership – and the conversations that have unfolded with other cooks when I've been wearing these fugly damn pants have been some of my favorites.

This is a Good-Hygiene Biz

Not all of us are FOH beauties, but we still need to wash those faces of ours, and brush our teeth. Every day. How can anyone learn the nuances of taste when each of their teeth is wearing its own tartar turtleneck?

While we're at it, let's all wash the rest, too. We're working in hot kitchens in very close quarters with other people, all of whom will quickly get sick of working with us if we smell like walking nutsacks. The way to avoid this – and really, the only way – is to shower and use soap and shampoo on a very regular basis. You can't just mask that funky musk with fragrances – those will probably be banned at any culinary school, and won't be welcome in commercial kitchens. So much of your palate and your accurate sense of taste depend on smell, often in very subtle and delicate ways, and fake fragrances will only get in the way of that. Ladies, pass on the perfumes and shelve the fake-scented toiletries. Gents, it's time to gift your Axe Body Spray to the nephew who just started finding chin hairs.

You know the phrase *it goes without saying*? People usually say this when they're about to tell you something really obvious in a super condescending way. They should actually just say, "Ready to think I'm a prickhole?" So, are you ready to think I'm a prickhole? Because this is the section where I'm saying all the things that *go without saying* – right up until you get partnered in school with the granola chick who lives in a campervan, or the scabby dude who does lines off urinals, or the itchy girl with year-round allergies, and suddenly stupid shit like "don't pick your nose while you're working in a kitchen" *does* need to be said. Cleanliness and health are important because we don't ever want to serve skanky food that's seething with pestilence. Simple, right?

So it's time to go to the doctor and sort out that runny nose or that persistent sneeze. It's time to break bad habits, like touching your face, or running your hands through your hair. This was the hardest for me to kick. I finally just cut my hair off so it wasn't getting in my face. Whether it's a grooming fix, a medication fix, a habit to break, or just a general cleanliness fix – fix it.

On the Rail:

- Invest in good shoes.
- Go to great lengths to keep your uniforms clean and avoid looking shabby.
- Be clean, and wash your body regularly.

*   *   *

WORK NEATER, CLEANER, TIGHTER

Look Clean at the End of the Day

If you met a line cook whose uniform looked like the ass end of a cat, would you want to eat the salad they just made? Cleanliness is a sign of badassery in kitchens. The Top Chef who finishes the quickfire challenge and is wiping down his cutting board with a bleach towel while his competitors throw shit onto plates as the timer goes off? That guy is the boss. Just like ease is sexy, cleanliness is also sexy.

And BE Clean Throughout the Day

Wash your hands, wash your hands, wash your hands.

I don't know if I've mentioned this yet, but wash your hands.

You know the old proverb, cleanliness is next to godliness? Cleanliness is actually way more important than godliness, which is of little use in most kitchens.

> *Kären Jurgensen, Chef Instructor:*
> You have to be clean; you have to make your hands itch when you've touched something. It's not just sanitation; it's being clean and organized.

> Clutter makes your brain slow down, it makes you more disorganized, and it will make your job harder. And that's probably the #1 thing that people hire – if I say that someone works clean, they get an interview.

It bears repeating: You need to be clean because we are serving things that people will put inside of their bodies. As a general rule of thumb, I think we can all agree that you shouldn't ever let a dirty-looking, scabby male prostitute put his penis in you. Likewise, you shouldn't let a dirty-looking, scabby line cook put his or her salad into you. These things aren't unsafe in *exactly* the same way, of course, but please don't make a habit of either one. They're both unsanitary, unhealthy, and grody.

As a line cook (and presumably not a male prostitute; at least until you discover how much line cooks make per hour), that means it's important not to look *or to be* dirty or scabby. Stay healthy and work cleanly. Wash yourself and your product and your station regularly. Sanitize compulsively. There are 57 thousand things that are allergens to people, and regardless of what you think or feel about that, it really is your job to keep them all separate if they're supposed to stay separate.

We're in this business to feed and nurture people, not make them sick.

This still varies from state to state, but there's a mantra in many cooking schools: No bare-hand contact with ready-to-eat food. It's on most tests for a ServSafe certificate or a food handler's card. So when you're in school, use tools and/or glove up, and be really diligent about it. People will be on this like hawks, which they should. We all need to be cleanliness police, with ourselves above all.

In the industry, there's a bit more debate.

We've all seen fools put on a pair of gloves and then proceed to do fifty seven different things with them on, including six-and-a-half unsanitary and cross-contaminating activities.

Lots of chefs strongly believe that working with bare hands that you wash religiously is far cleaner and more sanitary than gloves, which people tend to misuse because they're lured into a false sense of cleanliness. Our sanitation instructor in school verified that when bare-hand contact was banned and gloves mandated in our state, bare-hand contact went way down as an identifiable cause of food borne illness.

And cross contamination went way up. The overall rates of food borne illness? Stayed exactly the same.

There is bare-hand contact like crazy in actual restaurants, so don't get super bunched up about it to the point that you're scandalized and uncomfortable when you finally get the jobs that you're here to train for. But until then, you're in school to learn the best possible set of habits, so suck it up and get into those good habits. Think of this as embracing your purest most virginal state of being in a new industry. I mean that in a good way, not a pervy way.

Dirt is Inefficient

Beyond all the legitimate health concerns that being a total shitshow (and I mean that quite literally) invites, creating dirty or messy situations is also a totally inefficient way to work.

> *Becky Selengut, Private Chef:*
>
> Culinary school really helps teach you to work clean right from the get-go. If you're disorganized and you have shit all over the place, you stand out, and not in a good way.
>
> You can't have a clear mind if you have a dirty cutting board. Between every single job, you have to clean everything and reset. It does something to your brain that makes you a better cook. I can't explain why, exactly, but if you're dirty then you're muddled, and if you're muddled, you can't be tasting clearly or performing at your tops. You need to start fresh, each time.

If you don't make the time to wipe down and clean up at each step of the way, you're risking cross-contamination of allergens in your space.

Also, we'll talk later on about how to work with your body instead of against it, how to arrange your station so that you twist and lean less often, and how to deepen muscle memory by arranging your tools the same way every day. If you're working messy, you're probably not doing any of these things. Instead, you're probably working in one tiny corner of your board, hunching over, all cramped and reaching around and over things, and working more slowly as a result. All of these habits work together. Making the time to work cleanly also helps you stay organized, to spread out and use your uncluttered space, and to work faster as a result.

On the Rail:

- "If I say that someone works clean, they get an interview."
- Being clean is the best way to make friends and influence people.
- So be and work clean.

* * *

Part 2
Setting Yourself Up for Success

Becky Selengut, Private Chef:
It was the second day of culinary school when I thought, "This career is right for me." I'm not sure if I would've had that same experience working in a restaurant, because I've ended up in the teaching and private chef world, and wasn't aspiring to work in restaurants. I think some people could have apprenticed and instantly thought, "I love this, I want to live in a restaurant for the rest of my life." But for me the click had to be in culinary school.

The chance to attend culinary school is a gift.

Yes, you're paying tuition. Yes, you're investing a bunch of time and a ton of work. Yes, it's hard. But to be able to spend a chunk of time learning a new trade, practicing beside masters who are there to offer guidance, getting to make a bunch of mistakes in a lower-stakes setting, getting to ask a bunch of questions without getting shanked for annoying the shit out of everyone? Damn, that's some valuable shit right there. If you don't think that's an absolute gift, think again.

You might be making this happen – making the choice to go to school and working your ass off to carve out this time – but what an amazing and lucky break that you're able to do this! No matter how much willpower and sweat and pain and hard work you're putting into this, it's still super important to stay grateful that you're getting the chance to make it happen.

You can't start yanking out people's appendixes without attending medical school, but you can serve them perfectly-cooked salmon without attending culinary school. These obviously aren't apples-to-apples examples, but my point is that the time you're spending in school learning about the different types of salmon, talking about the sustainability of salmon fisheries, practicing various ways to cook salmon, learning to tell by temp and then touch when it's perfectly done – that's like someone pulling you aside and giving you a little present, all wrapped up in a bow. You tear it open, and it's all this knowledge that you'd still probably learn in kitchens or from cookbooks eventually, but in school it's all packaged up for you and easy to get into. It may not feel like this at the time, but I promise it will in retrospect, after a couple years of being a hard and wizened old line cook.

Culinary school is still considered optional in the field. There are some chefs who really appreciate hiring cooks who come in with that nicely-packaged foundational knowledge, who've had at least some controlled practice in basic cooking methods, and who've ideally learned some techniques and procedures properly instead of developing bad habits in higher-pressure work settings. There are other chefs who are totally disdainful of this type of packaged knowledge, who will need to break all the little culinary school habits that make you too slow or too precious in a real kitchen, and who can't believe you paid money to learn shit you could have been doing in a restaurant kitchen.

Whichever chef and kitchen crew you end up with, don't get uppity for a second about having had this opportunity. Plenty of talented people will succeed in this career without the chance to go to culinary school. If you get to – if you choose to – then appreciate it. Don't be uppity, but do be grateful.

> *Michael Jordan, Chef Instructor:*
>
> The key is making that commitment.
>
> I had that moment – I'd been in school, and we did an externship halfway through, so you go get a job for three months and then come back and finish school. In school, we'd learned beurre blanc[10] – I know they taught us beurre blanc. I was at work and the chef was going down in flames, he was out of beurre blanc, service was going to hell, and he pointed to me and said "Can you make a beurre blanc?" and I had to answer, "No." I was humiliated, because I knew that I'd been taught that.
>
> That was when I made the commitment, right there, to never allow that to happen again. That was my motivation: I would never say no to a chef. I would be the go-to guy in the kitchen at all times.
>
> I went back to school a madman, a fiend – focused, studying, sucking the life out of that school. And that was the springboard for me, into working

---

10 Check it out – this here guide has a glossary. Any terms that are randomly underlined like this will be defined in Part 5, way at the end. If you haven't encountered industry terms like beurre blanc, hotel pan, or dickwhistle before, flip back to see what they mean. If there are terms you wish I'd defined, or ones you feel I've left out, just email me through the website at www.NoBSguides.com and let me know. Or share your favorite kitchen language and swear words. I'd love to hear those, too.

for Emeril, being the key guy in his kitchen, getting the promotions, going to Vegas to move the company into a different state. It all went back to being that madman in school, way into it.

My brain clicked into a different place. The fear of ever having to say no to a chef again is still with me, and drives me. I didn't party as much. I went home and read cookbooks more often. Conversations tended to steer toward what was happening in school and cooking, rather than sports. Everything started moving in that direction, and doing the work was pleasurable, because it was something I was so eager to absorb. If you're into it, study isn't study – that becomes enjoyment, that's the downtime. So I'd say: Stop drinking so much, stop partying so much. Take some time off, and give yourself a break to really focus on this. You have two years. You don't get this back unless you're going to fork out another $20,000 to $60,000-plus for another two year education. If you want four years – at a private school, shit, man, you're looking at close to $100,000. Do you want to waste that money and get nothing at the end of that? When you're there, go for it. Trust the fact that it will pay off down the road.

Just showing up doesn't mean shit. That's the problem, is people just showing up. If you're not doing well on tests, go get a tutor. If you're not getting good grades, then make some changes in your goddamn life, and do something different, because whatever you're doing ain't working. I know that change is difficult. We get locked into our ways. But everybody can inch forward. With cooking and with craftsmanship in general, step by step will lead you to where you're going.

You have to make that final commitment to cooking. If you're really going to dedicate your life to cooking, culinary school is one aspect of making you a better overall cook. You have to give everything to your craft, become that craftsman. Because if you're the best cook, it doesn't matter what kitchen you're working in – you'll rise.

On the Rail:
- Don't ever get uppity about having the opportunity to go to culinary school.
- When you're there, go for it. Trust the fact that it will pay off down the road.
- Just showing up doesn't mean shit.

*   *   *

INTRODUCING INSTRUCTOR ICEBERG

In elementary school, you learn about the Titanic and then at some point, usually connected, you learn about icebergs. Sure, there's the part you can see, but then there's a way huger part of the iceberg underwater – so vast that you can't even guess from the surface how large it might be.

Your Chef Instructors in culinary school will show up, they'll design a curriculum that makes sense. They will then proceed to teach you a bunch of necessary and foundational skills and techniques that you'll need in culinary work, and push you hard to develop not only this sequence of skills, but a professional mindset and all the habits that we're talking about in this book plus a pile more.

If they enjoy teaching and the role is a good fit for them, they'll give it their all. And then they'll go home a little while after you do, and they'll put up their feet, and maybe have a bourbon or a beer because goddamnit they put in their years on a restaurant schedule, and isn't it nice to see sunlight these days? Or they'll go to another job, or they'll teach freelance butchery classes, or they'll hang out with their families. They'll enjoy the life that maybe they put on hold while they worked for years or even decades in restaurants.

During those years and even decades in restaurants, you better believe they've seen it all. Some of these stories will work their way into your classrooms – the occasional story about cooking with Emeril, or winning an ice-carving competition in Japan, or the line cook who killed a rat out back and then went all voodoo about it, or stories from an eating tour through Europe – and some of the many skills they learned, honed, and then taught their own line cooks will work their way into the curriculum.

The rest will stay below the surface – powerful and vast, but invisible from where you're standing. There's just not time in a culinary school curriculum – whether they have a two-week rotation, a quarter, or four years with you – for a Chef Instructor to even scratch the surface of all the skills and knowledge they've built over the course of a cooking career. It's not possible. And when you start working in the field, this will be just as true for your restaurant chefs, who haven't signed on to be instructors and typically have even less time for teaching in a much busier kitchen setting.

Michelle Nguyen, Chef:

My instructors were amazing. Culinary school teaches you the basics, and because you're there to learn, sometimes you can be more experimental. Often in restaurant kitchens it's so busy that you don't have time to make a mistake or review something.

Chefs have limited time – in a cruel twist of fate, as mortals, they're bestowed the same measly 24 hours a day – and far more demands on those hours than most of us. They may love to teach, but with such limited time you have to know they're running a quick calculation in their minds – how much can and should I invest in this person? Is this a student who will actually use and benefit from this extra skill? Is this a cook who's sticking around, or am I just training her for her next job? Is this kid going to retain new information, or has he maxed out, and I should just leave him on salad for the rest of his life?

My first restaurant chef was a natural teacher and loved the act of teaching itself, but I also have the feeling that once he saw how reliable and persistent I was going to be, he just figured he was stuck with me (and would feel too bad firing my ass when I was trying so hard), and might as well get me good and trained up.

My point is this: Your chefs will always know far more than they'll ever have the time to teach you. But there are ways that you can earn and invite more in-depth instruction while you're in culinary school, and you have nothing to lose by trying. You'd be foolish not to, in fact.

Kären Jurgensen, Chef Instructor:

As an instructor for many years, I've seen a lot of things. And in student evaluations, whether mine or anyone else's, there are often things written about favoritism. All that stuff is total crap – nobody is playing favorites. Some people are easier to get along with than others. So be the person who's easy to get along with, and it will be better for you.

So how do you get the most out of your time in school?

Ask Questions and Clarify

Start by giving your instructors the absolute and utmost respect. Start out the way you'll start at any restaurant job – with total deference. And keep that deference and respect over time, of course, but when you need clarification, ask questions. Ask follow-up questions. Don't just ask because you're a self-important jerk-off or you think it makes you sound smart – that just makes you an askhole. But do ask when you're genuinely curious, you're listening closely to the answer, and you want to know more.

It's also important to ask questions whenever you're not positive you've understood the instructions your Chef Instructor (or later on, your chef) has given. Or at least take a moment to repeat back to them what you think they've said. "Okay, so 20 count, small dice, then into the walk-in to chill," and then they can either say yes or they can say, "No, I said, throw out the fried rice before it makes someone ill!" and you've saved a bunch of time and product.

You know that little notebook that was on your list of things to have at the start of school? That goes in one of your pockets, along with a small pen, so that both are handy at all times. When your chef starts reeling off instructions, the plan for the day, a complex recipe, or a process with multiple steps, whip that little sucker out, and start taking notes. Scribble them in shorthand so that you can keep up; you can flesh out your notes in the following moments, when things are still fresh in your mind. Taking notes on the fly can help you stay on track and organized, and at the very least will convey to your instructor that you are listening and taking things seriously.

It's also perfectly fine to occasionally ask for quick demos. Because these can be more time-consuming, use more care when asking for this kind of help. For example, if your instructor just demoed trout fabrication to the whole class and you were late or zoning out, that's not the time to ask for a private lesson. But if you're assigned a complex or marathon-length task and you're genuinely not certain how to complete it, you have two solid options. First, ask your instructor to show you just one as an example. Or second, show them the first cut or the first one you complete. Let's say you've been told to bone out 72 squab. Finish the first one, take it to your instructor or chef, and ask, "Is this correct?" If they look at it and then brush you off with an impatient, "Yes, go," that's a *good* sign. You're on track to bust through the rest of the case. What you do NOT want is to have them roll over when you're almost done and notice that you've done 70 of them incorrectly and fucked up a super-expensive product.

Be The Good Bet

Be as strong a student as you can.

We'll go deeper into what this looks like, but it doesn't mean being perfect – it means showing up prepared and ready to work, and then working your ass off. It means being engaged with the theory, and paying attention the bigger picture. It means having a clean uniform and being where you're supposed to be at every moment of the day. It means being as focused and effective during clean up as you were during the cool demo when you got to bone out the chicken. It means respecting your classmates and demonstrating that you're a team player and in this for the long haul.

And when you can demonstrate that you're in it for the long haul, your instructors may start to invest a little more in you. Teach you a few extra things. Have those extra conversations with you that really poke at what you need to work on and where you should be focusing next.

Kären Jurgensen, Chef Instructor:

When you come to culinary school, your chefs can become mentors, and if you foster the relationship, they're happy to do it. Ask for an appointment. I've sat down with many students over the years. They'll come with a list of questions – these are some of the things I'm thinking about, who can I contact in the industry? I'm happy to have that conversation, and most of the chefs are. That takes probably 45 minutes to an hour, so you want to make sure the chef has time to dedicate to you. And then check back in when your career goals change.

One thing about mentorship – you can't just expect the mentor to hand you things. You have to come and ask, and it will spark suggestions like "Oh, I know this person," or "I think you should try this…," and then they're happy to respond.

My school started new cohorts of students every quarter, not just in the fall. My second quarter was drawing to a close and I didn't want to lose these brand-new skills over the summer, plus I needed to work and earn some money. So I went to my future third quarter chef, and asked him for ten minutes to get his advice on something. He agreed right then, and I asked him what kind of work he thought would prepare me the best to start third quarter in the fall, and where he thought a student like me with very little experience should look. I took his advice, and followed up with the places he recommended. When I started back at school, I mentioned our conversation and told him (not in a brown-nosey way; it was relevant to what we were talking about) that I'd followed up and gotten a job where I was learning the skills he'd mentioned in that brief conversation. And I noticed that the next time I asked him for advice, he spent a lot more time and gave me really specific and thorough help. I'm guessing that's because I showed him once that I'd listen and use it to the best of my ability.

Your Chef Instructors get asked for help all the time, so they must be running those investment equations in their heads, whether they're conscious of it or not. So be the good bet. Be the student they know is going to stick with it, do well, and reflect well upon the school, who will thank these instructors at awards ceremonies, and come back and visit with funny and scandalous stories, and in time become a mentor to others— and then there's no limit to the effort these instructors will make on your behalf.

As a general rule, people want to help. It's hard to ask for help, but 99% of the people you ask are willing and actually honored that you've asked them. So do your best, and then go for it – ask for advice and help and guidance, and see what happens.

On the Rail:
- Start with total deference. Practice "Yes, Chef."
- Your instructors will teach everyone and mentor a few. Work to be one of those few.
- Tip the odds in your favor by demonstrating now that you'll be a solid cook in the future – through your habits and attitude, not just your skills.

*   *   *

CLASSROOM VS. KITCHEN TIME

In most culinary schools, you'll spend some of your time sitting in classrooms, and some of your time up and around working in kitchens.

How this works will differ from school to school. Some schools frontload the classroom time. My friend Jen went to a culinary program where they spent the entire first quarter 100% in the classroom, and then never sat down again unless they were taking a written test. In most schools, though, every rotation, quarter, or semester will include both classroom and kitchen time.

It's worth clarifying what percentage of time you'll spend in the kitchen when you're researching your culinary school options, but don't just assume that more kitchen time is always better. Learning the math behind food costing and conversions, for example, will be crucial to your cooking career, and you might as well sit down and really focus on it. Some classroom time isn't going to kill you dead. On the other hand, cooking involves hands-on skills honed through repetition – so you also don't want to sign on to a program that defaults too often to sedentary lectures and book learning and doesn't provide you ample kitchen time to practice and practice some more. Both classroom and kitchen time are valuable, and you want to sign on to a program that balances them thoughtfully and strategically.[11]

The rules of engagement are different in the kitchen and the classroom, which means that your strategies for success should vary as well. You might have been Dexter

---

11   For more about decision-making strategies like these, if you're still evaluating schools, check out the *No-Bullshit mini-Guide to Considering Culinary School* that's on the website, www.noBSguides. com.

MENSA Pointdexter in high school or college, but kitchens operate according to very different rules and protocols. Having a high IQ doesn't always mean you get to keep all your fingers in this business.

So let's first talk about how kitchens work, and what rules, protocols, and hierarchies you need to be aware of in order to succeed in school and in professional kitchens. And then we'll turn to the classroom and talk about habits, hacks, and strategies that will help you kick ass at the academics you'll have to tackle.

KITCHEN RULES

In culinary school, you'll spend a lot of your time on your feet working in real kitchens – using real industrial equipment, creating real meals, often (ideally) for real customers. The equipment alone requires different rules. When you're sitting in a history class, the odds of losing a finger in the pencil sharpener are pretty low. In a kitchen, half the things around you can kill your ass dead. Add in heat, time pressure, noise, the need to work closely with so many peers – and suddenly you need a very different kind of classroom rulebook. And the way you interact and treat each other also needs to change. How? I'm so glad you asked.

Share Like You Couldn't When You Were a Shitty Child

Take a toy away from a toddler, and what's the reaction?

They completely fucking flip out. If you're an oldest child, you've practiced this so many times – don't even deny it. And if you're a youngest child, you can cry like any actress on *Scandal* at the drop of a hat – don't even deny it.[12] It's really hard to teach children to share. There are bazillions of parenting books devoted to why, but I'll save you some time and money: It's because children are assholes.

You're in culinary school, charting your path into a new and very adult career, so let's talk about sharing so that your teammates will respect you and not think you're a crybaby toddlerhole, which you clearly are not.

---

12   If you're a middle child, I just skipped right over you in that example, just like everyone else always did. Fuck all of us: you know you're the best. All quietly biding your time in the middle, about to bust out and be amazing.

Default to Yes (or Close To It)

Culinary school can be so goddamn stressful. Learning is bloody difficult, and most culinary school curricula is designed to quickly advance your skills and cram your head full of information by constantly pushing you beyond your current capabilities. That can feel overwhelming.

So you're setting up your station, and your mind is full of all the cramming you did the night before for the test at the end of the day, and you know you're already <u>in the weeds</u> on your prep, but at least you managed to squirrel away a <u>chinois</u> because you'll need it later. That's always the moment when a classmate will come and ask to use that chinois. And I can almost guarantee it – unless you're a *way* better person than I am, you'll *want* to say, "Go fuck yourself."

You should not say this!

First of all, it's not nice, and being nice is so vastly underrated in our society that it's a really noble and counter-trendy thing to be.

Second, it's not your chinois, it's the school's, and that annoying kid is paying the same tuition you are (but I hasten to add this advice would still apply even if it was something of yours – a knife, a <u>microplane</u>, anything in your kit).

Third, and most importantly, you're part of a team, and the overall goal is that all of you work together to feed all of the people who need to be fed. It's that simple. So if one of you goes down, you all collectively look like shitheels. This is why having a total idiot on your team is so frustrating, especially when they don't get weeded out in culinary school as fast as they'd get weeded out in an actual restaurant crew. But pretend I'm still trying to be nice.

When you're stressed or being pushed past your comfortable limits all the time, it's really easy for that little daisy of inner loveliness that lives inside each one of us to close up and grow thorns. It's easy to get a little grumpy and be bitchy. I find it easy to be bitchy on my best days, when my little daisy is basking in full sunlight, so you can imagine how much I struggle with this.

It's easy to default to no. You're in a rush, you don't have time to stop, so you just emanate thorny fuck-off energy, and the no is out of your mouth before you've even paused to actually consider the request / question / idea. And when that happens, it makes you a shitty team member. I cringe when I think about how many times I said no when I could've said yes – often realizing that right after the person walked away, when I looked at my prep sheet and noticed that I wouldn't actually need the chinois for another 20 minutes.

My first step in trying to solve this crappy tendency in myself was to jog after them, chinois in hand, and say "Hey, sorry – I'm a little stressed. I won't need the chinois for 20 minutes. Can you have it back to me by then?" That's okay, and better than nothing.

A better habit is to learn The Two-Second Pause. The moment when you think you have the least amount of time is the exact moment when it's most crucial to pause for a beat and give your slow brain a second to kick in and consider the situation. I'm still really trying to dial in this one tiny, repetitive habit: I'm really busy and someone's talking to me? Pause. Deep breath. How should I answer?

You might not always say yes. It's perfectly fine to say no. If I knew I needed that chinois in three minutes, and I jogged after them and asked them to give it back in 20, I'd be fucking myself. And, keeping that wider goal of the team in mind, fucking myself makes no sense if it means that all of us can't then feed all of them. But instead of a flat out no, I could *still* say, "I'm using it in three minutes, can I bring it to you right after I'm done with it?"

A rehearsed and ready catchphrase is another way to buy yourself the tiny bit of time you may need to execute the pause / deep breath / consider move. Come up with your own version of the phrase, "Let's figure it out." You're not saying no, but you're not committing to a yes that might leave you screwed if you actually need the equipment / space / time / or whatever you're being hit up to provide.

Hoard (Within Reason)

There is no culinary program in the world with unlimited resources – and no restaurant in that position either, once you get out and start working in the field. Some may have more space than others, or nicer and more equipment – but that equipment breaks and fails and the point is: There are probably not enough two-ounce ladles *on the planet* to meet the endless demand of culinary school students alone. Part of your success in culinary school kitchens depends on learning how to secure the equipment and the space you need to operate cleanly and efficiently.

If I ever ended up in prison (though I obviously hope I never do), once I got my bearings and settled in, I'd be the gal who could get you things. I'd dive into the cigarette economy, I'd be a bookie for tetherball matches, I would felt dryer lint into teddy bears that I sold for chewing gum that I traded for cough drops that I resold for Percocet. Whatever. So, big surprise: In my school two-ounce ladles and <u>ninth pans</u> were our cigarettes, and I could generally find one or two for you, if you asked real nice. I did this by being super strategic about pulling from the dish pit first thing in the morning.

One chef in particular tried to hammer it into our heads that equipment is <u>mise</u>, too. You don't peel one carrot, jog to the walk in for the second carrot, and then come back and peel that carrot – so you shouldn't have to stop and go get the pans and tools you need every time you start working on a new project, either. At the start of whatever time you'll have in the kitchen, you come prepared, you assess your needs for the whole day, and you pull ALL of the things you'll need for that day's cook. I took this to heart, and got more efficient and accurate in predicting what I'd need and tracking it down. I also pulled 110% of what I thought I'd need. If I ended up needing more of the smaller pans, for example, I had them, and if it looked like I was on track to have enough, I was quick to share. It was a win-win.

Our chef in the third quarter did a version of this on our behalf. He had a locked cart of equipment that was just for our kitchen, and he had a old-school football coach attitude about it: No one comes into our house and messes with our things. It was terrifying to be in any other quarter and have to come ask him to borrow something, and you KNOW he had an eye on when you brought it back and in what condition.

But even he said: Don't go overboard. The important thing is that the work gets done, by all of us, and efficiently. Stockpile too little, and you're wasting your time. Stockpile too much, and you're wasting everyone else's time. Hoarding all of the things will just compound the problem of many people using limited equipment. People will be annoyed, not impressed, if they have to check the storage rooms first, and then go find you every time, because you have everything of any use in the whole school squirreled under your station. Don't be a pain, just be strategic and proactive. And then share.

Help – But ONLY After Your Shit's Sorted

Culinary school is like an airplane with a loss of cabin pressure. You put on your own oxygen mask before you assist the passengers beside you. Even if they're children. And especially if they're acting like children.

I said it one minute ago, but it's so important I'm saying it again: You're part of a team, whether it's your cohort in culinary school or your kitchen crew at work, and the #1 goal is that all of you work together to feed all of the people who need to be fed.

If you go down, your team goes down. If you go down because you spent time helping everyone else, they're all still fucked, so who have you been helping? No one.

Have your shit together. And then, by all means, dive in. Your mise is ready, you've checked your prep sheet, you haven't overlooked anything, you're in great shape and not even popping a sweat? You're a magical God of Kickassitude. Jump in there and help all the mortals, and you will be beloved in all the land. Until then? Stay focused and get your shit done, which is the best way to serve your team's ultimate goals. Someone needs help? "I can totally help as soon as I'm set up. Can I come over in ten minutes?"

On the Rail:

- The overall goal is that all of you (the students) work together to feed all of them (the guests). Don't do anything that makes this harder.
- Equipment is mise, too. Come prepared to find and pull what you'll need for the whole day.

*   *   *

WHERE'S YOUR RUNG ON THE LADDER?

Kitchens are usually structured with very clear hierarchies. Therefore, most culinary schools also have hierarchies, since they're set up to prepare you to work in this industry. A clear hierarchy helps a kitchen function fast and smoothly when under siege. because that's what a lunch or dinner rush is: War.

Most kitchens use some variation of the <u>brigade system</u> taken right from the military playbook by <u>Escoffier</u> in the bad old days of cooking. From top down, the kitchen command is as follows (along with phonetic cheats in italics for the most commonly-used ones):

Chef de Cuisine (*kwee-zine*)
    Literally "chief of the kitchen"

Sous Chef de Cuisine (*soo*)
    The chef's deputy; literally "under-chief"
    The boss when the chef's not present

Chef de Partie (*par-TEE*)
    Manages a single station. Ranked roughly in order of seniority:

        Saucier (*saw-see-YAY!*) – the sauce-maker and sauté cook

        Rôtisseur (*row-tis-SOOR*) – roasts, broils, and deep fries
            Grillardin – the grill cook
            Friturier – the fry cook

        Poissonnier (*Pwah-son-ee-YAY*) – the fish cook

        Entremetier (*on-treh-met-ee-YAY*) – vegetables and eggs
            Potager – the soup cook
            Legumier – the vegetable cook

        Garde manger (*guard mahn-ZHAY*) – cold hors d'oeuvres, salads, charcuterie

        Tournant (*toor-NAHNT*) – the roundsman, who can pinch hit any station when needed

Pâtissier (*pah-tiss-ee-YAY*) – the pastry cook
    Confiseur – makes candies and petits fours
    Glacier – cold and frozen desserts
    Décorateur – makes cakes and show pieces
    Boulanger – prepares bread, cakes, and breakfast pastries

Boucher – the butcher

Aboyeur – the expediter

Communard – prepares staff meals

Commis (co-MEE) – A junior cook reporting to a Chef de Partie on any of the stations above

Plongeur – The dishwasher or kitchen porter

Apprenti(e) – An apprentice or student

Obviously, most restaurants don't have staffs this big anymore (although there are exceptions at the highest end of fine dining and in huge volume-cooking kitchens), but most of them still use some variation of this basic brigade structure to ensure that the division of tasks and responsibilities is crystal clear, and to establish expectations around how work can be delegated.

That's why it remains important to understand this basic pecking order. You don't make any friends in kitchens by violating it.

When I was a 4Q student, one of my FOH rotations was in the 3Q café. I "managed" two or three 1Q busser / servers. I worked alongside a 4Q expo, who managed the 3Q cooks as "head" of the BOH. Some of those 3Q chefs de partie (each running their own station) had a 2Q commis assisting them. When those 2Q assistants went back into their own kitchen the next day, they were learning their own station, and occasionally had help from a 1Q commis / assistant of their own.

So here's what that situation looked like, in that one kitchen, on that one day:

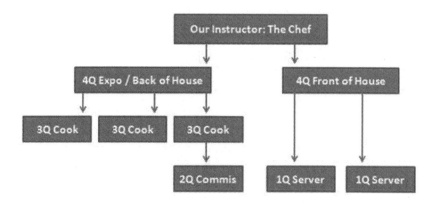

Those arrows are the direction in which delegation can happen. No other way. Why does this matter?

This is already a lot of people to coordinate, with the ultimate goal of getting hot food quickly onto the tables of hungry customers. And we're all learning, and not even close to being pros at this yet. So mess up the hierarchy, and shit goes all haywire fast.

So a customer asked one of the servers, "Where's my Brussels sprouts side?" So she walked into the BOH, right past the expo, stepped into the busy physical space of the line, and asked her friend in 2Q who was helping out the cook on the entremetier station whether he had a side of sprouts coming, and he shrugged because he didn't know, and started dishing one up to hand to her. That was about the moment when she got her ass kicked so hard, she might as well have been caught clubbing baby seals.

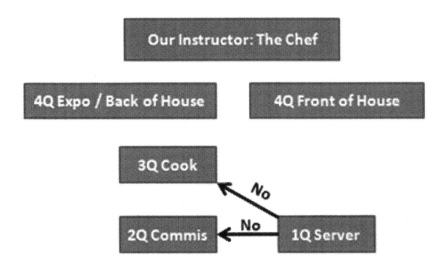

Why was this such a big deal?

First of all, any line is too damn busy for extra bodies, especially ones who aren't supposed to be there and that no one's looking out for – that's a great way to get burned or cause an accident.

Second, messing with the hierarchy breaks everyone's stride. If it's busy, the line cooks have their heads down and they're cooking their asses off. They're listening for one voice and one voice only: Their expo, calling out tickets. If they can tune out everything else, they'll work faster. Approaching them from a side and asking them a question they don't expect? WTF. Now they have to stop and think. "Don't *ever* make your line cooks think if you can help it," our chef would tell us, again and again. "Just let them work." You only have to be a line cook for a minute to laugh at how true this is.

Finally, pulling shit like this often results in waste. Say the cook sent those sprouts 30 seconds ago to the expo, who's just now checking her tickets to see where they go. She hands them to another server, and two servers approach the same customer with two sides of sprouts? It's not like it's the end of the world, but you look like disorganized monkeys. And then one of those sprouts probably goes back and dies in the window and gets tossed out, and wasted food is wasted money. Mistakes get made, but someone who consistently causes a lot of waste won't have a long career in kitchens.

So what should have happened?

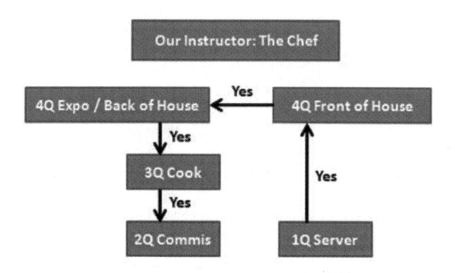

She should have checked with me, so I could make sure the customer had actually ordered sprouts and would be charged correctly for them. If I fucked up, I want to be the one to fix it, and fast.

Once I confirm they were ordered, then I'd ask the 4Q Expo (nicely, since she's my peer), "Hey, do you have sprouts coming for 33?" That gives her the chance to save face if she forgot to call the ticket out. Say she forgot the sprouts, she could say, "Oh, damn," real quiet like, and then call, "I need a sprout on the rail," which means *make this one fast*. If she hadn't forgotten, she'd just call out, "What's my ETA on sprout #1?" Or maybe that customer wasn't first in line, and she'd say "Where are my sprouts? I need two now, four all day," and then we don't end up shafting one patient customer to get all grabbyhands over a sprout for someone else further back in the queue.

Knowing and following the hierarchy minimizes fuck-ups. It lets the people at every step of an established chain of communications quickly check their own responsibilities, so even if it seems clunky at first, it actually keeps things moving faster overall, and it keeps food from getting wasted.

It also postpones that inevitable moment when your peers hate you.

That same 1Q student kept telling her 1Q peers what to do. She'd point out into the dining room and say, "That guy needs water," and then her classmate would go refill his glass and she'd stay put. Again, she was actually paying attention, and trying to identify a need and make sure customers were being served well. But guess how long it took everyone to think she was a lazy fuck? About two minutes.

We were slow, so I took the time to talk to the three of them, after I saw this happen a couple times, and said, "Listen, you can ask for your peers for help, but you don't give them marching orders. That's the quickest way to make them hate you." You should've seen how vigorously her two peers nodded. Turns out all three of them had tons of questions about the pecking order – who you can ask for what, when, and how best to go about it. This was their first quarter in school, and no one who'd been around longer had taken the time to lay all this shit out for them.

So, as a general rule, learn the kitchen hierarchy – they're all based on the same historical model, but the details vary in each specific kitchen – and once you're really clear on it:

- If you have any questions or needs, ask your direct supervisor first. Don't skip steps. If you're going way up to the chef first, you're narcing. Likewise, if the chef is skipping over your "supervising" students to deal with you, you've really fucked up. Incidentally, if there's a problem that's *not* a huge one, your chef will stick with the hierarchy, too, and tell a supervising student to correct you. So when they do, don't get all butthurt and shitty with them – they're probably just doing their job and relaying instructions from the chef.
- Maintain the FOH / BOH division up to the correct level. There are very few kitchens that appreciate a server approaching line cooks directly, and vice versa. In this example, only the 4Q FOH and the 4Q expo are talking across that divide, which may seem silly, but keeps screw-ups to a minimum. And *never* walk between the two physical areas unless asked, upon penalty of death!
- Only ever delegate down (respectfully), never sideways or up.

- If you're going sideways or up, you are *asking* very nicely for help or information. And when you're doing that, it should be very obvious that you are working as hard and intelligently as you possibly can, that you've exhausted your own efforts and knowledge, and that you're asking out of real need, not laziness or habit.

One thing to keep in mind, though: This hierarchy, which seems real and even important in school, is actually a very temporary and artificial one. The chef offering you an amazing job in the future may be the shy commis from two quarters behind you, who's pinboning your fish right now because you hate that job. So be firm and tough and honest, but don't ever forget to be respectful.

Kristina Glinoga, Line Cook:

I had classmates who could be good little boys to the chef and then turn around and be cocky assholes to underclassmen. Just because you're ahead a couple quarters in school doesn't mean you always will be. There was a guy who was a quarter ahead of me in school, so I was always his commis – doing his dishes, picking his parsley. At [the last fine dining kitchen I worked in], I trained him on his station. He had been very kind in school, and I loved him to pieces, so it worked out well. So I'd say: Be kind to each other. You're going to run into each other later.

School is a very short time to try to have a hierarchy. Have you heard of the Stanford Prison Experiment? A psych professor converted a building on campus into a fake prison and recruited random students to play prisoners and guards, and they had to cut that shit off because people were going nuts. Being in that environment so quickly dictated how people acted. Culinary school is like that. They'll put you in a hierarchy, but it only counts while you're there. Great, get into the role and experience what it's like. You don't need to break the fourth wall all the time – that's not the point of being there. Play along with it and understand how it works – but don't take that shit too seriously, because outside of school, everything changes.

On the Rail:
- Understand the hierarchy of your kitchen, in class and at work.
- Pay attention to and respect this hierarchy even – no, especially – when it's busy.
- Don't be a dick about it, though.

*   *   *

ROTATING OUT

In most culinary schools, you will have rotations that take you out of the kitchen.

You'd be amazed how much this freaks some people out. "I'm trying to learn how to be *in* the kitchen," they grumble, "so why do they keep pulling me out of it?"

Fear not. Your instructors have designed and incorporated these rotations for a reason. First of all, in the larger organism of a functioning school or restaurant, all these jobs need to get done, so why not by you? Second, and more importantly, each of these rotations offer you the chance to learn something else that's really worth knowing.

In my school, these included rotations through front of house, baking & pastry, and the dish pit, all of which occasioned much gnashing of teeth and rending of garments. So let's look at each.

Why Learn Front of House?

If your culinary program has a <u>front of house</u> (FOH) rotation, you're lucky. I know this isn't conventional <u>back of house</u> (BOH) wisdom, but trust me on this one.

I'm sure there are restaurants where the FOH and BOH work beautifully together – seamlessly, smooth as silk, each supporting the other, with the ultimate goal of serving customers ever in mind. I haven't been in any of those restaurants, but it warms the cockles of my heart to imagine they exist.

It's more common to see the FOH and BOH working together like a couple of dudes running a three-legged race at a company picnic – they don't really want to be doing it, and they're not drunk enough yet to be having fun. The FOH wishes the BOH would get the food out faster, not fuck things up, ask nicely for things, and quit cracking inside jokes and being dicks. The BOH wishes the FOH would quit texting, get the food out faster, and quit making three times the money for working one-third as hard.

67

So some conflicts of interest exist.

Ideally, learning a bit about FOH will help you bridge this divide. If food were all that matters in a restaurant, we could all use picnic tables and paper plates, and customers could pick up their own food and bus their own tables. If that's already your idea of fine dining, how do you like living in Seattle?

We're not all working at self-serve hamburger joints because the rest *does* matter. Which means that if you're ever going to take the reins of a high-quality restaurant, or – heaven forbid – open your own, you'll want to pay close attention to how a good FOH hums along. A chef who doesn't understand service well enough to provide FOH leadership better have a damn fantastic GM, or the restaurant's going to tank. And even as you're just starting down this path, having a handle on FOH expands your career opportunities. Lots of caterers want cooks who can talk to customers and cross The Great FOH/BOH Divide with ease. And with solid FOH abilities, you may be able to pick up some serving gigs as well. Once you have to get used to a line cook's pay, this might be a really welcome side job to be able to bring into the mix.

Julie DuRose, Business Owner & former Corporate Director of Catering

It's so funny how cooks can talk so much shit in the kitchen, and then they can't walk out and talk comfortably to the customer. Maybe it was just my school, but that was the hardest part for many. A lot of cooks are terrified to talk to guests, so you should reassure them that they're not as bad as they think they are in front of customers, and they'll get through it. Find someone who's in their element in the FOH and try to pretend you're that person, or ask them for help. Usually at the CIA those people were given a little more responsibility in the front of house, because there were real customers coming to eat at the four restaurants there, and you don't want to completely screw it up. But the first time I ate at CIA was before I had ever applied, and our server, man, was freaking terrified to open her mouth. She was sweating, and just operating from the assumption that she was doing a terrible job. And then I realized that was more common than not. Cooks don't want to have to be the servers.

One or two FOH rotations in school aren't going to make you a pro (believe it or not, there's way more to the FOH than looking *fantastic*), but it can really humble a lot of us BOH folks, and it's a good starting point for understanding the way a whole restaurant system functions.

If your school program provides you with a FOH rotation (i.e. requires it), throw yourself into it and learn as much as you can. Why not? Are you too good for FOH? I bet you will quickly find you are not, and that it's a whole new bunch of shit to figure out. And more importantly, it's one more chance for you to be part of a team. To hang in there with your classmates and get shit done in a new and different way. To work together while getting less Creole seasoning on your uniform. To practice being a problem solver, an issue fixer.

If you treat your FOH rotations as sick days, your peers will resent it. So be a team player, show up, and pull together to get this shit done just like you get all the other shit done – with an openness to learning and a winning smile.

Tom D., Culinary School Instructor:
For someone in culinary school just wanting to cook, why is a FOH rotation important?

It's half the business, maybe even more. This is the hospitality component. Two-thirds of customers who complain are complaining about the service that they get. They don't say anything about the food, even though that's what they're buying. Because they're actually paying for the whole experience, not just how the food tastes. They want to have a good time, and they go out to be treated well.

I have a wholesale food business that I bought a year ago, and I just visited one of my clients yesterday for the first time and introduced myself, and he was like "Wow, I'm so glad you're here. It's so nice to meet you. I have your competitor's product in my case right now, but I don't like them because they don't talk to me and I can't ever communicate with them." And that's just wholesale.

That's what you need in the front of the house, too – unless you just want to go through the drive-through or eat a nutrition pill for breakfast, and not have any human interaction.

I'm a one-man army for increasing customer service in this country. People should appreciate that aspect of the restaurant industry. Plus, it's very lucrative; you make more money in the FOH than in the BOH, you work fewer hours, you work less hard. But you have to have that passion to be in the front, and you have to be personable. A lot of people that work in the back are there for a reason – because they can't do the front of the house. And vice versa. But you can't have one without the other.

The skills and routines of FOH can be learned, but how much is just "being a natural" with people?

You have to be personable. I can teach you the skills necessary to be good at customer service, but you have to like to interact with people. That's probably innate, and it brings you to the front.

It's good if you like instant gratification. I got into the business because I like to cook, but I also like to see people eat, and say, "Wow, this is really good!" and you can't do that from the back of the house. I cooked for a long time, but eventually when I had my first restaurant, I was thinking, "What's going on out there?" I'd go in during the afternoon and I'd make fresh pasta or do prep, and every Wednesday night I would work the line, too, but I was always wanting to go out front and ask, "Are you enjoying your dinner? What do you think?"

You have to have it in you, to want to go out there. You have to be a little crazy or a little brave to go out into the dining room and throw yourself at the mercy of your guests, because they can eat you up if you let them. You have to be proud of what you're serving. If you are, and you're confident about your product, then it's easy to do, because you know you're doing the right thing. But if you're selling somebody else's stuff and you don't like it, then you're in trouble. If you're not proud of what you're selling, then you're just wearing a mask. That never works.

What things do culinary students do that totally annoy you?

When they don't know the menu, or make any effort to know about the menu – about what they're trying to sell to their guests, or even the most basic things like allergens. In school, it's so easy to bring fun things to the table when you're working the FOH because you can talk about where the product is from, how the product is prepared, how it's served, cooking techniques – because hopefully you've been in the back and you've actually cooked it. A lot of FOH people don't get that opportunity. Or they make it up and bullshit, and that irritates the hell out of me when people pretend they know what they're talking about, but they don't. Drives me crazy.

What are the most essential skills for culinary students to learn?

Attention to detail. The whole FOH is made up of a zillion little pieces of minutiae – steaming the silverware, polishing the table, having the chairs arranged, and the floor vacuumed, and the glasses polished, and the shirts pressed, and everything lined up. It's about being completely and totally prepared in every way – mentally and physically – with your *mise en place*, and the coffee made, the butter at room temp, fish forks there when you need them. It's about staying ten minutes ahead of the dining room, always knowing what's going to happen ten minutes from now, so that you can plan accordingly – whether that means fixing something before it ever happens, or preparing for it so that it's not a surprise. A lot of people don't get that.

It sounds kind of hokey, but you have to be a team player. There's a lot of work, and if you work together and communicate with each other, you can do so much more. You also have to be communicating with the BOH, and understand and have empathy for what's going on back there. That's why I think everybody should be cross-trained, and work both the front and the back for a while. Everyone should understand what it's like to be on sauté, when all the servers are standing there pointing at their watches and saying, "Table 23's been waiting ten minutes for their pork tenderloin, where is it?" and you look at the board and every single order is for pork tenderloin, and the guy's back there completely in the weeds. If you understand that as a server, it goes a long way. And, vice versa, when one server has the whole dining room, and they're screaming PICKUP. Hey, I've only got two legs.

There needs to be an understanding. Sometimes there is, sometimes there's not, but everything goes a lot smoother when there is.

Baking & Pastry

In my school, students in the Culinary program had two rotations through the separate Baking & Pastry program.

Our kitchens were hot, busy, sweaty fucking messes, with no windows and French tops and ranges and grills cranking heat out in waves, dish carts careening about, and a bunch of rushing and flailing students trying to learn how to be line cooks one day at a time. The bakery was more spacious, 23 degrees cooler, with large windows letting in daylight, the lightest dusting of flour coating everything, and huge pristine equipment that's designed to do quiet things like folding and proofing. The students walked slowly and with deliberate purpose. They stared into mixing bowls, watching things combining. Things rose. Other things fermented. Going over there felt like being an orc on a fieldtrip to where the elves live.

We called it Bakation. That was, of course, half because we loved it and half because we scorned it. It was nicer and more pleasant – and the pacing was a welcome relief from the heat and madness of our kitchens. But it was a little boring and less cool, too, and some of us kinda phoned it in. That was when you'd see people take absences, and I remember one of our chefs giving that his tacit approval. We understood his point: Miss a day on your grill rotation, and you screw the rest of the students on your line; miss a day of baking and you only harm yourself.

But you do harm yourself by missing it. A bakery rotation is like any other rotation – you can look at it as a requirement or as an opportunity.

I can't say I made the very most of my baking rotation. It took me a couple days to clue in to the fact that our baking instructor wasn't going to push us at all, but if we asked to learn specific techniques or methods, he was happy to run us through them. So I asked at work, "What are the basic baking techniques any chef should know?" and took a short list back to school. As soon as I asked, he showed me how to make a genoise (mine was lopsided and fugly), a chocolate mousse (a lot better), and an anglaise (dreamy).

Fast forward a little more than a year, and I was discovering that while I loved working in busy restaurant kitchens, line cooking may not be my jam. My chef was ready to promote me, and gave me a choice – do you want to move to sauté or baking? And I surprised myself more than anyone when I said baking. Our baker came in ungodly early and worked through a <u>prep</u> list of complex and interesting projects, and I thought, hey, that *way* of working might be a better fit for me than firing tickets to order. My little bakation rotations in school had actually given me just enough of a foundation in basic baking and pastry methods to come in handy in a new learning curve. And when I left to go work at my next restaurant, it was to do their baking, pastry, and complex prep – a job that felt like it was designed specifically for me.

So that "bakation" ended up being really core career training for me, I was just too dum to know it at the time. Good thing I didn't take a bunch of absences during those weeks.

The Dish Pit

"I'm paying tuition," I heard more than once at school, "Why do I need to do dish pit?"

My best friend went through the CIA (a program that in 2016 will cost around $130k without housing), and when I was talking about doing my rotation through the dish pit, she said, "The what?" So yes, if you're paying that much for school, then maybe you don't have to work in the dish pit. Otherwise, glove up motherfucker, because unless you're personally paying a dish pit crew in the form of your incredible tuition rates, *you* are the dish pit crew.

Our school had three main kitchens cranking out food for a student lunch program plus two dining rooms of paying customers, and all those pots and pans and dishes had to get done by someone. Why shouldn't it be us? If you're here learning to be a big dog in the kitchen, shouldn't that include the dish pit? That equipment is fast and hot and you have to be a real badass to run the pit well.

Working the dish pit well makes you a better team player. Everyone else does their shift, and you fink out on yours? Who the fuck respects that? You disappear for two hours in the middle of your pit day, and you think no one notices? Everyone fuckin' notices that shit, and they don't want to be paired up with you. Dish pit is another chance to show up, to pitch in. Don't miss that chance.

And believe it or not, working the dish pit makes you a better cook and eventually chef, too. First of all, you'll never make the two single douchebaggiest moves you can *ever* make in a professional kitchen – put a knife in the sink, or leave a hot pan unmarked. Those are great ways to injure your colleagues and get yourself hated and fired.

You work the pit and see a sheet tray crusted in <u>fond</u> come through, and you're just going to spray it into the water supply because some line cook was too lazy to deglaze and capture all that delicious flavor? You'll never be that <u>shoemaker</u>. You'll watch your <u>FIFO</u> better after you have to spray a bunch of fuzzy salad dressing out of a <u>bain marie</u>, or clean whatever the fuck that was at the back of the <u>Please Use shelf</u> out of a <u>sixth pan</u>. You'll cook polenta with a lot more care, and you won't let your risotto crust up a pan like a Jurassic goddamn fossil again. You won't send ridiculous shit like that to the dish pit in your restaurant either, if you ever do fuck up and burn the ever-living-shit out of something. You'll soak it and clean some of that shit out yourself, and your dish dude will like you better and the whole team will work a little better as result. Or you'll have the skills and practice to get into an excellent restaurant as the dish dude, to get your foot in the door and work your way up a more interesting ladder.

On the Rail:

- Your rotations outside of the kitchen are valuable chances to learn, so don't waste them.
- Yes, FOH earns more. Rather than (just) complain, learn it well.
- Kicking ass in the dish pit is hard. See if you're up to it.

*   *   *

KICKING ASS IN THE CLASSROOM

Every culinary school program involves some kitchen time and some classroom time.

The percentage of time you spend inside and outside the kitchen can vary a lot between various schools, and they'll all have slightly different approaches to how this works. In some schools, you'll spend a full quarter in a classroom before you ever step into a kitchen. Others move you into and out of the kitchen in distinct but shorter rotations. And in many programs, you're doing both kinds of learning at once, spending some portion of every day in the kitchen and in a classroom. So the structure will vary from school to school, but your basic strategy for each will be transferable.

So let's dive right in to some of the most common questions students tend to have about the classroom component of culinary school:

1. Why do we have to do all this classroom stuff?
2. Is it going to be hard?
3. Do grades matter?

Why require classroom time at all?

Because you don't need to be dripping sweat into a wok to learn <u>food costing</u>.

And because you absolutely must learn food costing.

One of the real benefits of culinary school over an apprenticeship in a single restaurant is the math and writing skills you will learn in the classroom, even if those are the things that might make you want to put your eyes out while you're there. Very few chefs have time on the job to teach you the math that underlies quick <u>conversions</u>, <u>scaling</u>, and food costing – and yet these skills are crucial if you ever want to move up from line cooking into positions of increasing responsibility.

Believe it or not, your instructors aren't assigning you projects involving research, proposal writing, and food costing just to torture you for no reason. They're torturing you for good reason. If you plan to stay and grow in the restaurant industry over the years, you'll end up relying heavily on strong math and writing skills, and you'll be in much better shape if you develop them now.

Will it be hard?

That'll vary for each person, but I've noticed that whether you're struggling or sailing right through, it really helps to remind yourself that this is vocational school. Any time you're rolling your eyes and thinking, "Why do I have to fuck around with this stuff?" stop and answer that question. Immediately. What's the on-the-job connection here? If the discussion or the task at hand seems abstract or useless, really think about how it could be relevant to a line cook, a <u>sous chef</u>, or a chef – on the job, during a typical work day. Most culinary schools are pretty good at honing the curriculum down to

75

cover vocational basics, so if you're not seeing a connection to workplace skills and outcomes, then take the time to ask or to dig deeper.

And if it is hard, stick around. The rest of this section will focus on specific tactics to hack your studying and improve your results without spending a ton more time that you don't have.

Do your grades matter?

Yes and no.

Yes, grades matter while you're in school. There were students every quarter who were strong in the kitchen but had to sit out a whole quarter because they didn't pass food costing or sanitation, and had to retake those classroom credits before they could move on. That's a flat-out drag, so if you're in danger of not passing any single component of your studies, grades matter a huge amount, and I'll talk about getting help and studying in different ways in this coming section.

At the other end of the spectrum, if your grades are really high, that will catch the attention of your instructors, which can be a good thing. High grades send them the message that you're both skilled and serious, and how can that be bad? If you're also strong in the kitchen, higher grades can make it easier for instructors to send cool opportunities your way. Imagine an instructor mulling over who to recommend for a cool _stage_ or volunteer opportunity. They might not want to send someone who's struggling – that kid should already be spending more time studying – so they send the student with high grades, confident that he or she won't fall behind in class as a result.

Here's the flipside, though – unless they're really low or really high, your grades don't matter much. For anyone whose grades are fine, your skill and attitude in the kitchen will be more important to most instructors, even while you're in school. And once you're out of school, a typical chef gives no fucks about your grades. They will only care about what skills you can demonstrate.

So work hard, and work your ass off if you ever fall into the danger zone of not passing a class, but keep the bigger picture in mind – success in culinary school is about building foundational skills and habits that will serve you well in the business, not about letter grades on a report card.

USE IT OR LOSE IT: FOCUS ON REAL JOB SKILLS

Learn The Math. Seriously.

Kären Jurgensen, Chef Instructor:
Cooking is math. Measuring is math. Figuring out how many people you need to feed at a catering event is math. Knowing your sales is math, and what your food costs are – math. It's all math. If you don't get math skills, you will always be working for somebody else.

Tom D., Culinary School Instructor:
How important is the math in culinary school?
Incredibly, insanely important. Ask any chef. It's great when I have guest speakers come in – corporate chefs, Mom & Pop chefs, bakers, GMs – every single one of them screams: Know how to do food costing, know how to cost a recipe, know what food percentages mean, know what labor costs are, know how to do this stuff. You can only work sauté for so long 'til your knees give out or you burn yourself to death. If you can't crunch a few numbers, you're never going to go up the ladder.

Conversions are the very first thing I teach in food costing class. If you can't convert, you can't cost a recipe. Students struggle with it all the time. Baking and pastry students do the math better, but they don't use volume measures very often, so they get tripped up doing that. Culinary students just struggle with all of it.

There are three ways in which you'll use math constantly in this business: Conversions, scaling, and food costing. Snap to it, now: We're going to talk about each.

Conversions
You'll be doing conversions from your first day of working in a restaurant.

In many restaurants, cooking isn't very seat-of-your-pants – there will be a recipe book, and you'll be expected to use it. The chef will provide you with recipes so that you can deliver on his or her expectations consistently, so pay a-bloody-ttention to them in order to do so.

As you use and scale recipes, you'll save time and increase your accuracy every time you can nail your conversations without having to stop and think about it (or reach for a different measurement tool than the one you have in your hand). For example:

- The best way to get a busy chef to want to slap you is to hold a tablespoon in your hand and measure out 1 Tbsp eleven times. Christ on a cracker. At your slowest, that's 1/2 Cup + 3 Tbsp. Or, if it's a recipe you can eyeball a little, it's a Tbsp shy of 3/4 cup.
- The recipe in front of you asks for cups of wine, but the bottle in your hand is 750 mL. How many cups is that? Nope, sorry – all the cup measures are in the bottom of the dish pit.
- Which products are weight-volume equivalent, and how can that save you prep time?
- The scale on your station is busted, but you have a little gram scale in your kit from back when you were waking up with molecular gastronomy wet dreams and sodium alginate sweats. You need one-ounce slices of cheese for your cheese plate – how many grams is that? Yeah, pull out your cell phone and Google it – we all love to watch the owner go apoplectic when he thinks you're texting during work hours.

Michael Jordan, Chef Instructor:

In modernist cooking, there's so much science involved, and it's all based on the metric system. Learn it now, and get it out of the way. I put 25 points now on every test that involve conversions from US standard to metric, Fahrenheit to Celsius. Memorize it now, because if you're the one guy in the kitchen who can convert standard to metric, you just made yourself a commodity inside that establishment. Even the craziest little pieces of knowledge you have can stand you above the guy to the right of you.

Scaling

Second, you'll also be <u>scaling</u> recipes constantly – adjusting them up or down based on the volume or portions you'll need to reach your <u>pars</u> and get through service (without getting so far ahead that food goes bad and you end up with waste).

Doubling a recipe is easy – anyone can manage that. But imagine one afternoon you step onto your line and you only have a quart of hazelnut vin, which means you'll need to make more. The recipe calls for five shallots and there are only two in house. Your sous chef wants to know how big an emergency this is – is she going to need to make a produce run, or can you squeak by? To answer her question, you'll need to be able to give your math muscles a very quick workout.

Since shallots are your limiting ingredient, how do you scale the rest of the recipe back, maintaining all the correct ratios?

- What volume will this reduced recipe yield?
- Based on how many ounces of vinaigrette you typically use to dress each salad, how many portions will this leave you with all day?
- Is this enough, or do you absolutely need more shallots?

These are the kinds of situations you'll encounter all the time in restaurants. They just happen to do double duty as the kinds of word problems you'll encounter in math class at school.

No one in a kitchen wants to wait while you pull out a notebook and do fifteen minutes of sweaty math to give them an answer. They also really don't want an incorrect answer. So you need to be able to think very quickly on your feet, and adjust recipes up and down based on what product you have in house and what <u>par</u> levels you're trying to maintain (based on the chef's best predictions of what volume of business you'll have on any given night of the week).

Food Costing

Third, food costing may seem abstract and annoying in school, but it's an essential skill if you're going to build a career in food – a notoriously low-margin industry, where keeping a firm grasp on costs can be the difference between a thriving restaurant and a note on your door that you've shuttered abruptly and thanks so much for the support, but see you never.

In many restaurants, food costing will become part of your overall responsibility at the sous chef level. You've been working your ass off as a line cook, from pantry over to sauté and up to grill, and you get promoted to sous, and all of a sudden you get hit with a goddamned tsunami of paperwork – from daily ordering, to creating order guides and managing vendors, to weekly and monthly inventory, to food costing specials and new menus, etc. It goes on and on.

I worked for a sous who had a hard time with food costing, and in a restaurant that ran anywhere from two to five new specials each night, it was a big deal. The owner ran her through it, but like many of us fine souls in the food business, he had the patience of a pissed-off gnat, and he made it really clear that she either needed to come in early and do her food costing, or she needed to get a lot damn faster at it. She did both.

You have an even better option – work the shit out of this at school. Learn it backwards and forwards. I know you will never feel like the food costing you have to do in school is a luxury, but it really is. This is one of those key moments when someone is walking you through a process – over and over, taking the time to break it down, and giving one rat's ass whether you actually get it – that your colleagues who don't get the chance to go to culinary school will have to learn on the fly, when they have fifteen other urgent things tugging at their attention. Save yourself time and struggle later on, and get comfortable with the process now. And then get faster. And then get faster than that.

Learn to Write

Please learn to write.

Cooking and writing were the first steps we took on that awkward stretch of evolutionary puberty from Neanderthal to Homo Sapiens, and you'll be doing your distant large-foreheaded ancestors a solid by learning to master both of these essential human skills.

Cooking? Great, you got that. Chase goat, cook meat, chew bones – modern human still like. Writing is also important, though, and throughout your long career in cooking the ability to express yourself clearly in writing will give you one more advantage in a competitive field.

While you're in school, your writing skills might be just as important as your cooking skills when you want to get funding. Lots of schools have money to give away, whether they make that information easy to access or not. My school was a community college that was sitting on a pile of foundation money, and grant officers came into our first quarter classes and asked – almost pleaded – for us to submit funding applications. I took a weekend and filled out the forms and wrote a 500-word essay about why I wanted to cook. The only way they could have made it easier was by asking me to draw a crayon picture of what I did on my summer vacation. I submitted it and got $1,800 in award money for school. Not a loan, just free help. And damn, it really did help.

I heard classmates whining in the locker room about how they weren't going to apply because they hated to write. "It's a whole page," they said in that it's-not-fair voice that stops being endearing around age four. I wanted to slap them. "Really? You wrote a page of homework on the 12 steps of baking bread last night – did our instructor give you $1,800 when you turned it in?" Bite the bullet, and if you hate writing every one of those five hundred words, imagine that you could get paid $3.60 for each one of them. *Playboy* doesn't even pay that well, and everyone reads *that* for the essays.

Apply for any scholarships that you can find. If your school doesn't have any, they suck – so start researching whether there are organizations in your city or state that offer awards. Do cooking organizations you've heard of have scholarship funds? Do local organizations who grant money to students also consider culinary school students for their awards? The few hours I spent working on scholarship applications made it possible for me to hang in there an extra quarter beyond what I could actually afford.

My BFF went to culinary school in the bad old days, and won an essay contest that allowed her to meet and cook with Julia Child. Hot damn, she thought, and entered and won a writing contest that sent her to the Aspen Food & Wine festival to cook with Anya von Bremzen. Not too shabby, right? Some of her most impressive wins came directly from her writing ability, and set her up well to work at Chez Panisse after leaving school. Where, not surprisingly, they said her cover letter scored her the audition. See the trend here? It was her writing that consistently got her foot in the door, where she could *then* show 'em she could cook the pants off anyone, too.

Once you're in the business, you'll be writing cover letters and resumes to get jobs. Eventually, you'll also be writing menus and specials. You'll learn in culinary school about the importance of the menu as a key business document – one that reveals your creative approach, sets the tone that your FOH should take, holds the keys to your food costing and operating budget. It's also one of the primary ways you're communicating with your guests – and have you seen how many typos are on most menus? How many crappy, ham-handed, unappealing descriptions you can find? Yes, one of the great joys of traveling to other countries is to post pics on Instagram of menus serving *Cowboy Leg* or *Cock Cola*. Tee hee. But you don't want your menu typos hitting Facebook in your own hometown. Sort that shit out! A menu is one of your primary sales tools, and it needs to be written well – accurately, concisely, even appealingly.

If you can write, will that open up entirely new ways to talk to people about the food you're cooking? Will you start to write articles and columns for a reading public that's inexplicably hungry for gossipy insider news from chefs and kitchen folks? Anthony Bourdain worked his way up through the regular old restaurant hierarchy, but he didn't become famous Anthony Bourdain by cooking. His writing skills brought him into the public eye.

What doors will writing open for you? You won't know until you work on it, get better and better at it, and see what opportunities it brings your way.

LEARN TO STUDY (IN NEW WAYS)

Every culinary program includes a healthy dose of regular old academic classes – tests, quizzes, homework, the whole drill.

You might be a fucking wizard in the kitchen, but you also have to succeed in the classroom in order to progress through any program worth its tuition. Every quarter my program held back students who were really strong in the kitchen because they didn't pass food costing, or bailed on sanitation, or had a classroom test average too low to move on.

Michael Jordan, Chef Instructor:

Students make a big mistake in the way they study. Culinary students feel like we should be cooking all the time, so the classroom tends to be a problematic area. I would highly encourage students to take their classroom work more seriously, because this is where we're really talking about and breaking down the methodology.

Study every day. Go through your notes for 15-20 minutes every day. A lousy goddamn 15-20 minutes of your life – give that, and you will find that you'll absorb the information, you'll take it with you, and studying for tests will become a no-brainer.

If you're entering culinary school right from high school, you might need to learn good study habits from scratch. Or maybe you're a career changer and you've been success-ful in other educational settings, but you're surprised at how different the academic components of culinary school are. You may also need to develop some new study muscles – for memorization in particular.

So I strongly recommend you try out the following strategies.

Nmaster Mnemonics

I was surprised how much memorization is required in culinary school. One metric fuck-ton, is how much. It makes sense – successful cooking is about attention to detail, so you have to be able to recall those details, and fast. You can't be a line cook firing a restau-rant's worth of chickens and pull out your textbook every time you temp them – you have to know immediately that they need to hit 165°F, and all those temps for all those other meats (at their various ranges of doneness).

Temping meats is an easy example, but there are hundreds and hundreds of facts that you'll need at the ready when your chef turns to you during a busy service and asks you to jump in on something new. The dudebro on sauté didn't mise himself out well – can you make a beurre rouge on the fly? Your chef's going to demo a sabayon – what mise do you need to grab quickly so that you're ready for her to come over? The prep cook is out sick – what are the basic ratios of a brine, and recommended brining times for the various hunks of meat you're staring at? You're on the phone with a vendor and they're out of branzino – what do you ask for as a reasonable substitute?

Of course problem solving and higher-order reasoning are important in kitchens, but there are so many plain-old facts that you need to know in order to solve many kitchen problems.

To get all these various details shoved into your skull, many culinary schools lean pretty hard on memorization. In most programs, you'll have tests that ask you to regurgitate plain old facts – name the four basic ingredients of a beurre blanc, the steps of creating a consommé, the equations for EP vs. AP costs, the various temperatures of egg coagulation, the five types of salmon and their characteristics, etc. etc. etc.

Mnemonics are memory aids that use the first letter of each word in a list or series of steps, and they are your friend. When you were a kid, did you use Roy G. Biv to remember the colors of the rainbow? Or the planets of the solar system (when I was a kid, before Pluto got booted): My Very Earnest Mother Just Served Us Nine Pickles. Or, if you went to my school, My Very Evil Monkey Just Shat Upon Nine Penises. Because (don't lie!) you remember the nastier ones better, don't you?

What are the five mother sauces? My classmate Charlie said, "Beth has VD."

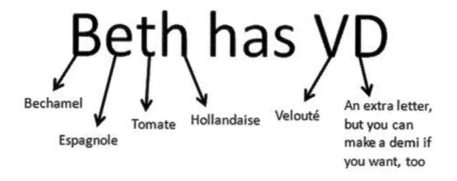

Poor Beth. But good for you for remembering them.

Those five kinds of salmon? Well, they each have two commonly-known names, so you're memorizing ten new terms – but that's no problem:

Kissing Scabby Penises Can Suck

| King | Sockeye | Pink | Chum | Silver |

also known as...

| Chinook | Red | Humpy | Dog | Coho |

Chad Rides Humpy Dogs Carefully

Really, humpy salmon? Sometimes these terms make mnemonic-lovin' easy.

Get creative about cramming these details into your brain – and then really remember them, not just to cram for the test, but to carry this knowledge into the kitchen during your cooking career.

Make Flashcards

Mnemonics won't work for everything, and they're time consuming. Save them for lists. For all those bazillions of other stand-alone details, you'll need another method.

Flipping through your class notes is passive. You're skimming the facts written down, thinking oh yeah, I know that, oh yeah, I'll remember that one. But your mind is just in browsing mode – you might as well be flipping through cable channels and mouth breathing.

You need more active practice that forces your mind to cough up the details it thinks it knows, and prove it. Use flashcards. If writing things down works wonders for your memory, then go old school and start making and carrying around index cards with you. If typing will suffice, bring your flashcards into the digital era with one of my favorite school tools, Quizlet (www.quizlet.com). Use it for free or pay for a very cheap upgrade, and make flashcards for each unit of school. Print up copies for the friends in your SWAT team (we'll talk about this in Part 3). Or print up copies and trade them for baked goods, or sell them for $5 to the lazy suckers in your class who aren't making their own. School isn't a competition – you can all pass with flying colors, and you'll be beloved of many if your first instinct is to help and not compete.

Make It Kinesthetic

Lots of the memorization you'll be doing – using both mnemonics and flashcards – will be processes, steps, and procedures. But we're not just brains being transported around on posts (I might have been in my last career, but I'm not anymore) – we use our whole bodies to succeed in this business. Cooking is intensely physical, and getting good at it involves lots of muscle memory and instinct. So when you're studying for your tests in culinary school, don't sit at your desk expecting your immobile brain to do all the heavy lifting – let your body get involved, because that's where the information will eventually need to make its way to be useful.

You've got a flashcard on the four essential ingredients of a beurre blanc: Wine, vinegar, shallots, butter. Maybe you have a mnemonic, too: **W**atch **V**ince **S**hit **B**ricks when I make this perfect beurre blanc. But take the next step: Visualize the process. You're standing there at the French top, off to the side where the heat is lower, and watch yourself adding the wine, the vinegar, the shallots. You let it reduce, then you pop in the cold cubes of butter one by one, stirring them in. Watch Vince shit bricks at you doing it so well! Better yet, while you're at home at night studying – stand up and mimic the process with your whole body, as if you were on your station at school. You'll feel like an absolute tool, but the process will start to live in your body as a known and familiar thing, and you won't just be cramming details into your brain that will fall back out as soon as the test is over. Most of us kitchen folk are physical people, so study with your whole body, too.

Our baking instructor wanted us to puke out the 12 steps of bread production in the correct order on our final exam. He just put 12 lines: Fill in the blanks, suckers. No context. Just write down: Scaling, mixing, fermentation, punching, scaling, rounding, benching, make-up and panning, proofing, baking, cooking, storing. We had a trial run on our midterm and I bombed it. I was writing things like punching, apologizing, making up, etc. Seriously, twelve? You can kick alcoholism in that many steps. That's too long a list for me to manage mnemonically, though two separate mnemonic phrases helped. The way I eventually remembered all these in order, though, was to visualize the spatial patterns of how I would physically move around the bakeshop in order to complete these steps. I stood in the middle of my room at home and gestured and fake-walked as though I was doing each step, bending, leaning, lifting, punching, carrying it this way and then over to there, etc. I got my body involved, and my body remembered the process better than my mind could.

Get a Tutor Early

Culinary programs move fast. They're cramming a lot of skills and information into a very short amount of time, so they chug right along. That means you can fall behind very quickly, and you can quickly get into a situation where you're just not able to turn things around in time to save your ass.

Ask for help early. Schools always have help available. And if the help isn't helpful enough, ask for more. You're paying tuition and you're working your ass off, so be a good advocate for yourself.

If you know you'll need support, asking for it early allows people to work with you instead of being pissed off at you. Imagine asking your instructor during the first week of class, "I know I have trouble with memorization. Is there a tutor I can work with, or do you have any other recommendations for how I can do well this quarter?" That's a clear request for help that shows lots of self-knowledge, drive, and a solid sense of responsibility. It gives the instructor the chance to offer options and think up solutions for helping you. It brings him or her onto your team, able and willing to help.

Now imagine saying, "Our final is next week, and I'm not passing the class so far. I need help right away, because I don't know this stuff!" I don't care if your instructor is Mother Teresa; she's going to think to herself, "You're just now figuring this out? What the fuck have you been doing the whole quarter? And now your procrastination is my emergency, and I'm supposed to hop to it and save your ass?" By waiting until you're in trouble, you're not inviting someone to work with you, you're just trying to save your own ass, and adding to their workload in the process.

So ask for help early, and be respectful but absolutely persistent about getting the support you need to succeed.

Kristina Glinoga, Line Cook:

The assignments they give you [in culinary school] are the bare minimum. The people who did the best went above and beyond. There was a guy in my class named Ian who didn't work outside of school at first, but then ended up working two jobs – one in fine dining and one at a diner – so he got his fine dining fix, and then he also cut his teeth on the line during crazy brunch rushes. So he got really good. He was a voracious reader of books, and just

> seemed to know everything. The program is there to guide you, but the people, like him, who got the most out of it were the ones who took it upon themselves to be really interested, read on the side, and go beyond the assignments given.

On the Rail:

- Get academic help early and often.
- If you need to, be persistent about getting the help you need.
- Study using the most active and physical methods possible, and try out new approaches.

* * *

EARLY ADOPTERS

Are you coming into culinary school straight out of high school?

Congratulations! You're entering this field at what most people agree is the "right" age. You are young enough to have at least ten more years of good knees and a strong back, a functional liver, an enviable level of energy, and hopefully a big and genuine openness to learning – excitement for it, even. You're young enough to get bossed around – you may not think so, but trust me, you'll be even less psyched about taking shit once you hit 40. Your cost of living is probably lower. If not, it's about to take a hit, but roughing it isn't as hard at this age as it will be later on. You'll need to trust me on that one, too.

Before I start sounding too much like yer mum, let me throw you some no-bullshit tidbits that you can take or leave, as you wish.

Be Patient

You want so many things right now. And you're probably a badass already. But this is a field that rewards time and repetition. Real basassery in a professional kitchen comes from skills practiced so many times over so many years that they've become muscle memory, first reaction, intuition. So be patient. This is the time to invest and work your ass off. The rewards will come later.

Humble is Hot

Closely related to that: Be humble. There is no end to how far you can get in this field if you can stay humble. How do you know where to improve? By having a very accurate picture of where you are now, so that you can see the gaps in your skills and the weaknesses you most need to address. Ego gets in the way of that. You're starting at the bottom, learning a whole new set of skills. So while you may be a badass, you can't execute every skill like a badass yet. Check your ego, be open to instruction and feedback, and keep learning.

Ask for help when you need it, too. A guy I knew at school said in the student lunch room once, "I told Chef that I haven't gone to college and don't know much about studying, and are there faster ways to get it done?" Of the students within earshot who heard this, not one gave him a look like "Dude, what a pansy move." Most of them looked at him like he was fucking genius, and why didn't they think of that? Humble is hot. It's also a good way to gain speed and efficiency faster than peers who are trying to tough it out on their own and look cooler than they are.

Desire Must Come From Within

Kären Jurgensen, Chef Instructor:
When you're right out of high school, so many times you don't really know what you're doing. If you love food, then maybe culinary school is a great thing to do. But sometimes it's good to go into the industry for a little while and work, and then come to culinary school. What works is different for everybody, but when you come to school because you really *desire* it, it makes a significant difference in how you perform.

Knowing why they're coming to culinary school is important for anyone, at any age – but it's even more important for you. You're at an age that's typically associated with pressure. You're stepping out from the protection, and maybe the household, of your parents or guardians. They genuinely want you to be happy, but most of them are also worried or even fearful – they want you to get your shit sorted as quickly as possible, because the world can be a scary and dangerous and expensive place to live. They want you to step into a life that's expanding and improving, not one that's narrowing and becoming harder every day. They want you to be proactive and create a solid future, not reactive, getting slowly crushed by debt or addiction or struggle or bad decisions. These are all good, big-hearted things to wish for you – but fuck, man, when I was that age it felt like all these expectations and wishes were going to crush me long before the big bad world got to me.

Like the rest of us, you're currently facing big decisions with limited information. You can't know what the future holds. You may be choosing between different options right now. If culinary school and cooking come right out of who you are and what you're most interested in, go for it. Just know that if you're going to invest your energy and your growth and your time in something like a school program, it needs to be your choice. You need to want it.

If you're not sure, or if choosing this type of school program feels like someone else's idea, then taking six months or a year to work in a good restaurant is a super smart thing to do. The world will not career off its rails if you take a gap year and test the theory that you might enjoy cooking. School will still be there in a year, and you'll be even more prepared to get the most out of it when you're more familiar with the industry.

Don't Fuck Up the Assets

Let's go back to my earlier crassly-ageist assumption: You've got good knees and a strong back, a functional liver, an enviable level of energy. Guess what the food industry is notorious for burning through? Yes, yes, those very things! Best ways to fuck up your knees? Offroad dirt biking, slalom skiing, restaurant work. Best ways to fuck up your back? Power lifting, championship limbo, and restaurant work. Best way to fuck up your liver? Serial voluntary chemotherapy, moving to Moscow, and restaurant work. Best way to sap your energy over time? Long-distance Arctic snowshoeing, marriage, and restaurant work.

See a trend? Working in restaurants may not be the single worst thing you can do to your knees and back and liver and your general youthful energy and joie de vivre, but this is a tough industry that can really grind down on you over time. It's your job to protect the very things it wants most from you. It's your job to find work in places that are set up in even slightly ergonomic ways – that use floor mats, for example, and invest in equipment that minimizes kneeling and stooping and climbing shelves. It's your responsibility to buy good shoes, and to replace them when you start slapping around like Hobo Joe in them. It's your job to at least try to eat a little bit healthfully, and get some decent exercise, and mostly resist the present and short-term allure of becoming a raving alcoholic like so many of the fun and lovely and unconventional people who work in this industry. This is not an easy job. It's almost as hard as the job of being a line cook itself. But it's even more important over the long haul.

Which bring us to... the long haul.

Killer Skills Kill Anywhere

The biggest difference between you and anyone older than you is that you can really play the long game – in this career or any other one.

Let's just say you jump into culinary school, you work in the field, and you ultimately decide it's not for you. That's a distinct possibility, however thrilled about this work you are right now.

Because this could happen, even on an outside chance, it's a good idea to get a degree. Go for a Bachelor's, or tackle the additional credits to get an Associate's instead of a certificate. Whatever next step is open to you right now, take it – even if it means another quarter or semester (or two or six) in school. You can work in restaurants while you're finishing up a more general degree, and having that under your belt opens up so many different possibilities to you in the future.

And then, regardless of what path your future self takes, take all the shit you learned in culinary school and by working as a cook, and bring it right along with you. You're developing shittons of good skills and habits, and I'm not just talking about your baller brunoise.

You'll learn and work alongside older career changers who are moving into the cooking field, who – unless they used to be miners – will get their asses kicked when they start working in professional kitchens. In contrast, if you decide to move into another field, unless it's mining, your ass may not stay kick-free, but you'll go in with some solid chops. When you hang out with office drones complaining about their hard jobs, you'll know what actual hard work requires. You'll know how to put in long days to get the job done, how to carry an impossible project over the finish line. You'll also know how much you can get done in 3.5 minute increments when you're focused. If you can carry this into your new field, you will kill with your productivity.

So if you ever decide to leave the kitchen, keep the work ethic, upgrade the fashion sense (and stop wiping your hands on your pants), be more careful about swearing and offering to fuck various things in mixed company, and go dominate another field like the badass cook you are.

The Long Game

Many of you will decide to stay in the field, though, and you're the ones who can really work the long game. You're the ones that Anthony Bourdain is talking to when he offers career advice – the ones who can put in ten years of insane work without many external rewards, who can live lean, who haven't made the sort of commitments yet to family and lifestyle that make it harder to miss holidays and special events. I'm not saying that's ever easy, but in an industry that requires – above everything else – an investment of time and persistence, you have the time. Develop the persistence, and you have a shot at reaching the top rewards the industry has to offer.

Your immediate task: Develop that persistence. Start with the basics. Dominate the fundamentals before you even think about moving on to the trickier, flashier business. Stick with me for a quick thought experiment. Let's pretend that everyone in this business bones 20 fish each week. With 52 weeks in a year (Haha! You didn't think you were going to get vacations, did you?), that's 1,040 fish a year. I started culinary school at age 38. I have maybe seven more years to kick ass in this business; during that time, I will bone 7,280 fish. You're 18, which means you have 27 years in the biz, during which time you'll bone 28,080 fish. Which one of us needs to learn the fundamentals more? Which one of us will get the practice necessary to do so?

Have you heard the rule of thumb that mastery means doing something 10,000 times? You're entering this industry at an age where you'll have the time to do that – and if you're pumped to hear that, this is probably a great field for you to be in. Say you hone your skills and can shave five minutes off the time it takes you to bone each of those fish. Over that many fish, you'll save 2,340 hours, or 195 12-hour workdays, or 32 and a half six-day weeks. Five minutes at a time. So don't rush things now. Every single skill that you learn to do right will snowball over time. Every efficiency you develop now will save you tons of time down the line.

Meanwhile, your short-term task will be to get yourself into the right kitchens with the right chefs to give you the most solid foundation possible. Culinary school is a good first step – these are chefs who will be willing and able to mentor you, and who understand the long game and can advise you on the best steps to take now. And finding work in excellent learning kitchens is another good step. The next *No-Bullshit Guide to Starting Your Cooking Career* goes into a ton of detail about why mentorship is so crucial early on in your career, how to find good mentors, how to get your foot in the door at the kinds of places you should be looking to work, and how to make a good impression once you're there.[13]

On the Rail:
- Be patient and humble, and you'll go so damn far in this biz.
- Cooking requires a commitment to hard work and a strong desire to kick ass, and both of these must come from within. Make sure this is your idea, and not anyone else's.
- You have the luxury of playing the long game: Lay a strong foundation and get strategic.
- The long game depends on protecting your knees, your back, your liver, your relationships, your deep well of youthful energy – all the things that restaurant work is especially hard on.

*   *   *

HEY, OLDER STUDENTS AND CAREER CHANGERS

Are you a career changer, entering culinary school at the venerable age of not-18?

You're in great company. As the culinary field expands – explodes, really – there are more and more opportunities for people to enter it at all ages, for lots of different reasons. The era when you'd roll into a culinary school and be the only student who wasn't an 18 to 20-year-old male is long gone. You'll find a diverse and varied student body in most schools now, with students of all ages enrolling and succeeding.

---

13   For more information about the second book, hit up www.NoBSguides.com. You can sign up to access a big-ass resources page, get updates on this and the next book, and send your questions my way.

I'm in your camp. I left a career in education and wandered for a while, until I decided I wanted to work in kitchens, and culinary school was the best way for me to feel prepared and confident enough to get my foot in the door.

Entering culinary school – and the culinary field – later in life is becoming more and more common, but that doesn't mean it's easy. I still remember the day that I was having a conversation in the student lunch room and realized my class-mate Micah was literally half my age. I was surprised at how much that threw me, for a little while (and how much easier on him I suddenly wanted to be, knowing that).

You'll have funny and empowering conversations about your age, and you'll have sobering ones that bum you out. Some days your age won't even cross your mind. Some days you'll curse the young and wish their brains would finally finish forming, the way a Jello salad finally takes shape. And some days, you'll feel old and tired and wish you had the energy of those same twenty-somethings.

Karen Nelson, Cook:

You think that you can keep up with the 23-year-olds, and that you won't mind spending 50 hours a week with them. There are a lot of really nice kids out there, but 43 is not the same as 23 – physically it's not the same, mentally it's not the same. If you have another life – you're married, you have kids, you have adult obligations – your life will be very different than the 23-year-old who can live on three hours of sleep and do nothing but drink. I could live like that at 23; I can't at 43. It's not realistic.

This lifestyle gets physically harder the older you get. When people who have been doing this a long time get into their 40s, and definitely into their 50s, there's a good reason they're not working the line anymore, or very rarely. There's a reason why people who have kids switch to working lunch, and don't work dinner anymore. Or they set themselves up with a schedule that's not 60-70 hours a week, if they can.

I can't predict what your experience in culinary school will be, but I can share some thoughts from my own experience as an older student, if you're interested in sticking around and reading this section. In no particular order...

Get A Chiropractor

Unless you're transitioning from a career in mining or rodeo, this job will probably be tougher on your body, so start putting a team in place to keep the old bones a'going. Jesus, this is tough work, and I don't care if you're fit as a fiddle, you will be amazed at the shit that 20-year-olds can pull off in kitchens without even blinking. I spent the first six weeks of my first restaurant job working and sleeping almost exclusively – I was so sore and so tired at the end of every busy shift, I felt like Old Mother Time. I worked with a guy in his 20s who would end his shift and drive to the mountains to go rock climbing after work.

Never Apologize for Your Age

You're there to kick ass, and you'll put in the work necessary to do so. End of story. You may need to ask for help occasionally, but guess what? Everyone needs help occasionally. If you need a burly coworker to help you lift a stockpot full of hot liquid, it's not because of your age, it's because of your upper body strength. There are younger men and women who'd need to ask for the same help, too.

Likewise, don't ever use your age to explain away poor performance – that casts you in a poor light that you can't change. You can work harder and come in more prepared tomorrow, but you can't come in any younger.

Don't Use Your Age as Leverage, Either

You may indeed be older and wiser and bring a whole previous career's worth of skills and abilities with you, but if anyone wants to hear about that, they'll ask. You are on equal footing with your classmates in school, regardless of age. So avoid coaching, advising, patronizing, or lecturing your younger classmates. Likewise, try to resist it if they ever cast you in a more responsible or even parenting kind of role – that doesn't serve any of you. You get to say, "Nah, we're all in the same boat here," and they get to learn to stand on their own two feet.

Beginner's Mind Can Be a Headache

I'm the crappiest wannabe Buddhist ever – I once got attached to a woman I met *inside a workshop about non-attachment*. But I do love the concept of beginner's mind – that even when you become an expert in something, you can stay open, let go of what you think you know, sweep out all your preconceived notions, and stay as eager to learn as you were on day one.

The tricky part is that accessing beginner's mind is really awesome when you're an expert, but it can be really disorienting and feel more like a bummer when you are actually, genuinely a beginner again. When Buddhists talk about beginner's mind, I wonder if they mean feeling clumsy and incompetent, starting to question your every movement, burning yourself a bunch, and crying softly at night sometimes – which are things an actual beginner often does in this field.

If you've achieved any little measure of success or seniority in your current career, you've started accruing rewards you may not even be conscious of. Do you have a title that earns you any respect? Do you manage any people? Do you earn a living wage? I hate to break it to you, but you're about to lose those things, and you're a far better Buddhist than I am if that doesn't cause you any pain.

Rachel Duboff, Personal Chef:

I had some real ego issues the first six months or so. I had a hard time telling people I was a personal chef. I was a suit-wearing power-monger kind of person!

I distinctly remember going into a client's high-rise building with a concierge. I used to be in property management, and the girls at the front desk were really snooty. And I was like, whatever; six months ago, I had a ton of those people working for me. They just think I'm like the help who has to come check out keys. And then I thought: Oh, wait, I do have to check out keys. I know I sound awful, but it was really hard on my ego. I had been at the high end of my game, and here I was, probably making ten bucks an hour in those early days. It was hard on my pride.

Now I have no problem. I talk to people about what I do, and they say, oh my god, how do I find that? And I say, you have to figure out what it is that you love, and build around that.

Karen Nelson, Cook:

When you're in your 40s, you don't want to be treated like a kid anymore – and that can be common in kitchens. I've worked with more than one yelling chef; they think that if they demean you, you'll do what they want you to do (if you can even figure out what that is). What adult

96

wants to be yelled at? It's not a good way to communicate, or motivate. Often when you're the new person, you're not treated with very much respect. It's assumed that you don't know anything. You may have a lot of life experience, even if there are gaps in your job-specific experience, and I think that can be confusing for some bosses to navigate. Sometimes younger bosses seem to approach this like, *Okay, you don't have this specific skill set, therefore I'm going to treat you like you don't know anything.*

I'd still say go for it, though. You'll probably find along the way that there are things you're not okay with doing – and that's okay. And you may have to figure out how to be humiliated and swallow your pride and put your head down and keep your mouth shut in a way that maybe you haven't had to do for a long time. Working in a kitchen is a lesson in humility. You have to be open to learning *everything*. If you're going to stay in this industry, you have to constantly try new things, and always be learning. You can't know everything.

If you're considering culinary school, or you're considering a new start in this industry, you'll learn a whole new set of skills, and that's always a difficult and risky and rewarding step to decide to take. The alternative is to armchair dream your way into a distant future that may never arrive, but you're making the move now. And that's ballsy and brilliant. You're never too old to learn a whole new set of skills, even if you feel rusty starting out as the newbie. Even if it's not always a painless transition.

Kären Jurgensen, Chef Instructor:
What drew you to professional cooking?

I'm naturally competitive, so the speed of being in the kitchen. I loved being around the people, and you can bang things around a little bit. From the time I was 14, I'd always had a part-time restaurant job, even though I had another type of career. But I didn't actually commit to a full-time restaurant job until my mother got really ill. And then I realized life is way too short, and I jumped in with both feet.

Are you following your heart? Are you throwing yourself into something you've always wanted to try? Then kudos to you – you're a badass. Thinking back, culinary school was maybe the second big decision in my life that I made solely for myself. I didn't even care, to be perfectly honest, if it led anywhere or if I did anything with it – I'd spent most of my life trying to follow a partner or build a career or "do the right thing" and fuck it, my culinary school experience could have led absolutely nowhere, and it still would have been one of the best things I've ever done. Because I did it for myself, purely out of interest and curiosity and joy and a love of learning. And those things are enough. I could beat myself up that it took until my late 30s to do that, or I could give myself a high-five that I did it at all, at any age.

This transition takes some bravery, and it's not always going to be easy. You're not bringing your job perks with you, but that doesn't mean that you're leaving all your previous job skills, talents, and education behind as well. As you navigate this new field, your challenge will be one of finding balance. What parts of your ego and your experience do you need to let go, even when it's painful? And what talents and skills do you really need to integrate in order to be happy and fulfilled in this new career?

> *Rachel Duboff, Personal Chef:*
> If you're coming to school as a career changer, ask yourself, what are the pieces of your world that you loved and that you hated, and how do you bring those in, in a way that supports you?

Yes, you'll learn a lot of humility in this transition. And yes, you may need to shelve some of your special snowflake sparkle to learn the ropes as a newbie in a tough industry. But for any long-term career to be rewarding and satisfying, it needs to jive with your talent, your character and values. You have to be able to show up with your whole, best self when you do it. What will that look like, for you?

Don't Candy-Coat the Income Issue

If you are coming from any career where making more than $35K per year was a given, you're in a very different field now. Our first quarter instructor used to hammer on the difference between a cook (shows up & does the job) and a culinarian (really knows cooking, and sees the big picture). Great. But then he'd always say, "Anyone can show up and be a cook, but if you're a culinarian, then you're valuable, and you can make up to $13-15/hour as a result." This was when the shoulders of all the older career-changing students would slump, and we'd be thinking: What the hell am I doing here?

When you start out in kitchens, you'll be making starting-out wages – the kind that can be workable in your 20s, when you spend it all having fun with friends and think that "401k" is a brand of breakfast cereal. It can be rough going to make a starting-out income in later decades, though.

Worse yet, that starting income will rise slowly in the low-margin restaurant business, and top off way lower than you might be used to from your work in other industries. And this may finally be changing, but you're less likely to be offered health insurance and benefits in this industry than almost any other. These are material realities that you shouldn't ignore in the excitement of starting fresh.

There are plenty of options to work outside of restaurants. I made twice the money in half the time doing personal chef work, and there are dozens of other options outside of line cooking. You can win the Lotto, or marry rich, for example. But do take the time to make a realistic financial plan, and don't underestimate how tough it can be to earn a much lower income (for quite a while) than you may have enjoyed in the past.

Make Sure Everyone's On Board

If you're a solo career changer, and you've figured out how to navigate the messy realities of starting over in a new career and making a cooking income work, then go to it. But if you have significant others, spouses, and/or kids, then it's extremely important to make sure that everyone's on board with you, because this transition will impact them (and all of your relationships) profoundly.

Sorting out the income issue is huge, but often the biggest ongoing sources of tension within relationships (once you move into the food industry) will be around scheduling. All those times when you guys love to go out and eat, whether to celebrate or just unwind? Those are the times when everyone else wants to go out and eat, too, which means those will now be work times. You'll rarely have holidays off, and you'll need to work very creatively to find cooking positions that will give you Saturdays off. You'll miss birthdays and anniversaries on a regular basis.

It's one thing to plan way ahead, or just schedule your life around an alternative "weekend," but in many restaurants you won't have a fixed schedule at all, at least until you've worked your way up the totem pole a bit. You may not know when you'll have days off until a few days ahead, depending on how often the schedule is drawn up. So how do you make plans with your girlfriend or boyfriend? Or how do you and your spouse divide up kid duties?

This doesn't always improve over time, either. The further you advance in a restaurant's hierarchy, the more likely it is that you'll be on call to cover for others' absences – so that day off to party on your friend's birthday, that you requested three months in advance? You may end up texting your friend apologies when you have to miss the party to cover pantry for the newbie who decided not to show up.

Karen Nelson, Cook:

The hours – and not just the number of hours but the schedule – was tough. My schedule was 3 PM to midnight or close, but most people would come in at 2 PM and work for an hour before clocking in, and I wasn't willing to do that. I might come in 20 minutes early, but if I'm there, I want to get paid, so that butts up against my values. And then we'd work until midnight or 1 AM depending on how busy we were or what night of the week it was. I didn't have a regular schedule, so my days off were rotating. Sometimes I'd work seven or eight days on, and then a couple days off. It was inconsistent, which was hard. I was putting in 45-50 hours a week, which was less than most people in that kitchen.

I would get off at midnight or 1 AM, and if it took me an hour to get home, it would be 2 AM. It would take an hour to wind down, and then I had to get up at 7 AM the next day to be there for my family. It burned me out a lot faster than it might've if my hours were different.

I was by far the oldest person in the kitchen, other than the owner. Most of my coworkers were in their early- to mid-twenties. There was a really nice full bar, so everyone was definitely having their shift drink. Sometimes there was one shift drink and then we went to get another drink down the street. Or I was waiting for my ride, so even if I didn't drink with my coworkers,

> I went to the bar down the street to have a drink. Maybe two or three. And then I got home and had maybe another drink or two. Pretty regularly, I was having between two and five drinks, five nights a week. And that started to slip into my weekend being like that, too. It was not a good lifestyle for me. I got into a pretty harsh burnout mode. I don't think that's unusual for line cooks, especially when your schedule is messed up. When you're 22 and you can sleep until noon, or even ten, that's one thing – but I had to get up at 7 AM because I have kids. That wasn't sustainable for me.

It's a beautiful thing to have a spouse who supports you in pursuing your interests, and in considering a potentially-dramatic career change. Be as honest with them as possible about what they're getting into. Have them read this book with you, and if they look like they've got a food-borne illness once they do, start having the hard conversations.

Sure, you're optimistic. What if you're the one who carves out a different path? What if, for example, you want to become a personal or private chef specifically so that you can achieve better balance in this field? That's great, but will you work in a restaurant for a year or two or three to establish the cred and the skills you need to do that? How exactly will you manage those years? You both need to be very honest – with each other, but also with yourselves – about how you'll manage the very real costs (the lower income, the crappier schedules, the missed events, the tired feet, the grouchiness, the tears, the late drinking with your kitchen mates, the rapid deterioration in your sophisticated sense of humor, how little you'll cook at home from now on, etc.). And have the *What If* discussions – what if you take that restaurant job just to pay your dues or earn your chops and you fucking love it? What happens then? Many people can handle disruption for one or two years, but there's no secret that the divorce rate among chefs is stunningly high. Folks who aren't in this business are often unwilling to put up with its shit over time, and why should they?

Of course, all this becomes more complicated when you're a parent – or when you and your spouse want to become parents at some point. Being on the same page with your spouse will be all the more crucial. If your kids are at an age where you can have very clear conversations with them about what you're doing, why you're doing it, and what might need to change as a result, that's an amazing gift to give them. This could get rocky for them, especially if they've been used to having you around. They'll see the costs soon enough, but keep in mind that they'll also see some real upsides, too.

Karen Nelson, Cook:

Being a parent is a pretty all-consuming job, and so is working in the food industry, and sometimes those things are in conflict with each other. For starters, no one gives two shits about your kids. That's a piece of the conflict I had working with twenty-somethings, who can work like dogs because at the end of the day all they have to worry about is themselves. They often have a mom or dad or sibling they can go to if things get shitty, but rarely do they have children at home that need to go to the doctor, need help with their homework, need you to be home when it's bedtime, or need you to get up at the crack of dawn to make sure they get to school on time.

I'm lucky enough to have a partner with a more flexible schedule and kids who are, for the most part, old enough to take care of themselves, but it fucking sucks to spend most of my time away from my kids, and then I can't even talk about them.

If they have a big project at school, and the teacher expects they'll work on it over the weekend, if you're not home to help them it feels terrible – like you're not doing your job as a parent, and like the teacher thinks you're just slacking off or not paying attention to your kids. So what I want to say to that career changer, the one who has kids, is be prepared to feel shitty. You'll miss your kid's birthday, you'll work on Mother's Day, you won't be home to give them dinner, or make sure they brush their teeth and go to bed at a reasonable hour. If you're lucky you won't work on Christmas.

What you will get, though, is the knowledge that you're teaching your kids it's important to work hard, and that sacrifice is okay, but most of all that following your dreams and being yourself is important.

Just know that when you're at work, you'll have to keep your stories about your kids to yourself.

On the Rail:
- This lifestyle gets physically harder the older you get.
- Starting over in a new career can be a humbling challenge. You'll get many chances to practice swallowing your pride and staying open to learning.
- Research restaurant incomes in your area and be prepared to live on those wages as you learn the ropes. No sugar-coating allowed: Have a realistic plan in place.
- This is an industry that's hard on relationships. Make sure everyone's on board and that they really understand what this will mean in terms of energy, money, flexibility, availability.

*   *   *

WOMEN IN THE KITCHEN (A PRIMER FOR MEN)

This is a section about the challenges unique to women working in professional kitchens – and men, if you skip over this and don't read this section, then you might be part of the problem.

This goddamn section has probably been the toughest one for me to write. When I started writing this book, I had no intention of including a section on being a woman in a professional kitchen. I'm a woman working in the food industry and this whole scrappy, cussy, opinionated goddamn book is written by me, so why do we need a ladies room break two-thirds the way through? Hello, 1996 called and it wants its section on *Women in Kitchens* back.

The industry is changing, though some say not quickly enough. I get as pissed off as anyone when some mainstream magazine still comes out with some *Best Chefs Ever* listicle and none of the chefs they name are women, or when food magazine roundups hover in the 10%-to-token female chef range. But many actual kitchens are changing, becoming more inclusive and less locker-roomy. And I believe the whole industry is poised for some seriously overdue changes as more and more people ask hard questions about why so few of us make living wages have and health insurance, etc.

I've been extremely lucky to have worked in kitchens where I felt like my gender just wasn't an issue. And I'm quick to give credit where credit is due – to the effort and thick skins of lots of kickass women who've blazed this trail long before me.

But I've seen things on various gigs that have made my career-changer jaw drop. There is still a metric fuckton of casual sexism that happens in many kitchens. Professional cooking remains a male-dominated field, so there are still many kitchens where just one or two women work, surrounded by men. Where, if a woman is hired, the assumption will be that she's a pastry or prep cook. Maybe pantry. Rarely will male cooks expect her to saunter over to sauté.

Interestingly, this was the moment in many of my interviews when some women stopped wanting to be identified by name anymore. We work to fit in, and complaining isn't valued in this industry. So women I spoke with suddenly went off the record right around this point, talking about otherwise-great workplaces where male cooks called each other "Sally" or "Mary" when they were working slowly, where the word "pussy" is the most common insult and used absolutely pervasively, where dishwashers cat call the women in the kitchen, and grab ass happens on the job. They talked about otherwise-awesome workplaces where line cooks talk in detail about getting blowjobs from servers in the locker room after a shift, in front of their female colleagues. One female cook was searing scallops (a pretty easy task, though one that uses expensive product), and looked around to see three male line cooks standing shoulder to shoulder like a tiny committee, observing her in a way that felt like they were just waiting for her to fuck up. In a way they never, ever would've observed another male cook.

Almost every time a female cook or chef told me a story like this, she qualified it quickly – maybe it was just me, maybe something about the way that I presented my skills or my skill level caused them to question me. And then she'd sit and shift uncomfortably, because that wasn't really what it felt like. It felt like being expected to fail, like being treated automatically as less competent.

I hate gender binaries. I don't think that all girls act pink and all boys act blue. But in kitchens that have been organized according to militaristic hierarchies and rules for centuries, you do end up seeing some classically male and macho behavior, and there are some women who succeed in this field by becoming tough as balls. When my peeps all headed into different kitchens around town, I started to hear all kinds of good gossip, and it's pretty common knowledge that two of the worst-nightmare chefs to work for in my town are women. Every damn time one of them comes up in conversation, someone will say, "Yeah, she came up through the old boy's club, and had to be balls hard to hold her own." And then everyone shakes their heads, like, yeah, that's the drill. These are chefs who are routinely abusive, who demonstrate terrible leadership, and the quick excuse is that they've learned to do that because they've needed to be tough enough to hold their own in male kitchens. Isn't it time to call bullshit on that?

Women acting like men within male-dominated kitchens is a temporary solution to a problem that's still systemic. Now, don't get me wrong – it can be so goddamn fun to work in a kitchen and feel like you're suddenly part of a pirate crew of cursing swearing buccaneers. I have personally used the term "pussy" about five hundred times, which makes me a little bit ashamed to admit right now, but can I admit that it's really fucking fun to be one of the guys sometimes?

> *Kristina Glinoga, Line Cook:*
> *Do we still need a section on being a woman in professional kitchens?*
>
> It's like any discussion about the equality of women – if things were really equal, we wouldn't have to talk about it. But obviously it's not very equal. A lot of chefs who are women would say, "You're not asking Mario Batali what it's like to be a man in the kitchen." Chefs like Dominic Cren would say, "Why are you asking me what it's like being a woman in the kitchen?" But it's still a thing. We're not post-sexism yet. You can't say it's going to be just the same, because it's not. And whenever you meet another woman in the kitchen it is like, "Oh my god, there's another one here!" And it's cool.
>
> Sometimes I do feel like I'll catch an attitude from guys I work with – not my current coworkers, but I *staged* at a butcher shop in town, and it was very much like, "Okay, Sweetheart, these are numbers. This is how the recipe works," and I wanted to be like "Fuck. You." That was the most sexist kitchen I've been in, a place where it was okay to have that kind of attitude.
>
> In another kitchen – where, again, I was the only woman – they were really nice guys, and they were trying to be really, really polite. So they would censor themselves a lot, instead of just being the dudes they are. If they were going to make jokes about dick or pussy or whatever, they'd apologize profusely about it, and I was always like, "What the fuck? I don't care." They were walking on eggshells and being on their best behavior because *there was a girl around,* which ended up feeling odd. I think if they knew they didn't have to censor

themselves, they'd be more open to having more women in the kitchen. If I wanted to censor myself, and be good and cute, I would have stayed in retail. That's what I like about where I work now – the guys aren't sexist toward me, but they don't censor their locker room men's talk around me either. They don't ever say offensive shit toward me, of course, but they also don't change their behavior around me. It's nice sometimes to feel like one of the guys.

The downside is that being one of the guys can create a huge amount of internal conflict for some women. Are you also supposed to call the slow cooks Sally or Mary? Surely that seems awkward and hypocritical, but aren't we all just fitting into the band of pirates here? And if being wimpy makes you a pussy, what happens when you have your most badass and brave day in the kitchen and you still have a vagina? Yep, it's still there! When a coworker tells you to grow a pair, and you "man up" and complete a task brilliantly – oh, hey, that vagina's still there, and you're still a woman! So do you chip away at yourself each time you toss off that slang? Or feel like you're passing when you have a good day, or all-too-exposed when you have a bad one? Do you have to work harder than the guys you're surrounded by just to be taken seriously?

Becky Selengut, Private Chef:

Look at the way we eat – standing up, out of quart plastic things! And it's a badge of honor. At the [super-high-end fine dining restaurant], I would sit down with the FOH staff to eat – me, the only other woman I worked with, and maybe one gay guy – the "weaker ones." All the straight dudes would stand at the counter, shoveling food in, grunting, and going back to work. And I decided that was bullshit. We're in this industry of appreciating food and goddamnit, I deserve to sit down and take a break, and eat a civilized lunch in the middle of a very long and not-very-civilized work day.

Having women in a kitchen crew is a very good thing.

And women *not* acting like men can be a very good thing.

Women tend to bring greater emphasis on balance, health, compassion, empathy, and relationships. A kitchen without those things can become a place where everyone stands and grunts and throws food down their face and tries to measure their dicks on the table. And it can become a place that can get out of sync and out of balance. My chef always wanted to make sure there were women in the kitchen because he felt it had a very good and very balancing effect on the way we worked, and I agree. Having a mixture of men and women in the kitchen makes for a much more successful kitchen.

Julie DuRose, Business Owner & former Corporate Director of Catering

I'll go into a kitchen and the first thing I want to do is count the girls, and then see how they all interact. It is really unusual to see many women cooking. It's one of those places where people haven't made it very comfortable; it feels like the onus is on the woman to be the thing that the men are expecting or needing, to make it a little easier on her. Instead of the men having to learn how to work with women differently or even understand that they work differently. So women often find other things to do in the industry.

What would that look like, if you put that onus on men? If you were writing the manual for men in a kitchen, what would you focus on?

For me it's about sharing ideas, and asking for feedback, but not getting competitive or being aggressive. When you have the guys you work with taste something, it can be like, "Hey, I made this – what are your ideas?" instead of being a deferential thing.

I'd add looking for cues that the conversation is uncomfortable. Cooks are a different breed – we'll talk about anything. So it's not about censoring. You don't want to be the one person who's preventing everyone from having fun, or from being themselves.

I feel like women are just a lot more inclusive, and more supportive. In some kitchens, it's more about trying to get people to mess up, and then making fun of them when they do.

On the Rail:

- A mix of men and women in the kitchen makes for a much more successful kitchen.
- It can be super fun to be "one of the guys."
- Also, women don't need to be "one of the guys."

*   *   *

EATING YOUR ETHICS

In kitchens, we eat things that have been killed – the more recently, the better – and we kill things ourselves, too. We butcher and break down and fabricate animals. There are always exceptions (more on this below), but at some point you will asked to do things that may push your limits.

I was reading a collection of assorted little tidbits of advice about culinary school and came across this advice:

"Be Fearless

… if your school is like my school, you will be required to slaughter a live lobster. Then cook it. And eat it."[14]

If your first instinct is to mock the shit out of this (God NO, tell me you weren't *forced to eat lobster*! How purely awful: How on earth did you tough your way through it? *eyeroll, finger-gag*) you're going to have an easier time working in kitchens. I'm not saying you're a better person; in fact, that reaction probably makes you a worse person, and you'll need to circle through insect lives for a lot longer than that writer above will before you reach nirvana. But you'll have an easier time in kitchens.

This is not to say that you need to be callous about the process of killing and preparing animals to be eaten. It can be rough work. Let me be very clear: I don't think anyone's weak for hesitating when they butcher an animal. It's okay – important, even – to stop for a moment and value the lives of the animals we eat, and be honest about own our own part in the process of raising, killing, preparing and eating them. This is some serious

---

14   S.J. Sebellin-Ross. *Culinary School: The 164 Best Cooking Tips and Tricks.* Amazon Digital Services, Inc. 2014.

circle of life shit, people. The real wussies are the ones who eat the cellophane-wrapped chicken in the grocery store and then get all squeamish and judgy about the dirty work they're not willing to perform – or even acknowledge – themselves. I went from working as a farmhand at an animal sanctuary to entering culinary school, and it wasn't a painless transition to go from rubbing sunscreen on pigs in the summer so they wouldn't burn to talking about getting a good sear on a pork belly. I'm fully aware that I continue to linger in some of my own uncomfortable ethical grey areas.

But in most restaurant kitchens, there are no grey areas, and very few people have time to talk over any hesitations you may have about the tasks you're expected to take on. Train you to break down chickens? Yes. Talk about how much you love chickens and how you're not sure you can do this? Not so much. You'll have a much easier time working in most kitchens when you don't blink twice before pushing the butt of your chef's knife down into a crab's brain to kill it quickly before it goes into the pot of boiling water, and when you're an omnivore who's blessed with a sturdy stomach and the desire to put into it pretty much any damn thing you come across, the weirder the better.

So what if you're vegetarian or vegan?

I'm not going to go all Anthony Bourdain on your ass and tell you to stay out of the biz. Fuck anyone who says you can't succeed in the food industry *at all* just because you're not planning on doing it the regular mainstream way. There are vegetarian and vegan restaurants in every big city these days, and there are towns of all sizes where people would welcome more of these options. The full range of these offerings is growing all the time, to include everything from fine dining right on down to falafel stands and fast food. Healthy convenience foods is one of the fastest growing segments of the food industry right now, but strictly vegetarian offerings are still a tougher sell to mainstream consumers. Which is all to say, this is still a small segment of a very large industry, which means that you may face much stiffer competition to find work in these kinds of kitchens. You'll need to be even more creative about building good solid relationships to get your foot in the door or (eventually) open your own doors.

Can it be done? Hell yeah.

Do these vegetarian and vegan restaurants need great cooks who know their millet from their amaranth, and would rather scavenge seabeans than slaughter sheep? Yep, and that can be you.

The road there can often feel a little bloody, though, so it's important to pause and do some hard thinking, to get really clear at the start of this new career adventure about what kinds of things you will and will not do in the service of your culinary learning.

With more people considering culinary school than ever before, a wider range of choices, options, and alternative programs are becoming available, with schools and programs focusing on sustainability, vegetarian cooking, nutrition, Ayurvedic diets, spa food, etc. etc. etc.[15]

In most mainstream culinary schools, though, vegetarian cooking may only be the topic of a single rotation, or even a single lecture or practicum assignment. Or perhaps it will only merit a glancing mention. In the culinary program I attended, the "Why would people choose to be vegetarian?" discussion and slide lecture I remember most clearly was bookish and benign, resting softly on the assumption that "people" meant "your eventual diners and customers" and not "you folks here in culinary school." By the time we cycled through the various permutations, from pescatarian to ovo-lacto to vegan to macrobiotic, the general level of politeness frayed a bit. By the time our chef was describing the limitations of a fruititarian diet, the jokes started and some students made disparaging comments. Everyone took the practicum more seriously, since we faced the challenge of pulling together a satisfying, nutritious, elegant, and interesting entrée without a big hunk of animal protein in the starring role (a very good exercise for anyone wanting to develop serious cooking chops in an industry where most folks are content just cooking chops). But that was one assignment out of almost a dozen in the quarter, and all the others involved practicing our skill in fabricating and cooking meats.

That's because cooking meat is a big deal in this country – which means that learning how to cook it properly is a big part of culinary school and of the business as a whole. A friend of mine was a vegetarian when she started culinary school, but she realized right away how much she'd be missing out on, just in terms of developing her palate. So she tasted everything, even if she immediately spit it out. She said she got ridiculed for doing so – and within a couple weeks, she gave up, and now eats everything. Her advice wasn't to quit being vegetarian or vegan, but raises a good question:

---

15 For links to and more information about various culinary programs, check out the rad resources page on the No-Bullshit Guides website, www.NoBSguides.com.

How will you navigate decisions like this? If a big part of culinary school is developing your palate, and much of that involves tasting meats and animal products, how and to what extent will you participate? I don't have an answer for you – these decisions and boundaries are totally personal – but do think it over, so that you're not caught off guard or feel cornered into making inconsistent decisions on the fly.

It's also important to understand that in most culinary schools, you won't get a hall pass or a *Get Out of Butchery Free* card for being vegetarian or vegan. The school I attended had two tracks – Culinary and Baking & Pastry. During my time there, I'd wager – and this is just based on anecdotal evidence and student lunch room conversations, not actual survey results – that fewer than 5% of culinary students were vegetarian or vegan. I'd guess that number was up to 15-20% in the Baking & Pastry program.

Here's the catch: Those Baking & Pastry students had to do rotations into our kitchens at least two or three times, and these were meaty field trips indeed. In their first culinary rotation, their cutting boards were set up directly across from the second-quarter culinary students working on their butchery rotation, breaking down subprimals of beef and pork, fabricating chickens in various assigned ways that included deboning them into big skin-n-meat sheets to roll up into galantines, and filleting, skinning, and portioning whole salmon. The pastry students would stand at their boards, shifting foot to foot waiting for the chef to have time to get them started, as the smell of fresh raw meat slowly took over the area.

When the chef did come over, it was with two rabbits. Breaking down bunnies was always the first task in the rotation (and we did it on the Culinary side, too) because the anatomy of the rabbit and the step-by-step process of fabricating it is a pretty good model (in miniature, and with much cheaper product) for breaking down a lamb. The vegetarian Pastry students, of which there seemed so many, didn't get out of it – these were skills they had to demonstrate in order to pass this rotation, this quarter, and ultimately this certificate and degree. Some complained, and some were deathly quiet, but they all worked through it if they wanted to continue on in the program.

A skinned rabbit looks slender and long – very much like you'd imagine a skinned cat would – so at some point, without fail, a culinary student would pass behind them and "Meow." Because we're giant bastards.

On the Rail:

- In culinary school and in most professional kitchens, animals are butchered, broken down, and fabricated every day.
- In most schools, students who are vegetarian or vegan still need to complete the parts of the curriculum that involve fabricating and cooking meats.
- Most towns have vegetarian and vegan restaurants that need skilled and creative cooks.
- Cooks are giant bastards.

*   *   *

Part 3
Seeing the Bigger Picture

Kären Jurgensen, Chef Instructor:

It's an evolution. Students come here [to culinary school] and they're all about their own stuff, and trying to get their own work figured out, and it's a very selfish thing. But they *have* to be a team. So they have to learn to be able to look outside of themselves, and that process of getting there – is annoying.

So we've talked about the shit you'll need to get sorted right away – your kit, your knives, your sparkling clean uniform. And we've talked about the basics for starting off on the right foot – respecting your instructors, being aware of the very different rules and hierarchies of kitchens, taking your other rotations seriously, and kicking ass in the classroom.

Now it's time to step back, lift our noses from our cutting boards, and start looking around. You don't want to do okay in culinary school. You want to thrive there, and learn so many skills and gain so much insight and information from the time you spend there that you never look back and wonder whether it was worth it.

So I want to look at some of the ways that you can start to really excel in school, with an eye toward how this will build the right foundation for your future cooking career. It's time to:

1. get peeps,
2. get comfortable,
3. get a job,
4. get serious, and
5. keep getting better.

Ready? We're going to dig into what I mean by each of these.

GET PEEPS

There's good reason why this comes first –it's the connections you make here in culinary school that will make this experience most valuable over the long haul.

You will never succeed in this industry alone. Every success and every failure you experience will be shared, for better or for worse. Working in the food biz – and especially in restaurants – is always a team effort. There's just too much shit to get done in too little time to try to go it alone.

> *Tom D., Culinary School Instructor:*
> This business is designed to be managed by a team; it's not designed to be run with a bunch of independent thought. There is one goal: To make our guests happy with food. It takes a lot of people to do that, and they all have to work together. If they're all thinking independently, it probably won't happen. If they all say, "No, I don't want to do it that way," then the system breaks down, the customers get pissed off, the servers don't make any money, the cooks don't make any money, and eventually everything dries up. But if everyone gets on the same page and they share that same goal, they'll all do a good job, and they'll get to go home at the end of the day satisfied that they made somebody happy and that they have some money in their pocket.

Now maybe you're thinking, "Fuck that noise! Ima get a food truck and make smoked pigface beignets all by myself!" That'll work for maybe six months tops. Either you'll call it quits or, if you should meet with any little measure of success and try to sustain the operation all on your lonesome, you'll start wishing that truck would just run you down. This is a team sport. There's a food truck in my neighborhood that does grilled cheese sandwiches – so not exactly rocket science – and they've got four dudes in there, all elbows and asses. They're inexplicably good fucking sandwiches, and like magic, all of a sudden they have a restaurant line's worth of guys in ten square feet just to keep up with the volume of customers who want to pay 10 fucking bucks for these things. And that's a *good* problem to have.

If you're going to be stuck in a team sport, you want to be playing with the best roster possible. Food industry folks have to spend a lot of time thinking and talking about and planning their staffing. They need to get the right people into the right roles, and they need to keep doing that because this is such a high-turnover industry – in large part because the work is hard and the pay is low anyway.

Now, I don't care whether you live in Buttnugget, Nevada or New York City – the restaurant business is a small one. People talk. They trade war stories, they drink too much together, they gossip like middle school girls, they say things, they hear things.

In culinary school, you'll probably be in a cohort of anywhere between three and 53 classmates at a time, let's randomly guess. My cohort was 28 at the start, and got smaller each quarter as people were either weeded or took time off to work. The people in this cohort (and the one or two on either side of yours) will remain your peers in the industry, throughout your entire cooking career. Some will bail or move on to other things, but the ones who stay in the business will scatter into restaurants all around town. They'll work in great restaurants and they'll find learning kitchens with chefs who dig being mentors. They'll leave jobs when the chef is a nutsacky asshat instead, or the owner cuts corners or doesn't pay for safe equipment, or the GM is doing shady shit. They'll work in fast, high-volume restaurants and learn badass speed, and they'll work in higher-end restaurants and learn precision that will blow your mind.

And when you keep meeting up for beers every once in a while, probably on Monday nights since that's the day that most of you will have off, at that little shithole dive bar y'all used to go to after class on Fridays? They will tell you these stories. If they respect you and like working with you, they'll help get you in the door at the great restaurant and, just as importantly, they'll warn you when they experience or hear about the other kind.

That's it? You might be thinking, this is just gossip – how is that valuable?

Let me ask you this: Do you want to hear about the nutsacky asshat chef second-hand? Or do you want to take a new job, all excited to work for this guy, only to have him rip your throat open halfway into a Saturday rush and shit down your windpipe? That's a hard choice, but I'll pick the gossipy story over a beer with a mate. You?

As soon as you start school, you're building your network of contacts, peeps, and eventually co-workers. If you do well in school (and you know by now that I mean working hard and learning solid skills, not just getting good grades – no one but yer mum gives one fuck about your grades once you're out of there) and your peers know you're solid, they will help you throughout your whole career in cooking, just as you'll help those you dig and respect.

So here's my very best advice. If you take one thing away from this entire book, let it be this: Approach culinary school like it's the longest job interview you'll ever tackle. You're not only being interviewed by your instructors, you're being interviewed by your peers.

I had a classmate in culinary school who was (and is) totally lovely, but bless her little heart, she was quick to delegate, quick to narc, and not nearly as quick to clean. And I don't remember what particular little thing had ticked me off at the time, but I do remember the day I looked at her and thought to myself, *I will never hire you.*

Is that arrogant and ratbastardly of me? Yes, absolutely. Do we all think things like that when we have to work closely with people in stressful, fast-paced, high-pressure situations? I'd bet my mother's teeth the answer is yes.

As soon as you realize how hard kitchen work is, and how important it is to have a solid team in place to tackle a busy service, you're going to start evaluating your peers.

And guess what? They're doing the same.

The Three Questions Everyone's Asking

When you're first working with people in culinary school, and then later in restaurant kitchens, they're going to be wondering three things (even if it's just subconsciously):

1. Can I count on you?
2. Do I enjoy working with you?
3. Can you cook?

"Can you cook?" is #3. You're in culinary school to learn to cook; you'll get better and better at it. You'll enter kitchens green as fuck, and your cooking skills will skyrocket if you're serious about learning them. As long as you hang in there and stick with this work, that question will start to answer itself.

But the other two? Those aren't as easy to teach, and that makes them more important.

Show Up. And Then Keep Showing Up.

The #1 thing that your classmates, and later your kitchen crew, will want to know is: Can I count on you?

Ideally, you'll end up working in a kitchen that pushes you – that's busy and innovative and creates lovely food and demands the very best of you. That's how you grow and improve, because the only way to pull off that level of consistent achievement is to work as a well-oiled machine – each of you serving your own functions effectively, and then working together smoothly. Every night, always.

If there's a star in a kitchen – a hot shit chef, a rising prodigy, a TV personality, an award-winning genius – that person is succeeding because he or she has put a team in place that functions beautifully. A kick ass chef needs a pirate crew of killer cooks. Every kick ass line cook needs a badass dishwasher. All the parts of the machine function together – there is no solo talent in a kitchen, because any brilliant idea needs to be executed again and again, brilliantly every time.

So the number one question in any kitchen is: Can I count on you?

The most basic version of this is: Can I count on you to show up on time for your shift, clean and reasonably healthy and ready to work? Nobody in a kitchen crew wants to spend one single second of brain power wondering if you'll show up. You want to be the kind of line cook who is so dependable and so reliable that if you're ten minutes late, your coworkers skip right to worrying that you're dead.

Tom D., Culinary School Instructor:

It's a crazy business, and you never really know who's going to show up. Hopefully your guests always show up, but you might not have a full crew working. You have to communicate with each other and form a game plan, whether you're in the FOH or BOH.[16] You have to get organized and do it together – if you don't, you'll get crushed, buried under the onslaught of business.

The biggest hit to your reliability score is called a no-call no-show, when you don't show up for work, and you don't have the nuts to call and give them a heads up. Even with a couple hours notice, a sous or a chef can call someone else in and shit can keep

---

16   Check it out – this here guide has a glossary. Any terms that are randomly underlined like this will be defined in Part 5, way at the end. If you haven't encountered industry terms like BOH, finger condoms, or French top before, flip back to see what they mean. If there are terms you wish I'd defined, or ones you feel I've left out, just email me through the website at www.NoBSguides.com and let me know. Or share your favorite kitchen language and swear words. I'd love to hear those, too.

rolling along. Do this a couple times and you'll still be out of a job, but you're not fuck-ing the whole kitchen. But no call at all? Ten minutes into your shift, and they're having to call around and see who can drop everything and get in as soon as possible? The chef who just worked 11 days straight needs to come in on her one day off? The owner needs to get a chef's jacket on and work pantry until they can find someone to cover? That's when you've burned a bridge, and the food industry in most towns and cities is a smaller world than you might imagine. Word gets around when you show people that you can't be counted on.

I overheard an interesting conversation at school once. A student asked one of our Chef Instructors for a recommendation and she flat-out said no. I was surprised – he was a stronger student, had experience in restaurants already, and wasn't a total mouth-breather. Why no? As it turns out, he'd once confessed to her that he'd pulled a no-call no-show at a kitchen job. I never heard the details, but he'd probably been fired and eventually told her why. Now, months later, she was still totally unwilling to give him a job reference. He'd violated the core principle of teamwork (show up), and she didn't trust him not to do it again – which meant she'd be damned if she was going to put her name forward and recommend a guy to a kitchen crew that he might end up letting down.

But this is just school – everyone plays hooky once in a while, right?

Yep, they sure do. But if culinary school is like an extended job interview with your peers, why act any differently in school than you'll act when you work in kitchens?

When your classmates are absent or disappear on you for a while, when they think of their dish pit rotations as sick days, or don't show up for cleaning days at the end of the quarter, you notice, don't you? And if you're like me, there's some part of you that's thinking: Fuck you, I showed up for this. What are you, too good for the dish pit? And does that make you better than I am, because I showed up and I'm working my ass off today?

When you graduate and you get a rad job in a great kitchen, and your chef says, "Hey, do you know X? He's applying for a job here and it looks like he went to your same school," that first reaction – in that one second, when your chef is looking right at you – matters. If it's someone who let you down in school, and you shrug and say, "He's okay," that speaks volumes.

The whole point of culinary school is to prepare you for professional work, right? So start practicing the simple habit of showing up now. Be the one who shows up, even for the shit jobs. Be the one who's so dependable that people love being partnered up with you on rotations and projects. When a chef asks an old classmate of yours, "Hey, do you know so and so? She's applying for a job here and says she went to your school," you want them to say, "Oh cool. she's awesome. The dude you always wanted to work with on group bullshit."

Showing up is the first way you demonstrate you can be counted on. But once you're there, the teamwork really starts. That's when your classmates and coworkers are wondering:

- Can I count on you to hold down your station like a pro, and not disappear for no reason? Or take a longer lunch than you need? Or be out smoking every time we get <u>hammered</u>?
- Can I count on you to work your hardest, so that you can help the rest of us when we're <u>slammed</u>?
- Can I count on you to <u>mise</u> me out when you're on the shift before mine, so you've set me up to succeed, and not fucked me from the minute I clock in?
- Can I count on you to stay and clean up well, so we're all ready to do this again tomorrow?

There are a million more examples, but you get the idea. When real, no-bullshit, super-effective teamwork is what gets you through rushes that can make this job feel like you're fighting a war instead of serving plates of yummy food to people, you need to become a strong team player.

Which is equally to say – if you are already a strong team player, and your default is already to be reliable and responsible, you have a huge leg up in this field, even if you're a total noob. Even if you can't <u>julienne</u> to save your life. A culinary school instructor – hell, one of your peers – can teach you a specific knife skill in ten minutes, and with enough practice you can have it basically dialed in that week. Way easier than trying to get through to the dude (we all know one) who never quite learns to be reliable or act responsibly. So if you're feeling overwhelmed about all the information and techniques you'll learn in school, keep the bigger picture in mind. People who already know they can count on you will take the time to teach you anything else you need to know.

Kären Jurgensen, Chef Instructor:

Teamwork is everything. There are very few one-man shows.

One example: If you don't set up the cook coming in for their shift well, the whole business can go down. You get the restaurant reviewer in that night, and you've had to 86 everything, you've lost money. If the dishwasher doesn't show up, then you're doing dishes. There is a hierarchy in the kitchen, but each part of that brigade is *crucial* to the rest of the system.

There's also teamwork between the FOH and BOH that has to happen. This gets lost a lot. Cooks are always quick to blame somebody who's not in the kitchen, but if you had to go out to that table and tell them why their meal was burned, or not the way they wanted it – you should be grateful for the FOH, right? Trying to put yourself into someone else's shoes really plays into being a better team member.

Michelle Nguyen, Chef:

We're always helping each other out.

In kitchens, you're always doing multiple things at once. You might have a stock going, and a sauce, and something is braising. Teamwork means that everyone is aware – if you notice a stock is starting to boil, you turn it down. If you hear a timer, you check the oven, even though it's not yours. It's not big things, it's little things – keeping an eye out, looking at what's on the stove. If something looks like it's about to burn, you pull that shit off, you don't just stand there and shout "Hey something's burning over here!"

You pitch in. If you're done with a task it's not the time to say, "Alright, I'm done." You go around and you ask, "How can I help you?" At my last restaurant, we had two sous chefs, and my co-sous and I worked very well with each other because we always tried to do something for each other.

We never really worked the same shifts, but when it came down to the prep work we had to do, we would always try to find ways to get through what we needed to do and then help the other person get set up for the next day, too.

Teamwork is not just looking out for yourself, but also looking out for others, and then everything goes way more smoothly, and it's way less stressful. That translates into the food being better, too. If everyone's working really well together, it's like a symphony – it all works well and sounds beautiful and tastes beautiful.

When things aren't a symphony – how do you get through those shifts?

You get through the shitty days, and then you make yourself a strong drink – and sit down and decompress a little bit, and always think it over. Any time I have a bad experience, a bad day, a bad *whatever*, I analyze it, think critically about it. What should I have done better? Where did it start to go wrong? I work backwards and think about how I could have prevented it, or what I'd do differently next time. A chef is constantly problem solving. That's how I get through a really bad day – a stiff drink and then think back, analyze, solve it in my head.

Be Rad (or at least Don't Be a Dick)

The next question people are probably asking themselves is: Do I enjoy working with you?

I'm not saying you need to be inspiring, pleasant, joyful, even likeable – if that were required, every kitchen in the land would be radically understaffed, and most of us would be home eating Hot Pockets. Kitchens are like pirate ships. You might be a foul-mouthed, STD-ridden band of misfits, but you get the job done and you have a decent time doing it.

I can't tell you how to be enjoyable to work with – you have to decide what that means to you, and how to go about being your best self more often than your worst self.

For me? I don't like working with dicks. That's where my bar is set in kitchens. I prefer the pirate version of professional and cheerful – yes, our communications may be peppered with cuss words and funny insults and might be more direct than I was used to before working in kitchens, but there's a basic respect underlying things. We value being on the same team. We're working together, not against each other. When one of us fucks up, the rest jump in to keep shit rolling. That's ideal for me. You might have a totally different ideal. But I think we can probably all agree: Start by not being a dick.

My definition of dick isn't necessarily yours – which is good, since you really don't want a grumpy lesbian defining what dick is for everyone else. We're going to drill down more deeply into dickitude in greater detail in the sections that follow, so don't worry that this is pretty general. We'll talk about sharing, delegating, and communicating with jerks and with friends. We'll talk about what to do when things go wrong, and when things go right.

As you read through all the various scenarios that follow, though, personalize them. I don't know you yet, so I'm reaching out the best I can to offer advice that will help you kick ass in culinary school – but these ideas come out of my own approach. Make them yours. If you read a response and think, "I'd never say that," no worries. What would you say? What's your best response? And how can you prepare yourself mentally to respond that way under stress, and not with your worst possible response?

When I ask, "Do people enjoy working with you?" I'm not looking for a right answer, or a checklist of do's and don'ts. I just hope you'll keep the question itself in mind every once in a while, think about how you move through school and kitchens and the world, and evaluate whether you're putting your best out there, whatever that may mean to you.

On the Rail:

- In this business it's all about the team. Make it a priority to learn to play nice with others.
- Approach culinary school like it's a super-long job interview, and understand that you're actually being interviewed by your peers.
- Being reliable and working hard is more important early on than knowing how to cook.

*   *   *

THE TRIBE

I've used the word tribe a couple times already, and that's intentional.

Cooks and chefs and all the various folks who work in restaurants, catering companies, food suppliers, vendors, culinary schools, and all the other weird corners of this massive industry are like a tribe, and a brilliant one at that. Did I mention that I love food industry folks?

> *Michael Jordan, Chef Instructor:*
>
> We tend to feel we are – and historically we have been – the dregs of society. Until Escoffier, this was not a job that anybody wanted. You would be *told* to go work in kitchens. You might be from prison, and you might get beaten – it was terrible work, rough and rowdy work, and male dominated. You put guys together, and it's of course about who's the toughest. Although there's not just one type of approach – you see the down and dirty, you see the prim and proper, and they all do well in kitchens. It's not necessarily who you are, so much as loving what you're doing. And I love that about it, too.
>
> I have to be careful at school, because I have a potty mouth. And every chef I've ever worked for did. That's the fun of it, too. You're in the back, and you can swear and cuss, and you're working hard – it's a wonderful melding of common labor and high artistry. You don't find that combination very often. It's a very unique mentality.
>
> That subculture drew me to restaurants – this offbeat society – and I really enjoy the underground type of mentality that cooks have. Hell, we don't even *start* drinking 'til midnight. In New Orleans, we'd get off at midnight, get home around six, go back to work at one o'clock – it was a total lifestyle, and it was fun.

This is a big industry – one of the biggest – so it's easy to forget that it's still a tribe. That you can belong in it, and also that you can fuck up enough to basically be run out of it. That's a really important thing to keep in mind. In any given city, the food industry is smaller than you might imagine. You'll start seeing the same folks over and over again. You'll start to learn to spot the menus, restaurant styles, career movements, and vocal opinions of chefs in town, for example. You'll start to hear gossip about which of these chefs are great to work for and which ones are total <u>douchekazoos</u>. Which ones run tidy ships and which ones run sloppy and shitty <u>FIFO</u> graveyards of rotting food. Which ones love to teach, and which ones love to scream.

All of that is also happening in the tiny parallel universe of your culinary school. As the 50, 150, or 300 of you come together to work and to learn, you'll start to form opinions about your peers. You'll be psyched to be partnered up with some of them, and you'll dread working with others. You'll learn a ton from some, and others will seemingly exist solely to fuck with you.

You will carry this knowledge into the rest of your cooking career – as will they. That's why, even though you're all in school together to learn, you need to put your best foot forward.

Second quarter in my school program was when we got turned loose for the first time into the main kitchen, and our job was to make student lunch for everyone in all the other quarters. That was just our official job – our real task was to get used to moving around and working in a commercial kitchen without killing ourselves or anyone else.

We were partnered up for the whole quarter with the same person, moving from station to station together. I was paired up with a Turkish guy named Oğuz (sounds like Ohwz). He came into the program with more industry experience than anyone else in our class, so this was a clear career move for him. He wasn't dinking around trying to decide whether he liked cooking or not. He was all in.

He was fast as shit, and I started to have such complete faith in his ability to bang shit out that I could let go of a lot of my "Are we going to finish this?" anxieties and just focus on getting it done. He could sometimes over-rely on his speed, though, and end up running fast, but in circles. I had more practice with organizing and planning, and he never seemed to mind when I offered ideas or strategies or even direction. Our skills complemented each other, and we worked really well as a team.

Most importantly, we were both really hard workers, who were in the habit of trying to look around and see what needed to be done, and not shy away from doing it. If I needed to find him, and I could see his prep was done or his food was rolling fine, I'd look for him at the sink because he'd be doing the dishes and pans that piled up when everyone else ditched them there. Fast forward to fourth quarter – I'm standing at my station and I look over and see him still banging through other people's pots and pans at a different sink in a different (and much nicer) kitchen, and I think to myself with such crystal clarity: There is nothing I won't do to help this guy succeed. He's the real deal. If I can ever work with someone to start something, I'll go to him first. If I can ever help fund something, it'll be his project or restaurant. I'll be loyal to him my whole cooking career because I respect him and I believe in him, because he showed up and he worked his ass off, and because he was never too good to roll up his sleeves and do the dishes. He took his job seriously, and he demonstrated over and over again that he had my back, and that he's a team player in the best possible way.

Did he make mistakes? Yes. Did I occasionally want to smack him upside the head with a spatula? Yes. Am I quite certain he felt the same way about me sometimes? Oh yeah. I'm not saying that Oğuz was perfect, or that I was anything close to perfect, or that you have to be perfect. We're all in school to make mistakes and occasionally over-reach and fail and fuck up – and better to do that here in school than in a restaurant job – so quiet your inner perfectionist and take those risks and put yourself out there.

You don't ever have to be perfect. But you do have to show up with your best self. Show up with your work ethic. Show up with your openness to learning and the best of your problem-solving abilities.

Keeping showing up – for yourself and for the people you work with.

Becky Selengut, Private Chef:

I've had some rough experiences, but in general people are very family-oriented toward other people in the industry. I feel very connected – it's almost like the feeling you'd have for the people in a small-town high school. So anyone in your age group, say plus or minus five years – you've all moved through various jobs, you know each other from those jobs or from culinary school, you've met their friends and hang out with them at weird hours, or you've met them through common connections. The only currency we really had in the restaurant world was stoking each other out when we'd go to each other's places. So it felt very connected.

There's also that high school feeling because there's a lot of fracturing – there is so much addiction, and a lot of people get messed up and drop out.

The bonding in restaurants was much more intense, but I also feel connected to other teachers and private chefs now.

On the Rail:
- This may be a big industry, but restaurant folks talk. Earn a good reputation.
- Start now, with your peers in school. You'll travel the same paths together for years. Many of them will be your future colleagues, cooks, chefs, food critics, meat suppliers, produce vendors, etc.

*   *   *

BUILD A SWAT TEAM

Have you ever seen that show *Survivor*?

You're probably thinking, "Have I lived under a rock for the last fifteen years?"

If you've managed somehow to avoid this pop-culture clusterfuck of a show, it's a bunch of people dropped in some tropical location who have to survive, both the harsh conditions and getting voted off weekly by the devious frenemies surrounding them. The last one standing bags a million bucks. The filthy, increasingly-malnour-ished victors usually persist by forming strong (or even passable) alliances, which is not a bad strategy to take in culinary school, and later in your cooking career (which, on a bad week, can feel like a crappy survival drama, minus the million bucks).

Get some peeps. Look for ways to help them – whether it's finding and stashing that 2oz ladle for them because you know that as <u>saucier</u> they'll spend half their day trying to pass kidney stones through a chinois, or reminding them how hot to keep the pizza oven so they don't turn their flatbreads into charcoal their first time through. Help them study, prepare for tests together, prepare your kitchen plans of action and mise sheets together – whatever ongoing assignments and repetitive preparation routines you need to get in the groove of tackling in your culinary program. Have their backs, and they'll have yours.

Grow into this industry together. Start by sharing notes:

- Where are each of you working outside of school, and what are you learning there?
- Can you help each other find <u>stages</u> and jobs outside of school, either at res-taurants where one of you gets in the door, or just by forwarding job postings you think might be a good fit?

- What products and techniques are you each getting exposed to outside of school, whether by working, volunteering, or just exploring and researching on your own? Can you get together on your days off and exchange demos, teaching each other these things?
- How can you work together to gain practical experience – like catering parties for friends or clients, or taking on volunteer gigs together? Lots of cities have regular food bank and feed-the-homeless events, and would kill for help. Pitching in together can make it more fun.

Use care when you start bringing together this team.

You'll start hanging with certain classmates organically at the start of school – you'll naturally gravitate to the people kind of like you, or roughly your age, or tatted up in the same places you are, or you'll just get more comfortable with the people sitting around you or scheduled in overlapping rotations most often.

That's a great way to start getting to know people, but when you're taking the next step of building a close support team, take more time. Stay patient, and be choosy. Seek out peeps whose style in the kitchen and whose work ethic you admire, who encourage you to be your best self, and who help you get even better. Which is to say, choose peeps who are focused, work hard, have creative ideas, like to talk about the big picture, are in this for the long haul, and are serious about continual improvement.

Share Strategy

We had one rotation in second quarter when we got free reign to cook whatever we wanted for student lunch. My partner and I worked fairly independently on it, and discussed our plans very little. Some students seemed to approach the week aiming for the easiest possible workload. That wasn't of interest to either of us, but it turned out we had really different approaches. I decided to work on time management. Could I accurately plan the time I had, and arrange my tasks throughout the week in a way that would allow me to tackle multiple recipes that required more than a single day of prep? I wanted to create complex recipes with real depth of flavor, and thereby impress my classmates with super yummy and unusual food. I didn't articulate this at the time, but that was basically my goal.

I spoke with my partner after the fact, and he had taken a totally different approach. You learn cooking by repetition, but in cooking school you might only have a day or two on each station before you move on. There's very little time to get comfortable, get your flow, and get a lot of repetition working with certain products. You might make risotto twice. A consommé? Just one time. It depends on your program, its rotations, and just plain old luck of the draw, but you could graduate from culinary school having seared three steaks, or rendered two duck breasts. Total.

So he chose the most expensive product that our chef would agree to purchase for him (a surprisingly high bar, actually), and seared 20 duck breasts in a single day – more than I'd end up working with throughout the whole program. It was a genius way to get experience and even a bit of repetition on product that would be way too expensive to buy and practice with outside of school.

As soon as he told me this I was like, <<facepalm>> I wish I had thought to do that, too! It hadn't even occurred to me, and I know that if I'd asked him ahead of time, he would've happily shared his plan. I'm not describing this situation because it created any tension while we worked together, but just to point out that being really clear about your intentions and strategies, and sharing them with others, can also be super helpful.

You Will Likely Cry. Really.

While I was in school, I was part of a fairly "formal" SWAT team of peeps. There were eight of us who were all women, all career-changers (so all a bit older), and all jumping into this new field pretty committed, if occasionally freaking out about it. I call it formal because we had an email list all set up to share info and make plans, and we met up pretty regularly. The primary thing we did was drink – we had happy hour wired – and we kvetched and gossiped and bitched and did all (okay, fine, at least a couple) of the really helpful and productive things I've just recommended. But one of our most memorable and helpful conversations was, "What do you want us to do if you ever cry at school?"

Now don't get all uppity about this being a gender thing – I saw guys break down in school too, so you can still do this exercise with your Men's Culinary Drumming Circle, and if it helps you take it seriously, you can substitute the phrase, "What should I do if you start losing your shit, bro?"

It came up because one of us – let's call her "Karen" – had a rough day and started *sniff* getting all red-faced and then full-on tearing up, and a student farther along in the program just touched her shoulder and said very matter-of-factly, "How 'bout I get you a glass of water?" And she left, and came back with the water, and damn if it didn't help, Karen reported.

So two or three drinks in, we actually went around the table one by one and said what we wanted the others to do if we ever started crying at school. Since we'd just heard Karen's story, most of us went with hand on shoulder / glass of water. Only one person said hug, at which point everyone else recoiled at that being the worst possible thing. One of us – we'll call her "Jen" – told us to ignore her completely, not even make eye contact. And "Jess" said, "So help me God, if you see me *about* to squeeze a tear out, punch me in the fucking FACE. I'm serious: Punch me as hard as you fucking can." She might've (hypothetically, of course) had a military background.

Fast forward to a few months after we had this conversation. I was broke. I mean, shit ass Charlie-Chaplin-style-pants-pockets-inside-out fucking broke. I was working as a line cook, I was always exhausted, and with so many hours of my week in school, I couldn't add more shifts to make ends meet. I was so goddamn broke, I had to ask my parents for a $600 loan to bridge the gap, and I am WAY too old to be doing that. And not just a loan. A how-fast-can-you-get-this-money-to-me loan. So I'm waiting for a check to come in the mail (*No sense of urgency, these people!*) and I get a big-ass box at the post office instead, and I haul it home on the bus wondering what's in it, but mostly praying to anybody's random god that there's a check in there, too. There was no check, but there was a brand new copy of *Modernist Cuisine at Home*. Which was lovely, and thoughtful, and at 120 bucks, not something I'd ever buy myself.

The next day I'm in school. I'm tired, I'm still worried, my mind is anywhere but at school, and so of course shit's not going well, and my partner Morgan says I seem distracted and what's up? And I start to tell her about the box and the check and the book and it seems like it's just a story until – *oh fuck, it's that flush and my face is hot, and I'm too old for this and too broke for this, and what am I doing in school, and I used to have a "real" career, and everything about that lovely, glossy, <u>Modernist</u> cookbook is disconnected from how I cook and how I eat and how I live and definitely how much I* *live on, and I couldn't afford the equipment to make even one recipe in there, and why would I want to glue chicken or spherify pea juice anyway? And suddenly this lovely and thoughtful gift seems like this emblem of disconnection, or maybe this pressure to be the kind of cook – no, food scientist! – that feels impossibly out of reach to a pantry-level line cook, and of questionable desirability anyway –* and I'm literally suffocating trying not to cry before Morgan smiled, put her hand briefly on my shoulder, and said, "Why don't I get you a glass of water?" Which was a great way to tell me: Hey, you're losing your shit. So I bugged out to the bathroom and hid for a minute until I could get it together – and the glass of water that was waiting for me when I got back? The best, most calming water ever.

This one conversation proved helpful so many times in school. There are just those days – when you haven't slept enough, you're emo for some totally unrelated reason, you're hungover, you can't get your shit together, you're <u>in the weeds</u>, you're fucking up, your instructor is riding your ass, the dog ate your mise – whatever the fuck – and all of a sudden you feel that flush come on. Having a friend in that one moment touch your shoulder and put a cup of water alongside your cutting board suddenly makes this a hilarious moment. I guarantee you will laugh, at least a little. Even if you cry a little anyways. If that involves snot, please do us all a favor and hit the hand sink and sanitize that shit up, would you?

Know how to help each other. Shit just gets real sometimes.

Most of All, Think Big

The benefits of building a solid SWAT team of peeps extend well beyond school.

At some point, you'll start working in the field. Later in this section (see *Get a Job*), we'll talk about when to start looking for work, and how much work makes sense for most culinary students. But for now, let's just pinkie swear that at some point, you will work.

I'll keep going back to the idea that culinary school is like one long-ass job interview. It's so important, I'll be harping on it like the fabulous but bitchy mother you never had (or maybe did). Here's the payoff, though – if you build a solid enough team of peeps in school, it might get you out of having to do so many of those "real" job interviews down the road.

There's high turnover in kitchens – even the good ones. This is hard work and it's not typically well paid, and people move on for all kinds of reasons. Most restaurants hire new cooks fairly often, and I've never been in a kitchen where one of us lowly line cooks knew an applicant and the chef didn't seriously ask what we thought of them.

Kristina Glinoga, Line Cook:

During most of school, it didn't matter. I was getting jobs on my own. People would ask me, "Oh, how'd you get that job?" and I was like, "Craigslist, how else?"

But I got a good job when Johnny C. was leaving to go work a cruise ship – they needed a line cook and he recommended me. Johnny's a great cook, so if he says you're a good cook, that means something. I didn't even have to *stage* there – they just asked, "When can you start?" Isn't that crazy?

It's important to value the relationships you build in school. It's a small industry, and so much is based on who you know. I've definitely gotten jobs for friends, by being a reference and telling a chef that I'd love to work with them again.

Becky Selengut, Private Chef:

Did the connections you made in culinary school matter?

In my particular cohort, not so much – but connections to the school, to the chefs, to classmates in other cohorts? Absolutely. For example, Toby was in a cohort later than mine. I knew him because I came back to teach in a different program. Immigrants and refugees would learn English in the morning, and then cooking skills at night, and I was teaching the cooking skills. I did that for two years. It was Tom D.'s old job, and when he stepped down he recommended me for the job because I knew him through his wife, Diana D., who was one of my Chef Instructors. So you can see these connections.

> In that job, I would come in right when school was ending, and got to know Toby. He told Jerry Traunfeld, the chef at The Herbfarm, where he was working while he was in school, "There's a woman named Becky who's teaching. I see her working in the kitchen and she seems great – I encourage you to give her a *stage* day."
>
> I came in, I shook the chef's hand and said, "I hear great things from Toby about working for you. I've been teaching, but I really want to learn from you, and I'd love to do a *stage*."
>
> He said, "Great. Come tomorrow." He never looked at a resume or asked questions. I did my *stage*, I did a good job, and he said, "I'd like to offer you a job."
>
> I said, "Great."
>
> Who I knew got me in, and then my performance on the *stage* got me the job.

A good word from someone you work closely with at school can get you into a kitchen faster than a lot of things, which is why you often see alliances form in this industry and the same people working together again and again as they move around town and also move up the ladder in their careers.

So when you think about forming alliances and building a close group of support, think big: You're not just helping each other through school, you might be working together for years.

On the Rail:

- Form alliances. Get peeps.
- Do well in culinary school, and your peers will be the ones recommending you and getting you into jobs down the road.
- You might cry. Come up with an emergency response plan in advance.

* * *

THE TRICKY BITS

Dealing with jerkoffs can certainly be challenging, but it might surprise you to realize that dealing with friends can be even harder.

You get peeps, you form a SWAT team, you have each others' backs, and most of the time – genuinely, the vast majority of the time – it's as smooth sailing as anything in cooking can be. Many of my favorite memories from school have to do with working with classmates who became friends.

Every once in a while, though, shit bounces off the rails. You mess something up, you let down your peeps. Or sometimes your friends screw up, or aren't carrying their weight, or annoy the hell out of you during service. This shit just happens. So let's talk about what to watch out for when working with friends – when things go well, and when they don't.

Chattiness

The quickest way to piss off most chefs and all instructors is to be chatty. That's tough for a big blabbermouth like me. I loved working with friends in the kitchen, but sometimes it was hard to turn off the part of me that wanted to chat and catch up and, you know, be friends.

> *Michelle Nguyen, Chef:*
> Somebody who talks too much bothers me. I'm always, "Less chit chat, more chop chop."

You're in the kitchen to be a line cook first (or assistant, or classmate, or whatever your role is at the moment), not a social butterfly. Kitchens are hot and intense places where you need to summon your best focus to manage multiple techniques, processes, and pieces of equipment, many of which are dangerous. Oh, you're not firing anything at the moment? Well, the folks around you are, and they need to summon that same degree of focus, not chat with your bored self. And anyway, isn't there something you could be prepping or cleaning?

Communicating More Clearly

Ages ago, I read one of those short "How to improve your relationships" lists – probably on Facebook when I should've been doing real work – and one of the suggestions has stuck with me for years: Let others win with you. It was strange phrasing, and caught my eye.

When I'm working with someone and it's not going well, I can almost always trace it back to poor communication. And almost always that cycle of poor communication has been kicked off because one or both of us is expecting something to happen, but hasn't bothered to actually say out loud what / when / how / why.

You can only control what you're bringing into the dynamic, so if the way you're working with someone is feeling clunky and frustrating, it's worth asking yourself: What are you expecting to happen that you haven't talked about? Because making that clear in a calm and positive way allows people to meet that expectation (if they so choose), and win with you.

I'm not talking about delegation – we'll talk about that in a minute, because that's trickier, and there are tons of unspoken rules in kitchens about who can delegate what to whom and why.

I'm talking about laying your cards out on the table in a really clear way that fosters good teamwork. Let's say there are two of you on entremetier, and you have a huge prep list to bang through before service. Taking a few minutes to talk and collectively work up a strategy will save you a ton of time and frustration over the course of the day. It's totally fair to jump in there and say, I've never gotten a chance to work on X, and would like the practice. Or I hate doing Y, and I'm wondering if you'd mind doing that. It's also fine to get into the details, since that's where miscommunication often happens – are the sunchokes large or medium dice? Are the romanesco spears just chopped off the stem, or are the tips carved into points with a paring knife? You're two equals sharing ideas, comparing notes, negotiating tasks, and making a plan together.

Another important time to communicate (when it might be easier to shut up and look away) is when you think a classmate is screwing up. Use care. No one likes being told they're doing something wrong. It can sometimes help to start with a question, like "Are we supposed to be [tourneting the potatoes, not dicing them? Insert expectation here]."

135

It's easier when your chef has articulated clear expectations that you can just refer to. But if it's your dish and you want something done differently? Then that becomes your job, and you still need to jump in and redirect. If you're talking to an assistant, you can say something like, "I'm sorry I didn't demo this. I'd like them done like this [walk over and show one or two as an example]." When you're talking to a peer, a more delicate approach might be better, like "I'm worried that X won't cook evenly. What do you think about doing Y?" And give a well-reasoned argument for whatever change you're requesting, so that you don't just come off like a control freak.

Giving Feedback

Your friendship is not solid if it's not based on honesty, trust, and a genuine concern for each other's well being. Which means that sometimes you just need to nut up, and act from that place of honesty, trust, and genuine concern. Be brave about giving feedback when it's needed, and be sure it comes from a good place of concern and not an ooky place of competition or jealousy.

I'm always wanting more feedback about how I'm doing. If a friend takes the time to talk to me about something that I could be doing better, he or she is doing me the best favor ever. That doesn't mean that part of me might not be a little bit butthurt to hear it, though. Taking criticism is hard, and since we all know this, offering criticism is super hard, too.[17]

If you're really going to be good friends and effective teammates to each other, start to establish patterns of honesty. You don't have to bust their nuts in the heat of the moment, but when you get a beer after class, don't dodge the day's events. Do the old, "Hey can we talk about how that all went down today?" thing, and be honest. Try to be humble about it, since your view of how things went really is just that – one person's subjective view. And try to really listen, with an open mind, because there's always going to be shit that you could've done better, too.

Think about your timing, though. Feedback isn't always helpful, especially in the heat of service, and it doesn't always come from that good place right away. If you're

---

17 When I finished a draft of this book, I sent it to a couple of good friends and told them: Don't hold back. I'm serious. I'd rather hear hard shit from you in private than from strangers in sucky reviews. What do you think, now that you're this far in? Were they sugarcoating things when they said I had a solid future as a middle school boy?

like me, sometimes it takes you a little while to get past the ooky impulse and into the good place, so give yourself that time. If you decide that something still needs to be said or resolved so that it doesn't fester – great, have the conversation when you can do it with a generous heart, not a pissy ego.

Carrying Your Weight vs. Carrying Others

Forming a SWAT team of peeps is a great way to support each other, but is there a point when your support might be too much?

For 90% of the time, you should be looking for ways to be a more supportive team player. But there will also be times when making yourself a little scarce, being less available, or letting folks figure out their own shit is actually being more helpful in the long run. Every one of you is in school to learn, so make sure that when you offer support, you're supporting their learning – not doing shit for people that deprives them of the repetition and practice that provides them that learning.

When I was partnered up with Morgan, we tried to do a really careful job of dividing up tasks. I remember lots of times when one of us said something along the lines of "I'd really like more practice at doing Z, can we swap jobs today?" or "I hate doing X and I know you can do it better, but I should get my ass over there and practice it." If she did all the shit I hated to do (or vice versa), that might have been a nice thing to do, but it wouldn't have been actual support. She was one of the best partners I've ever worked with because, among many other fantastic habits, she was relaxed and honest about offering feedback, and careful about how she offered and accepted support.

If you have a friend or partner who's less careful, and whose help starts to feel intrusive, don't get quietly resentful about it. It's your job to have good boundaries, so that's when you can say – ideally in a calm and not aggro-weirdo way – thanks so much for your help, but I've got this.

I had a friend who was in the weeds on the garde manger station, and I jumped in to help out, which solved the short-term problem. Instead of thanking me, she said, "I need to do this. You can't just jump onto my station." And I thought she was a cow for saying that, and I hated her for five whole minutes, nurturing brief fantasies of letting her sink. And then I realized, yeah, she's right, so I stopped hating her and became a slightly better partner because of that valid criticism.

On the Rail:
- Most chefs hate chattiness.
- You can almost always communicate more clearly. Start practicing the skill now, while the stakes are lower than in busier and more dangerous restaurant kitchens.
- Both giving and receiving criticism is hard, but honesty is super important in this field.
- You can be too helpful – give others the space to learn.

* * *

THE KILLERS

Becky Selengut, Private Chef:
Don't be cocky. Don't be cocky. Don't be cocky. God, the students in my school who were so cocky. You will know more than someone, and you'll know a lot less than someone else. Don't put it in people's faces. Don't make people feel bad that they don't know something. Be humble.

We've talked a lot about good habits. Now let's talk about some bad ones.

There are times when you really shouldn't need trial and error. There are just some things – like buying a ferret, or tattooing your face – that consistently cause such instant remorse, you should just leave them for others to experience. If I can save you the pain and heartbreak of trying them out yourself, how could I not share this information with you?

So let's talk now about the shit you want to avoid. These are the killers – habits that are so annoying or counterproductive that they're the teamwork equivalent of the pox. If you pull this shit enough, it will make it very difficult for you to regain the respect and regard of your peers.

If culinary school is like interviewing with your peers for future jobs, this is the kind of shit that *at best* will get you a chilly "Don't call us, we'll call you" cold-fish handshake.

Shortcuts and Disappearances

If you ever think to yourself, *no one will notice this*, please know that they will.

Sure, there are small things – you didn't glove up just then, or you went ahead and used the ingredient with too much char on it, or rinsed that oversalted shit off in the sink when the instructor wasn't looking. Your peers will notice these things, though, so really be honest about your performance each day. Instead of chuckling to yourself that you got away with it, make a genuine plan: How can I work tighter tomorrow? Where am I cutting corners or screwing shit up, and how can I plan or manage my time better tomorrow? You don't want your peers to start thinking of you as a messy or corner-cutting person.

> *Julie DuRose, Business Owner & former Corporate Director of Catering*
>
> There was this ex-Army guy in my class – I don't remember his name, but I can picture him – who used to love showing off the things he could get by with. It wasn't like "I need to save time here; I'm just going to do this shortcut in stealth mode." He would really revel in the fact he was getting by with something. He'd do things like instead of mopping the walk-in when it was his turn, he'd put a bucket of bleach water under the produce. The chef was an older guy who was super sweet, and we all loved him because he was so kind and we learned so much from him. He'd walk in and smell the bleach smell and think, yeah, that's a clean walk-in. And then our classmate would look at us like, "Aren't I amazing?"

You think anyone rushed to help that dickbag get hired after graduation?

Disappearances are also killers. Think you'll just slip away and have one more smoke, since your shit's all sorted out? Think no one will notice you're not around?

In my cohort there was a guy who'd disappear for two hours in the middle of service. Occasionally our chef would ask "Where's J?" and no J was there, and he'd shake his head or throw up his hands in frustration. But the other students? We were onto this bullshit right away, and the worst thing was to get paired up with this guy. Our disappearing girl was M. She never showed up for a dish pit rotation, or she'd check in and then vanish for the next three hours.

Were there reasons for these disappearances? Probably. Were we empathizing about that? Nope, without any real information, we were just gossiping. Are you struggling? Are you sick or addicted or facing some terrible adversity? There is such a thing as too much honestly, but it probably won't hurt to tell folks (just the once!) what's going on, and what you're doing to deal with it. And then either (1) try your best to be reliable and trustworthy anyway, or (2) hold off on school, take the time to get a handle on whatever other stuff is going on, and tackle culinary school when you know you can be reliable and trustworthy again.

If your colleagues and coworkers can't count on you to show up, it's not ultimately going to matter *why* you're not showing up. But being honest and up front with people might help, and might buy you a little goodwill while you get your shit together, if people see you're working your ass off to do so.

But just assuming no one will notice? Will never work, and will always backfire.

Blaming & Passing the Buck, or Ratting & Pointing the Finger

In culinary school you'll often be partnered up on stations or in projects, and sometimes you'll also have assistants from newer cohorts in the program who are rotating into your kitchen to learn the ropes and give you a hand. So you'll constantly be talking to your peers about how to execute tasks, and occasionally even managing them as they do so. We've already been talking about good communication – and you can *always* aim to communicate better and more clearly – but let's also focus on the kinds of shit you really want to avoid.

Things go wrong in kitchens. And when they do, your reaction will show your peers a lot about you. What you *don't* want it to show them is that you're a blaming ratbastard self-protecting throw-us-under-the-bus turdburgling little narc.

So, first off, blaming and passing the buck are out.

When you work a station – whether in a restaurant or in culinary school – you'll be responsible for a specific number of items to prep and to fire, and you'll need to do this with speed and accuracy. In restaurants, all these divisions of duties are usually clearer, because they have to be. In culinary school, though, you might be sharing your station with a classmate and dividing up tasks verbally, or your prep sheets or the necessary mise won't be as clear. Tough shit. If you and a classmate communicated poorly, or there was a misunderstanding, or they straight-out fucked up, and your chef comes to you and wants X and there is no X, or wants Y done right and Y was done anything else but right, take that fucking bullet. If it's your station, it's your bullet. Make eye contact, don't look away, and take it.

The quickest way to inspire the hate and enmity of your peers is to try to dodge responsibility in that moment – to blame others, or to throw anyone under the bus. It genuinely wasn't your fault? Fuck it. Your moment of discomfort will pass, but your reputation for being solid will last.

Kristina Glinoga, Line Cook:
I remember when an instructor in school said "Welcome to *It's Your Fault.*" Oh, was your sous chef supposed to fill your plate warmer? Oh, was your partner supposed to get sani buckets for you? Oh, was your commis supposed to chop your parsley? Welcome to *It's Your Fault.* To this day, if my line partner lets me down, well shit – I should have checked that before service.

Similarly, ratting and pointing the finger are also out.

Let's say you have an assistant for the day. Awesome. You can make them do all the shit you don't want to do, and you could use the help because you have a monster-long prep list.

So let's say you told your assistant 20 minutes ago to do X and Y, and you haven't checked in since. You're cruising along doing your tasks, and all of a sudden your chef is looming over your assistant (who's probably shitting themselves if this is their first time in this kitchen) and saying the equivalent of "What the hell is this business?"

Everything an assistant does for you is *your* responsibility. If someone is helping you out and they're doing something wrong, it's *exactly the same* as if you yourself were doing it wrong. Because at any moment, you could've stopped them and shown them how to do it differently.

So the ONLY acceptable responses are ones like:

- "Yes, Chef, I'll fix that."
- "I'm sorry, I didn't understand that. We'll redo it."

- "These onions were on the <u>please use shelf</u>, but yes – I chose to use them. I'll fix this." (This is as close to "not me" as you should skate. It's anonymous – you're not blaming an individual who cut the onions – and you're still taking responsibility for the decision to use product that wasn't prepared well. This does NOT work if you say, "Joe cut these, but I chose to use them." That still makes you sound like a fuckwit).

Unless you want to spend the rest of your cooking career working at the Douche Canoe Palace, you won't blurt out things like:

- "I didn't cut these." (But you *did* choose to use them anyway)
- "My assistant burned this rice." (Why weren't you supervising him / her better?)
- "Jack did this." (If your Chef's looming over you waiting for an answer, it probably means this dish is your responsibility, not Jack's).

When you throw your helpers under the bus – however experienced or inexperienced, fast or slow, accurate or downright dim-bulbed they may be – then at best you look like an ineffective and crappy manager. At worst you look like a petty twit.

Don't Shit Where You Eat

Ah, the joy of a phrase that works well both literally and metaphorically.

This is, taken literally, excellent advice: Please do keep food and poop separate! That test you'll need to take for your ServSafe certification? And for your food handler's card? Just remember: Don't mix poop and food! See how easy that is?[18]

I first heard the proverb "Don't shit where you eat" in Turkey, and it's a great metaphorical caution to act with great care in the places (and with the people) you'll need to spend a lot of time around. Our proverb "Don't burn your bridges" means don't leave people so angry that you can't go back and interact with them again. But what if you don't have the luxury of choosing whether or not to go back? What if they're the

---

18   We had a sanitation instructor in first quarter who was wacky funny. "Look back through the entire stretch of human history," she told us one day, gesturing broadly, "and the real disasters? Every single one comes right back to sex or poop, alright?" Her advice when traveling in places with questionable sanitation was, "If I'm gonna eat poop, I want it fried, alright?"

people you have to keep on seeing and working with, day in and day out? Then you *really* better be careful about stinking the place up.

When Turks roll out the "don't shit where you eat" proverb, though, what they *also* mean is don't fuck your colleagues. And that's definitely what I mean.

Culinary school is intense, and all that teamwork under so much pressure means you will make some really good friends really quickly. Take your time, so that these intense and quick friendships don't get too close too fast. School can be really fun! And sex can also be really fun! But both of these usually stay more fun over time when you're doing them with different (groups of?) people. So do try to resist the urge to multitask in this particular way.

Most of us are either super positive or super drunk at the very start of a relationship – this person is amazing! And sexy! And interested in me! And has a pulse! Taking your time to explore all this great newfound information is important, because you're going to be working with your cohort of classmates for months, even years. And the last thing you want is to jump into something in a hasty way that eventually ends badly, creates ages of awkwardness, and starts to divide the team that you and all your classmates (or coworkers, since this advice applies equally in restaurants) need to create and sustain. Because when shit like this goes down, everyone gossips about it, and if shit goes south, everyone is affected.

Conflicts in kitchens are already difficult to manage without attaching any other awkward and heavy dynamics to them. So, while your clothes are still on, imagine for a moment that you're the student sous chef for the day, and you're supposed to be managing all your peers, and service is going really badly because some of these peers aren't pulling their weight. You're trying to be professional and slightly intimidating, as you stare down a classmate who's screwing around and about to sink the whole ship – do you really want that to be a classmate who's seen your O-face and knows where your awkward birthmarks are? Or, imagine *you're* the one having a rough day and causing service to suck. Do you want the person "disciplining" you to be someone who knows your deepest insecurities and your gossipy thoughts about other classmates – and recently broke up with you?

Nope, nope, nope. You really do not want either of those things.

If the chemistry and respect and interest is real, it'll still be there when school's over. In fact, if it's meant to be, it will have grown to an epic tension by then, and be a million times more intriguing. Get your certificate or degree, thank your instructors, have some beers with your classmates, and then by all means, fuck any or all of them to your lil heart's content. But try your very best to wait until you're all out of school to do that.

On the Rail:

- If you ever think to yourself, "No one will notice this," please know that they will.
- Welcome to *It's Your Fault*. Also, get comfortable with *The Buck Stops Here*.
- Don't shag your classmates until you're done with school.

* * *

GET COMFORTABLE...

This is such a physical line of work you're getting into, that it's really important to learn your body, to work with it, and to take really good care of it. Instead, lots of restaurant cooks take a work hard, play hard approach, and abuse the shit out of their bodies. It's easy to do. In fact, it's much harder *not* to do that.

You're in culinary school to learn the best way to do things and to start building good habits from the start, though, so let's look at some really basic habits you can build now that will be helpful to a long cooking career.

Walk Faster

Our first quarter instructor used to bark at us, "Sense of urgency, people!"

His kitchen was the farthest away from the rest of the "main" kitchens, probably so that as total noobs we wouldn't get hazed quite as badly by the nefarious students in more advanced quarters. Watching him walk the long hallway between these kitchens was always a delight. Put this dude in a roadrunner cartoon and all the other characters would look like they were standing still.

Don't ever run in a kitchen. That's just idiotic and dangerous, and makes you look disorganized and flustered. Conversely, sauntering usually doesn't make you look hip and way ahead of the game; it often comes off as lazy, and you just get in people's way.

If you do have to walk somewhere, do it at a good clip. There will be generally-accepted traffic patterns in your school and in the kitchens where you work; pay attention and follow them, and then keep moving. Walking with quick purpose conveys intention and purpose, and a sense of urgency that instructors and chefs typically want to see.

Move Less, ya Giant Spaz

I said "*If* you do have to walk somewhere," because the goal is not to be doing quick laps around the joint. The goal is to cook, and that requires a different type of physical energy.

In culinary school and then in the restaurant biz, you're going to be spending long days on your feet, and everything you're doing will be intensely physical. So you want to learn to be super smart about how you use your energy and your body.

First, develop efficiency of movement away from your station.

We talked about this a bit already in the "share like a benevolent and wise adult" section earlier on, but always try to come into the kitchen prepared, and set yourself up well at the start of your cooking time (which is a good habit to carry right into how you start each restaurant shift). Be mad efficient about this. Our chef who hammered on this point the hardest had us write up our product and equipment mise sheets in the order we'd actually move around the kitchens. If we had our shit together, we could make one circle through the dish pit, the pots & pans room, the kitchens, and the various walk-ins, and in less than eight minutes have all the product and equipment we'd need for the whole day. If you're always running around like a chicken, stop it. Put more time into your preparation, and join a gym after school if you want to jog in circles. You'll save time, and you'll save your knees.

Second, develop efficiency in movement at your station.

You've hustled all this product and equipment back to your station like some hyper-efficient hunter-gatherer on crack. Now, set up your station to minimize unnecessary movement and maximize muscle memory:

- Set up your core kit – your basic two or three knives, your bench scraper and peeler, or whatever you use the most each and every day – exactly the same way around your cutting board, every single time. Once you get the hang of where you like to have things, lock that in and never vary it. Eventually, when you need your paring knife, for example, your hand will start moving for it before you even think about it.

- Everything you'll need the most of / most often stays closest to you. Everything you'll need rarely is further away. That's true for both product and equipment.
- Use your space super efficiently, and find the best-sized pans for your mise, so that you're decreasing the number of times you need to reach and lean. Use the space overhead, if you have hooks above your station. Ditto on any shit in your <u>lowboys</u>. Can you set things up so that you're not constantly bending over or going down to a knee? In the tiny kitchen I worked in, we couldn't – and after months my knees hurt terribly, all the time.

Once you get your station set up, and you roll into service, make fewer movements:

- Get in the habit of moving efficiently and even strategically. If you've got multiple tickets in, and you can reach up for three pans once instead of one pan three times, you're a ninja.
- Any time you're making a lot of extra movement – flailing, walking and then stopping, turning literally in circles, dropping shit, tripping, etc. – it's probably because you're in the weeds and you're totally flustered. Your mind is flooded, and your body is responding to the silent command center with random hurry. This is when you're most likely to injure yourself. Try your very, very best – this will really only come through genuine practice – to stop and take a breath and try to regroup. Those seconds you spend pausing will save you so much time if you're able to get back on the rails. Over time, try to catch yourself earlier and earlier – deep breath, take stock, still the body, reengage the mind, and figure out *just the very next step* you need to take to get back on track.
- You probably won't become ambidextrous, but what's it called when you make equal use of both arms? Ambi-arm-ulous? Become that. It will help you twist and reach less. I took a bartending class outside of school about halfway through my program, and I couldn't believe how much this one change – using both arms easily instead of always defaulting to my dominant arm – increased my speed and efficiency. I felt like an Aikido-octopus.

All this leads right into...

Work With Your Body, Not Against It

There was a woman in my culinary school who was painful to watch. She'd be doing something super simple, like standing at a cutting board with plenty of space to work, julienning a pile of carrots – and it would be like watching a one-person game of Twister in progress. She'd somehow have the inside of her right wrist practically facing the ceiling, her body at totally the wrong angle, her elbow shoving into her appendix. If she was a cartoon character, she'd be *The Anti-Ergonomitron! Awkwardly Sowing Physical Discomfort Across the Land!* You'll be so surprised to hear she was slow as fuck and relentlessly inefficient – probably because she was always working against her own body. Don't be like that. If you're always feeling twisted up and sore, talk to your instructors about changes you can make, and start paying more conscious attention to untwisting.

In third quarter, our chef led us through a demo on how to break down round fish. We each had a couple trout to fillet, and he talked us through one before setting us loose and walking around the room coaching. Third quarter, you're asking? Yeah, pretty late: Most of us had broken down plenty of fish before that.

But the demo was a revelation to me, because he started it well before you'd even reach for your knife: Where are your feet? What's the angle of your hips? How far forward should you lean, and what motion does your whole body make to enable that smooth follow-through you need? It was like a guru descended from a misty mountaintop and taught me The True Yoga of Fish Boning. It turns out filleting a fish is a whole-body thing, and when you get your physical flow right, it becomes easier and you get a lot more accuracy over a much longer period of time. Who knew?

A heads up to the women in the kitchen – we'll sometimes have to adjust and adapt these lessons we're taught, or find mentors who can show us how to tackle some of the things that won't be immediately obvious if we're working or learning in a sausagefest setting. I am really goddamn strong, and it still makes me crazy to see how much dudes who are way scrawnier than me can lift straight out in front of them. My center of gravity is so much lower that I often need to get some hip into things.

Julie DuRose, Business Owner & former Corporate Director of Catering
    I had a mentor who really taught me how to move heavy things. It's difficult to explain in writing, but women just can't carry the same amount of stuff in the same way. She was graceful but systematic, and said, "We have to learn how to move things differently." Her overall advice was to get as much bone as you can under whatever it is, and use your hips and your legs so much more. I often move heavy things using my thighs as a supporting structure.
    Guys will just carry something out in front of them, because their arms and shoulders are stronger. We just can't do that, and we don't *have* to do it like the guys are doing – you don't want to work in a kitchen where they're going to make fun of you for moving something differently.

This is a physical job (duh, right?), so it's really important that you develop the habit of working with your body, not against it. This is the point when I really want to advise you to exercise regularly and do yoga classes, or take up martial arts of some sort. Have I done any of this? I have not. Should I? I absolutely should. In this field, we all absolutely should.

So I'm telling you that all this is important, but I can't really teach you much more about how to do it. I only found out that I *have* a mind-body connection about three years ago. Up until that point, by body was an abstract set of occasionally-malfunctioning parts that existed to transport my brain to places it wanted or needed to go. So learning how to work with my body has been a process for me, one I'm still learning.

Here's what I see, though. A lot of kitchens aren't designed in helpful and <u>ergonomic</u> ways that will help you to protect your body and develop the endurance you need to work in this field over the long haul. So that's going to be your job, and it's not one you can ignore. I see a lot of young line cooks working their way up in kitchens at the cost of their own bodies – it's like they're cutting out chunks of their future bodies and selling them now. They're giving their knees and joints and shoulders to the cause. If they're drinking a bunch to have fun and to come down from a busy shift, and then shooting quad shots of espresso to gear up for their next shift, they're putting their own livers and kidneys on the menu, cutting them out and serving them up in their restaurant, bit by little bit.

If you're older, entering kitchens as a career-changer, you'll notice this shit because you'll be quicker to get sore, tired, and even injured. No one should wreck their bodies for a job, but you don't even have the short-term luxury of pawning off spare parts like the 22-year-olds you'll be working alongside.

So while you're in school, start paying attention to your body. If you don't have a yogini-like instructor who can walk you through the ergonomics of the tasks you're learning, ask questions. Pay attention to how your best instructors stand during demos. When they break down a primal cut, you're probably looking at their knife, but where are their feet? Their hips? Their shoulders? That smooth motion that makes the process look so easy – how is their body moving to execute that again and again with such accuracy?

On the Rail:

- Sense of urgency is a big deal in cooking. Show some hustle.
- Develop efficiency of movement, both in setting up your station and in working it.
- Start paying attention to the physical flow of tasks, and learn on a muscle-memory level how to work with your body, not against it.

*   *   *

...BUT NOT TOO COMFORTABLE

Don't Touch People

Kitchens are dangerous places full of potential hazards, and as you learn to navigate your way through them, the last thing you want to worry about is other people running into you. That's why there are so many audible calls in kitchens: *Corner, Sharp on your right, Hot behind* (to which some smartass, often me, will *always* say, "Thanks man, you too!"). It's crucial that we know where people are so that we can all avoid potentially dangerous collisions. Someone careening around the kitchen like a drunk person will raise everyone's stress level a ton.

The only time I ever lost my shit at school was on the one-woman Twister I described above. She also seemed to be missing that mental GPS card that pinpointed where her body was relative to other people. As a result, she was constantly running into people. Constantly. Even typing this (years later!) fills me with rage. I'm working on that.

So one day in particular, she runs into me three different times – mostly in my quarter's kitchen, where she doesn't even need to be. So I'm standing at a sink, leaning in and washing something, literally as far out of anyone's way as I can possibly be, and she runs into me from the side, and I wheel around and say, low and furious, "You have run into me four fucking times today," and she gapes at me, like some wide-eyed Weebles Wobble, not even aware of having done so, "and if you touch me one more time, I'm going to punch you in the throat." I do not advocate doing this! Christ, I probably could have gotten expelled for threatening another student with bodily harm, so I'm definitely not advising you to try any shit like this. But I think it's interesting that she never ran into me again. Right?

My point is, if you're running into people or colliding with them, you're doing it wrong. Bring your attention to where you're going, call out your positions, and get that inner-GPS working.

Oh, and if you're friendly, be friendly from far. Kitchens are hot and sweaty, they're fast and occasionally frantic, and they're hotbeds of sexual harassment. So be nice from over there. And if someone is being friendly in a touchy way, it's perfectly fine to tell them to back the fuck up, because you're here to work.

Injuring Yourself

For every time you cut yourself with a knife, you'll have five or six more injuries on totally dumbshit things – you'll pinch yourself with plating tweezers, slam your hand in a reach-in door, split your whole finger open on the flat and totally innocuous-looking edge of a hotel pan. I once injured myself on a baguette. Nope, not with a bread knife – with the fucking bread.

Not to be Captain Obvious about it, but injuries are inversely related to focus. Less focus = more injuries. Great, you're probably thinking, what an epiphany, that you should focus! Now that we sorted that, we'll just all focus and kitchens will be the safest spots on earth. This no-brainer equation is, of course, a little more complicated in real (rushed, noisy, busy, fun) kitchens. You're well into a 10- or 12- or 14-hour shift and getting tired, your friend's chatting, you hear a loud sound, you start daydreaming, you're worried about the test later, you got laid last night and you're thinking back to the— that's when you lose your fingerprints in the meat slicer.

You won't always be focused and perfectly present and mindful, but try to sleep enough, try to drink enough water and eat, try not to be perpetually hungover (and please never still actively drunk). Try to get in the habit of consciously summoning your attention when you open the oven, pick up a knife, turn on the meat slicer, drop a fryer basket, climb a ladder, etc. Servers in one of the restaurants I worked at used to say "I'm here" instead of "Behind" or "Corner" or all the various ways to call attention to your location in a small and busy kitchen. I mentioned this to a friend who cooks, and he admitted (somewhat sheepishly) that whenever he's just about to do one of the many knife / slicer / fryer / ladder-type tasks he has during any regular shift, he says to himself – not out loud, though his lips move with the silent words – "I'm here."

We got to trade stories then, because I already had my own silly word rituals at work. Whenever I had to climb shelves to reach the vinegars that were stashed way above the ice machine, I used to say with every step (out loud, since it was a back storage room), "Safely." This started after my foot slipped and I almost fell in a way that could really have fucked my shit up. So up I went, "safely, safely, safely, safely," and back down the same way, like Rainman rappelling for vinegar. It was part command (to myself, to use more care? To the universe, to please conspire in my favor? Who can know what I was thinking?), and part wish / prayer / manifestation / whatever woo-woo way you want to think about it: Please let this dumb thing I have to do right now not fuck me up. I'm paying attention. I'm doing my part to make sure this goes well.

If it helps you focus and stay really present in a job that has more than its fair share of dangers, come up with your own little rituals.

Also, in no particular order:

- Never try to catch a falling knife. This sounds idiotic, but it's just a reflex. Train yourself to throw your hands up don't-shoot-style any time a knife falls to kick the temptation to reach for it.

- Never put a knife into a sink. It doesn't matter if it's full of water or not. You drop a knife in an empty, dry sink, where it's clearly visible. Other people drop pans and dishes that cover it. Someone comes along and runs water and soap into it. Someone else jumps in to help clean up, reaches in, and cuts his hand open. A friend's brother needed reconstructive hand surgery, he was cut so badly in exactly this way. Any knife stays in your hand – you wash it right away and carry it back to your station, blade pointed to the floor, calling out "sharp behind" as you go.
- Never leave a hot pan unmarked. In my school the signal was to tie a paper towel around the handle. It took three seconds and two free hands to do it, but it can prevent terrible burns. Also, no pots or pans still holding pools of hot oil or melted fats go onto the dirty dish racks for someone else to accidentally splash on themselves. Dump that shit into the compost and give your hot pans a quick rinse before you stick them on the dirty dish racks, and tie them with a paper towel.
- Always have one bone-dry towel tucked into your apron and another one in your hand when you're learning to work a hot station. Professional pans aren't like the ones at home, with rubber insulated handles. They get screaming hot, and if you try to pick one up with your bare hands, you'll feel it. Sixth pans on the edge of a French top get hot. Tongs hanging in the wrong place get hot. All this shit's metal, so have a dry towel handy for when you need to grab things. A damp towel will work for about four seconds, and *then* you'll get the steam burn.
- Learn the double-touch pick up. When you reach to pick up anything on a hot station, get in the habit of a light-tap-then-grab move. It only takes milliseconds longer, and once it's a habit, you won't even notice it. The light tap will tell you if something's hot before you're holding it firmly enough to burn your hand or having to drop a pan full of something that can splash and burn you or the people around you.

Injuring Other People

You think injuring yourself is bad? Injuring other people feels ten times worse. The worst goddamn day of my culinary school experience was the day I injured Angela.

We've already talked about the pecking order in culinary school, and when you're in the thick of it, it matters. She was in her last quarter, and her big final project was in two days. It was crunch time for her, and she needed shit to be rolling just right.

I was in second quarter, and tasked with using up a bunch of please-use plantains by frying them up for student lunch. They spit up and spattered, and I was still scared of the deep fryer, so I was leaning away from it and doing these crappy hesitant drops. I can think of five better methods now (lower them in with a spider, use the basket better, etc.), but I didn't think of them that day. Angela slid in next to me to use the other side of the fryer. I leaned in to drop the plantains, the oil spat up at me, I flinched and pulled back at the wrong moment, and the oil splashed up bigtime – not on me, though. On her. I burned the shit out of the inside of her wrist, up her forearm, maybe her palm. All the sensitive bits. She cursed loudly, threw her tools into the fryer, and walked off. The fryers were in the center of noisy, busy, interconnected kitchens. They all went quiet.

Hurting yourself on the job is a bitch, but hurting someone else feels worse. I was like a zombie. I fished her tools out of the fryer, I just threw away the rest of the fucking plantains, I went and finished something else, I took some shitty looks from her friends, and when a lot of time had passed, I found her and I apologized a lot. I was so upset that that's when I got all sniffly; she isn't someone who appreciates sniffly. She was gracious about it, and far more forgiving than most people could be. But who of her cohort of classmates would be psyched to work next to me after that?

If you hurt other people, from speed or from carelessness, or even by accident, it's hard to be a valued part of a team. I haven't hurt anyone since, whether that's from extra care, a lot of fear, or just luck. I think about it a lot, though, and try to be constantly aware of where I am and what I'm doing relative to others, so that nothing like that happens again.

Alcohol

I can't write a book on succeeding in culinary school, and in the restaurant world in general, without talking about alcoholism and drug abuse, because it fucks up some of our best and most creative talent.

I know through the grapevine that there are kitchens where drugs are the norm and not the exception, though I've never encountered one of these myself, nor have my closest friends from culinary school. What I see a lot more of is a lot – a lot – a lot of alcohol consumption. And it's totally understandable – you get off work at 1 AM, all amped up from the rush of a busy service, and what the fuck else is there to do but hit a bar with the peeps you work with (who are probably awesome, and one of the reasons why working in a kitchen is so fun)? And you drink a bunch and have a great time and you're wrecked in the morning, but you're young and you do it all again the next day. And the next day. And there's nothing wrong with this, once or even a few times. But you have to know your body, listen to what it needs and what's fucking it up, and decide to take good care of it, because that shit will take a toll over time. When the kid at the movie theatre asks you if you want a senior ticket and you're 35 years old, that will be such a sad day for you. Don't let that day come.

Kären Jurgensen, Chef Instructor:

Get sleep. Don't take that <u>shift drink</u>. Save it for the weekend. Save it for Friday night. The restaurant industry is so bad for vices. You serve people all day, to the point of exhaustion, and then you get to sit down and be treated. And it is so tempting, but it's so bad for you. Take your treats on a day when you can absorb them. Otherwise, it just breeds alcoholism and poor functioning, and you don't get what you want out of school, and you don't get what you need out of work.

You work insane hours all the time, and then sometimes it's also seasonal. Maybe you went through Restaurant Week, or you're catering in the summer and you've got events stacked up, you're working all night long and getting three hours of sleep anyway, and then to turn off you drink alcohol. It doesn't help.

If you have addiction issues, seek help early and often. Alcoholics Anonymous has groups in so many cities and towns and villages – in a tiny hamlet of six or more adults, two of them have probably formed an AA group. And if that's not your jam, they'll be able to point you in the direction of other groups and resources.

On the Rail:
- Less focus = more injuries.
- Develop routines to summon your full attention whenever you do any of the high-risk tasks your days include.
- Alcohol and drugs fuck up some of our best and most creative talent. Don't let 'em get you.

*   *   *

GET A JOB

At some point, you'll start working in the field – which is the point of all this, right?

I'm continually blurring the lines between culinary school and early line cooking, since most of you will probably work a line at some point, even if that's not your ultimate goal. Culinary school is meant to be vocational training, so blurring that line is useful. Getting tunnel vision – whether that means letting your skills plateau because you're stronger than your classmates, or getting caught up in school drama – won't serve you as a cook, or in any other food industry role. I know the title of this book is *Succeeding in Culinary School*, but that's not the end goal – that's just the first step.

Unless they advertise and offer specific alternatives, most culinary schools are structured with the aim of preparing you for restaurant work. The food industry has expanded so much that there are now many more options for working in this field – from personal and private cheffing (and variations on those that include working on yachts, trains, in resorts), to food styling and photography, food writing, recipe development and consulting, importing, purchasing and sourcing, food advocacy and nonprofit work, television production, teaching gigs – the list goes on and on. As a very general rule, though, starting out in restaurants will earn you a lot of cred with industry people, whichever direction you take later on. So many folks who end up in the remote corners of food-related wonderland still have a gig or two as a line cook under their belts.

Restaurants remain the beating heart of the industry. They employ far and away the most people, and they set the tone and the pace of mainstream food trends. Knowing how they work from the inside is valuable. So whether or not it's your primary goal for attending culinary school, really consider doing some restaurant work. It's fun and intense, you'll learn a shitton (about cooking and about yourself), and it does lay a good foundation for any kind of involvement in the food industry.

In my cohort in school, I'd guess that about 60% of us wanted to go into restaurant cooking and about 40% didn't, but almost all of us planned to work in restaurants during or right after our schooling. Very few of my peers had no intention of ever working in a restaurant. So of course we had a million questions at the start of school, like:

- How do you find good jobs?
- How on earth do you get your foot in the door with no experience?
- What's a *stage*, and why would anyone work for free?
- When should we start looking for work? Right away, or once we learn more in school?
- How much should we aim to work?

Blurring the lines between school and work is good, and even important, but as soon as I started writing and interviewing peeps in the field, I realized I had way too much material for one book. So my intention is not to be slimy sales-y, but looking ahead, I want to let you know that the second book *The No-Bullshit Guide to Starting Your Cooking Career* will leave off where this one ends – that imaginary moment when you step out of culinary school and start working in the industry (which, of course, can and probably will overlap with your time in school). I'm kicking off that book with a way more in-depth look at *staging* and mentorship than I have room for here, then going into the nuts and bolts of finding and getting that first or second restaurant job, and then looking at the bigger picture – how to do well in that job and make the important early steps that will underpin a successful cooking career.

Since this book is focused on succeeding in culinary school, I'm just going to zero in on those last two questions here, and talk about achieving a balance between school and work that will allow you to succeed in both.

Happy Birthday, Go Get a Job.

Michael Jordan, Chef Instructor:

I started cooking because in my family when you turn 16, you go get a job. That was the way it was in Iowa, growing up. My birthday card said: "Happy Birthday. Go get a job." I wish I still had that card.

There was a McDonald's opening up, and I figured the easiest job to get was at a brand new restaurant. So I went in and they said, "Do you want to work in the front or the back?" and I looked at those polyester uniforms and said, "I'll work in the back." I didn't want anyone seeing me wearing that.

At that time, McDonald's was very organized, very clean, very efficient. It was actually a great place to have a high school job. And after that, the easiest job to get was – more cooking. After a while, I just fell in love with restaurants. I fell in love with restaurants first, rather than the cooking. I just happened to be good at the cooking side of it. I dropped out of regular college a couple of times, because that wasn't for me, but always went back to cooking. Finally my mother found the <u>CIA</u> in New York and it was when I went to school that I fell in love with the rest of it and all the pieces fell into place. I love the craft of it – the workmanship, the physicality, the primal essence of what we do. And it's taken care of me; it's paid the bills.

At some point, most of you will get a job in the business. The smartest of you will have worked in restaurants before rolling into culinary school at all, to be sure that you'll enjoy and want to stick with this kind of work. But if you're like me and *didn't* do this, you'll probably get your first industry job while you're still in school.

Some schools include an externship component. They'll help you nail down a restaurant job, hopefully in a good kitchen where the chef is willing and able to do some teaching along the way. You'll go off and work in the field, learning at a restaurant pace that's impossible to recreate in a school setting, and then you'll come back to school to finish your studies.

But in most programs, work is something you'll need to balance with school. I didn't have much choice whether to work in school or not; I needed the money, and I wanted the experience. Most of my friends and classmates worked, too, and I noticed some general rules as I compared our experiences.

On one hand, working while in school can be great for your learning. Work will offer you lots of chances to practice your skills, to bring any abstract learning from school into really concrete application, and to get a better sense of how restaurants really work. All of this will help you stay focused on the bigger picture – that culinary school is a means to an end, so dive in now and get the most out of it that you can.

Rebecca Cooley, Farm Apprentice:

I could directly apply what I was learning in school to my work, and I brought what I was learning at work back to school. It worked both ways, and was really helpful.

I was working as a prep cook when I started school, and I already knew that I didn't want a typical restaurant job. I didn't want to be a line cook or a chef in a restaurant kitchen, because I knew what it looked like – long hours, hard work, little pay. If I were younger, hell yeah, I would totally live for the thrill and the challenge of busting my ass every day for this art, busting my ass just to show myself that I could do it. But I knew I was too old for that, and I wasn't willing to put up with that shit anymore.

So when I started school, I thought maybe I'd go in the direction of working as a private chef or a nutrition consultant. I never really saw myself in a restaurant kitchen long-term. Restaurant work for me was to gain experience that I could use for something else.

On the other hand, working too much can make it tough to get the most out of culinary school. I did have to work, but I was able to work part time, and this seemed like a pretty nice sweet spot. I didn't have the time to volunteer very often (there will always be tradeoffs), but I got a lot out of my work experience. My friends and colleagues who either had to or chose to work full time during school were total gladiators to be able to pull it off, but often talked about not having the luxury of being their best at school, and missing out on some of the opportunities that others could participate in.

Josh Gaylor, Sous Chef:

The whole time that I was in school, I was working full time. So at certain points, I was just getting through the fucking day. I was an insufferable asshole around finals or midterms. I know I was hard to deal with. I didn't know until I was almost done with school that a lot of the underclassmen called me Angry Josh. I was kind of offended by that, but then I thought, actually, yeah, that was probably right. I was pretty fucking angry most of the time. I wouldn't pull any punches with people – you want me to yell at you, or do you want me to grab the chef to come yell at you?

But having that real life experience and going through school at the same time – as hard as it was, it made me so much better. The way I handled things, approached food, approached flavors – I could take all the stuff I was learning at school and immediately see how it was applied at work. I could see at work, oh, this is wrong – or is it wrong? Is it just a different way to do things?

Michelle Nguyen, Chef:

I definitely wasn't a favorite in my class. I was known as "the bitchy one." I was in culinary school and working full time in a restaurant, and I was exhausted. Sometimes we were doing things I already knew, and I was doing them again at school and thinking, "Why am I wasting my time doing this?" But looking back, it was really good practice. I'd learn a certain technique or fundamental skill in culinary school, and then at my job I got to practice it over and over again. That's how I got quicker and better.

Kristina Glinoga, Line Cook:

I worked full time during school because I was paying out of pocket. It sucked a little bit – I never got to go out with everybody, and I was always so tired and having to do homework at crazy odd hours. In fourth quarter I took a job in fine dining, and it was interesting to see the difference between "play" fine dining and "real" fine dining. But I would get out at one in the morning after scrubbing down, and the guys could go out for drinks, and I would have to go home and do homework and sleep and be up at seven the next morning for school. It was hard. But I got to work at cool places, and I also got some smug satisfaction from being such a hard worker. When I apply for jobs, I can say I know what it means to work 14-hour days all the time.

This is a career where there will never be any shame around working hard. You proved you can bust it out and work your ass off? Props to you. Your work ethic and persistence are the most important foundations for a successful career in this industry.

While you're in school, though, be strategic. There is no shame in working less if you're gaining more from it in the long term. So be careful about falling into the "of course I have to work full time" mindset. Your time in school is so short. Are there any other things you can do to lighten your financial burden, so that you can work less and use your time and energy to get the most out of your schooling? It can be hard on the ego, but can you ask your family for help? Can you live with five roommates, instead of having your own place? Can you move to a cheaper area, even if it's less fun and takes you more time to get to school? Can you use public transportation and ditch your car expenses for a while? If you're a career changer and earned more in your previous life, can you work fewer hours and make just as much by sticking with that skill set for just a little while longer? Can you set aside a weekend or two and churn through some scholarship applications? Your school, if it's worth any tuition at all, will have advisors you can talk to who can help point you in the direction of funding and scholarship opportunities.

It's true: Sometimes you just have to buckle down and do what needs to be done. I didn't talk to anyone who worked their ass off throughout school and concluded therefore they shouldn't have gone to school at all – they all kicked butt, and got tons out of it, and are doing very well in the industry now.

But at least *ask* yourself questions like: How much do I *really* need to work? What are the benefits and costs of this work schedule? Is this the right balance for me? Take the time – each quarter, or each month, ideally – to think super strategically about how to achieve your own best balance between the demands of school and work.

Becky Selengut, Private Chef:

I had a Chef Instructor who was a mentor to me, and I assisted her on so many gigs and jobs. I have to be honest, though – there's a lot of privilege going on here. There was a point in culinary school when I decided that working was keeping me from taking some of these opportunities. I was able to ask my family for help, so I quit my restaurant job, just did school, and then threw myself into volunteering and interning with whatever mentor needed me.

Not everybody can do that. A lot of my peers couldn't do that. Some of them were working pretty shitty jobs with no mentorship, and I was cooking for famous chefs at a television station because I didn't really need the money. It's not going to be easy for everyone to do those kinds of things. But whenever you can, do whatever you need to do.

That also meant I was able to get my sleep, study more, and get better grades. Which, frankly, makes you stand out more to the teachers. Which, frankly, leads to more opportunities. If I were working a restaurant job the entire time I was in culinary school – exhausted, not able to study, not getting good grades – I wouldn't have stood out as much.

Kären Jurgensen, Chef Instructor:
What's the key to getting the most out of the culinary school experience?

I think you have to carve time out. You're putting money forward, and it's a big commitment, so you have to be able to pay attention. Avoid everything that distracts from that. Even though we want you to get experience on the job, if you're not present or you're too sleepy or worn out to get your homework done, you're not going to get what you need out of culinary school. Put away as much outside distraction as you can. Plan on four hours of study for every one hour of lecture, so that's a lot, not even counting the physical demands of the kitchen.

Would you advise people to work part-time during school, or to clear the decks?

A part-time job does help you hone your skills. We throw all of this stuff at you, and you only have four days [on a particular station] to master it, which is not realistic. So having a part-time job is really practical. And then when you finish culinary school, you've already formed those relationships on the job, and you usually find that you get promoted pretty quickly after your schedule frees up.

I don't know that I would start out working part-time right off the bat – maybe by your second or third quarter you can. But it needs to be a part-time job with reasonable hours. That fluctuates depending on industry needs, but we have lots of culinary grads in the industry, for example, and they're fairly understanding about how important the education is. The exception is if you know that you struggle with testing or math – then maybe you need to carve out more time for that.

I know it's a struggle for lots of students, especially moving to the city and finding that rents are so high. But if you can apply for scholarships, get roommates – it's a short period of time, in reality, that you're in school.

Yep, It's Still Who You Know

Your Chef Instructors are incredible career resources, especially early on. We've talked about approaching culinary school as though you're interviewing with your peers, but when you're all just falling out of the culinary school nest, none of you have any helpful connections. That network will become more and more valuable, but it will take time. Right at the start, your instructors are the ones who can help you get a foot in the door.

Becky Selengut, Private Chef:

One of my Chef Instructors in particular connected me with so many opportunities. She got me work as a cook for a television station. They had all these famous chefs come in for a cooking show, and needed one cook to come in and prepare the chefs' food as they came through town on their cookbook tours. She knew I was interested in alternatives to restaurant work, and said, "There's this opportunity, this is what it pays, it's during the summer, you'd be great." It was awesome. I met all these well-known chefs and saw their cookbooks, and it inspired me to move forward in my career.

If you work those connections with your chefs, who have major connections in the city you live in, you will get all kinds of opportunities. If you're a punk and they don't ask you to do that kind of stuff, you're not getting out of school what you could be. So much of the value of culinary school is in those placements. I could've probably learned the same skills that I learned at culinary school by apprenticing, but I might not have gotten all those various different placements and opportunities.

Kristina Glinoga, Line Cook:

One of my instructors in school taught a butchery class on the side with a fourth-generation Italian butcher, who taught us <u>seam butchery</u> on a side of pork. I ended up interning with him over the summer for a whole week – he just let me hang out in his butcher shop, which was such a cool place. I never would have had the chance if I hadn't talked to my chef at school about what I was really interested in.

Your Chef Instructors will have connections in town that can get you instant interviews, but like your peers, they need to be absolutely willing to vouch for you and completely sure that you'll do their name proud if you use it to get in the door.

They'll also be able to give you great advice, once they've seen you work for a while. If your instructors don't set up one-on-one meetings with you once a quarter or semester or so, request a meeting in advance and schedule it with them. Come prepared with notes and questions. You're not asking them for connections or even referrals – those are for them to offer, if they think well of you and want to help you out. You're asking them for advice, and might come with questions like:

- What do you think I need to work on next? What gaps in my skill set do I most need to correct? What resources do you recommend for doing so?

- Are there habits or mindsets you've seen from me that are working against me? Why, and how do you recommend I change these?
- What kinds of places or types of work do you think I should be going for?
- If you were running a restaurant right now, would you be likely hire me, based on what you've seen from me this quarter? Why or why not?

You don't want to fire awkward questions at them like you're writing a book report. Come with some prepared, and then go with the flow of the conversation as it unfolds. Mostly, listen, with an open and grateful mindset. Their expertise and insight is like gold to you at this stage of your learning. They can save you a lot of time with a few very clear observations, and you'd be an asshat not to pay a-bloody-ttention if they're willing to share this kind of information with you.

Becky Selengut, Private Chef:

My Chef Instructor Diana D. was a mentor to me, and I assisted her on *many* of her gigs and jobs. I don't know how I scored it. I don't think I was the only one she mentored; she was a teacher, so she had lots of us. But I think I just put my head down, did what I needed to do, tried to make her laugh, and just kept being persistent – saying, "Whatever you need, I'm there. Would love to help you." I'd be the first to raise my hand.

And then I watched her, and learned from her, studied her professionalism, the way she treated other people. I just sucked it in like a kid looking at a parent. I did my job, but my eyes were wide open; everything she did, I was watching. I still don't think I've ever been able to emulate how polished she is, and how together she always looked – and how clean! I think I look a little schlubbier. She was always so very professional and calm. I knew that was the way I wanted to be as a chef – professional and calm. I always want to let people feel that I'm in control – I have their best interests at heart, they can put their trust in me, and it's going to be a fun evening.

Josh Gaylor, Sous Chef:

All our instructors in culinary school were phenomenal. They were people with real life experience. I felt a huge jump forward after I worked with my third quarter Chef Instructor. He's a fucking line jockey. I still use some of his mannerisms. I still talk like him. Someone's doing something wrong, and I'll just say, in that tone of his that was so calm it was almost flat, "Please stop." And they stop and they look at me, and I say, "I need you to do this, in this way, and don't ever do it another way. Please. This is wrong. This is right, and I'll tell you why this is right." I still cut my fucking lemons in the same way we cut them for the Caesar salads. It's a fucking lemon. I still hear my instructors in my head. Especially when I'm just trying to get by with something and I hear my second quarter Chef Instructor waving his arms around going, "What are you doing???"

On the Rail:

- Working while in school is great practice, and helps remind you that culinary school is a means to an end. Too much work can make it tough to get the most out of school, though.
- To get the most out of both, be strategic about balancing work and school.
- Don't hesitate to schedule meetings with your instructors to ask for guidance.
- Consistently demonstrate the skills, focus, and work ethic that will make it easy for your instructors to recommend you for jobs and opportunities.

*   *   *

GET SERIOUS

Working in the food industry is quirky and different. It can be an all-encompassing lifestyle, and for a long stretch of this career – maybe all of it – most of us will work really fucking hard and not make a whole lot of money or get famous for doing it. So the work itself should be interesting, and we should love what we're doing and learning and working on. But what does that really mean, and what does it look like day to day?

Do You Have The Right Traits To Succeed?

Take even a quick browse on the interwebs, and you'll find a ton of ~~porn and kitten pictures~~ advice about what traits you need to succeed in the food industry.

Are you the right *type* of person to succeed as a cook? Do you have the character traits necessary to become a chef? They'll provide lists, or even charts. You have to be a passionate and creative person, a patient person, an organized person, someone with stamina and a good fitness level. Someone naturally comfortable with taking direction and criticism, with no delusions of grandeur.

This is total bullshit. Look into kitchens – do you see this perfect specimen, this *übermensch*, at the helm of every successful restaurant? Fuck no, you don't. If you needed all these inborn traits to succeed, we'd have two restaurants on earth – the one that <u>Eric Ripert</u> could run by himself, and the Nelson Mandela café, and the rest of us would have to just fuck off home and feed ourselves.

Kitchens are such great places specifically because such a crazy mix of people work in them. Every successful chef is sometimes patient *and* sometimes impatient, creative *and* slavish, totally humble *and* occasionally secretly desirous of grandeur. We're complicated people, and there's room for all the various *types* of us in kitchens. Extroverts *and* introverts. Even those Geminis and Pisces, and you know about *them*.

This focus on imaginary "types" masks a deeper truth, too. Habits matter, not inborn traits. You're not an organized person? Well, don't hang up your chef's coat just yet. Be honest about where you're at and work your ass off at developing systems, rituals, and (eventually) habits of excellent organization.

You're super creative? Great. Keep a notebook of ideas for when you work your way into roles with more responsibility and leeway – and in the meantime, practice learning to deliver on someone else's creativity with accuracy and precision every time. Develop the habits of consistently flawless execution, so when it's your turn to be creative, your skills can keep up with your mad visions.

You're messy, you bristle at criticism, you hate taking direction? Great, join the club. It's called being human. Start working on getting better habits in place. Experiment with routines for keeping yourself and your station cleaner until one or more of them start to work. Start planning and practicing responses to criticism in advance – here's one: Try "Yes, Chef" – so that when all the blood starts to flow into your head, you can just respond from habit in a productive way that buys you time to chill out. Start practicing the *learned* ability to discern between helpful and unhelpful criticism – even if it's just taking one moment to determine which kind you're hearing before you decide what to do next. Come up with your own phrases and literally practice them ahead of time, along the lines of "I hear you, how can I do it better?" or (to a coworker or classmate, not to a chef), "Your tone is kind of aggressive but I know you're trying to help. What changes do you want here?"

Start practicing the *learned* ability to see direction as a gift. This chef or instructor or even colleague is taking the time to show you something and help you learn it. Your ego might be rearing its little ugly fangs, all pissed off they're saying you've done something wrong. Fuck it. We all do wrong shit sometimes. Don't let that little butthurt flood of ego wash away a moment when you could be learning something and getting better. Practice the *learned* habit of hearing you've done something wrong, and staying open to learning and growth anyways.

Start building and practicing habits around taking deep breaths, around managing stressful moments, around letting shit go. If singing two bars of Katrina and the Waves "I'm Walking on Sunshine" in your head helps you mentally leave behind the dumb shit someone just said to you, great. You don't want some negative response sticking like a sliver in your brain for the rest of your day.

There's a side benefit to focusing on habits instead of traits. Habits are hard to form. They're hard to stick with, and it's hard to practice them enough that they actually become your default response. So if you're making headway on all these habits, it means you're forming the best habit of all: Persistence. My grandma called it grit. If you can become one gritty motherfucker by relentlessly developing the habit of persistence, you'll be fine in this (and any) career.

With enough persistence, you'll find and work your way into the parts of this industry that make you the happiest. You may eventually lead others, which often happens when you've developed good habits that propel you into positions of more responsibility. Leadership comes in a million different forms and styles, and they're all learned. No one is actually born a leader. They may start out with great qualities or talents, but they've figured out – through lots of practice and often through mistakes and adversity and tough lessons and failures – habitual ways to teach, direct, and manage others while continuing to learn and grow themselves.

Is Your Heart In It?

Oprah tells you to follow your passion, career gurus tell you to find your calling and live your dream, your friends ultimately don't care what you do as long as you're not a trainwreck all the time, and your parents (if you've still got 'em) probably just want you to be financially secure enough that they can spend whatever money they rightfully earned and eventually peg off peacefully without worrying about your ability to survive unaided in this cold, harsh world.

So, follow your passion, live your dream, don't be a wreck, and ride it into financial security. That's all. Shouldn't that be easy?

If you're like me, you've gone through times in your life when that advice might as well have been: Fuck woodland fairies! Do lines off unicorns! Find a leprechaun, follow him to his pot of gold, form an LLC, and then buy a winery!

Let's get more real here.

First of all, fuck passion. Can we all just be honest about this for one hot goddamm minute? If I hear one more career "guru" telling me to follow my passion, I'm going to bury a microplane in my own eyeball socket. Passion is for great home cooks, and folks who decide on a Saturday to post pictures of the gorgeous scones they just baked with their very-most-favorite Instagram filter. If you want passion, go sell shit on Etsy.

Trust me, it's not passion that's going to get you through the last eight hours of your line cooking shift. Your smartphone probably has longer battery life than most people's "passion." Yes, you absolutely need to love what you do in a deep-down and core way, and have a deep and abiding interest in and curiosity about this work. But you don't need to be passionate about it – that's an unsustainable state of being, and it's a stupid thing to expect if you really want to last in this business.

I will go to the mat on this, but okay, let's say you insist on calling it passion. That's cool, there's about 57 million other people in your corner on this. You want passion! You want to make sweet sweet love to your career and you'll settle for nothing less than a *passion* for what you do!

Fine, you big perv. But please understand that passion isn't going to come out of nowhere and light upon your arm like a gentle butterfly. Finding a genuinely pre-existing passion is so rare it's like hen's teeth, horns on a horse, milk from birds. In interviews, super successful people will often say their passion came first, propelling them into their wildly successful career. I think this is just hindsight talking. They're being asked to explain how they got where they are, so they look backwards and create a good story. Persistence and sweat and luck aren't as sexy as passion – so they talk about the passion.

Most people, good stories aside, don't fall deeply in love and get married on their first date – lust can be instant (and often unsustainable and disappointing), but real passion comes once they get to know each other, learn their lover's quirks and secrets, and get through setbacks or conflicts in ways that reveal deeper truths. Why would a passion for what you do be any different? The more knowledge you learn about a topic, the more interesting it becomes. The more skill you develop, the more you can take on. You start to see the complexities, the nuances. In fact, I bet most successful people started with curiosity, not passion. Curiosity is a great starting point.

If passion is actually something you need to work your way into, then this whole "find your passion" advice leaves most of us totally fucked. We're looking *right now* for something that might not exist yet – but that doesn't mean it won't exist in the future. We're demanding passion too early, and then we're disappointed when the first steps of learning a new set of skills feel difficult and slow and even dull. Isn't this supposed to be exciting? Aren't we supposed to be radiant, growing exponentially every day, running through sunlit fields like those women in tampon ads?

No, we are not. That's a stupid expectation, foisted on us by the Oprah-industrial complex, a media wet dream that has nothing to do with how actual skills, deep engagement, and eventually mastery develop. So instead of asking "What am I passionate about?" ask yourself questions like:

- What am I curious about?
- Where can I be useful?
- What direction would give me a long runway for learning?
- Where can I imagine not being bored for a long time?
- What skills do I think are awesome, and would find interesting to develop?

The false expectations that "follow your passion" heaps on us are really a damn shame, because if we could just let our curiosity and the hard work itself feed us for a while, we might get somewhere that feels like genuine passion. But to hang in there long enough to develop real mastery, you need to discover a gritty and persistent and almost inexplicable satisfaction from the work itself that has very little to do with the glamorous and sparkly feeling of passion. And then, by the time a real passion does grow and develop, you may not need it as badly anymore. It'll be icing.

Josh Gaylor, Sous Chef:

Thomas Keller says that your desire is what keeps you going when your passion fades. I just want to cook. I've never been happier than doing this. I've come back to this multiple times; done other work for five, six years, and come back to this. I'm more comfortable here than anywhere else. I love cooking for people. I love breaking bread with people. I love to sit down and eat and talk. I love to eat by myself. Fuck yeah, I dine alone, and I love it.

Carpe Diem: Seize the Carps!

If what we're actually aiming for is interest, curiosity, and engagement, then it's time to get into sleuthing mode. Think back to times when you've experienced these states of being – what kind of jobs you've enjoyed, what work environments, what kinds of colleagues and how many of them, etc. Don't screw the pooch demanding passion right off the bat – just put your radar up for curiosity and interest, and start taking notes. In writing. Really.

Some of you might be wondering, "What if my little Geiger counter of desire is flatlining?" If your desires and interests aren't already obvious to you, how do you find them? Maybe it's because I've always been a late bloomer, or because the set point of my internal happiness thermostat (if you believe these sorts of things are innate) hovers just above zero degrees Kelvin, but I have definitely gone through long funks when I felt like nothing interested me, and may never interest me again. Isn't depression fun and exciting?

I'm not a psychologist (though by god, I've supported a number of them!), but what I've seen work for me and my friends has simply been a numbers game: Try a bunch of shit, and see what sticks. It's not scientific, it's not sexy, it takes time and lots of effort (like everything in this guide – do you see a theme?), but if you put yourself out there and try lots of new things, you're increasing the odds that you'll dig one or more of them, and that something will capture your interest enough that you'll want to go deeper, learn more. Once you get past the initial awkwardness of trying any genuinely new thing, you'll start noticing that curiosity, interest, even contentment.

Trying new things throughout school is also a great way to deepen your friendships, impress your instructors, become invaluable to future mentors, and expand your skill set. There's no downside to trying new things, as long as you're getting enough sleep not to become a zombie. Your school and your instructors will regularly offer volunteer opportunities and extracurricular activities. Do them. Figure out how much time you need to study effectively and take care of yourself (those are priorities), but beyond that, get involved in as many ways as you can. Volunteer. Show up.

> *Becky Selengut, Private Chef:*
> Take advantage of all the extra stuff that goes on, as much as humanly possible. That's almost more important than getting good grades. If they're going to bring a pig in for an event they're doing at school, and they ask for a couple volunteers to help break it down an hour before school starts – be one of those two people. Get in there. Get your hands on as many different opportunities to do different things as you possibly can while you have that time to learn.

I've already talked about how our bakery rotation (aka, Bakation) ended up being way more important training for me than I anticipated at the time. Similarly, things that feel like "sideline" activities – volunteering gigs, extra-curricular and purely optional activities – might lead you in totally new and unexplored directions.

> *Rebecca Cooley, Farm Apprentice:*
> I'm discovering that I'm more interested in growing the food than cooking it. One of the reasons I chose the school I went to was the farm program. We had the opportunity to work in a rural area with people from

school and our instructor, learning how to use what was available locally and seasonally, and how to make the best of that. And how simple it was to make really amazing food. To me it was a humbling experience – why do we have to make food so complicated? We learned how to ferment and can foods, milk goats, make goat cheese. One of my favorite things was the foraging – there is so much food that we walk by every day! That was the most exciting – the berries, the Oregon grapes, the watercress and the little pine nuts, the chickweed salads...

As I interviewed students, graduates, instructors, and chefs, one of the things I heard again and again was: The time you spend in school is so short, in the grand timeline of things. At the risk of sounding ancient – *You kids get off my lawn!* – you'll look back at your time in school and it will feel like it all flew by in a minute. So make the most of this early and fascinating part of your learning curve. This is your time to explore, so try everything. You're not on a path or in a rut – take every chance, try every new thing. You never know when a yes will open up a whole new path.

Quitting Time

Culinary schools will always want you to finish their whole program.

In fact, they are required to publish statistics for how many students do so. A low completion rate looks like a bad thing – and in some areas of study, it definitely is. You can't start being a nurse without going to nursing school, so when you look at a nursing program with a low graduation rate, it's probably safe to assume they're not preparing people well for the career. Or there's not enough academic support, the instructors are jerks, the admissions folks are bad pickers, or it's expensive and many students run out of funding midway through. All crummy things, right?

For culinary schools, though, a different story is possible. Cooking isn't like nursing; you don't need a certificate or degree to get into the field. So culinary schools can also show lower graduation rates because they aren't strong programs or they're too expensive, and people opt out as soon as possible. But they may also show lower graduation rates because they're preparing students well to work in the field – and those students are going ahead and doing that.

I'm glad I had the chance to go to culinary school, but I also want to make it really clear that I decided not to finish my program. That's right – you're reading a How to Succeed guide written by a dropout. Oh, the irony! At my school you earned a certificate by completing five quarters plus summer; I completed four quarters and then decided to leave.

I loved my culinary school experience, but left early for two very specific reasons.

First, I was going flat-out broke. The tuition wasn't the hardest part for me; having the time to work only part-time while in school was the bigger hit. I couldn't add more work, but every month it got harder to make ends meet. For someone who doesn't want a life focused around money, I was spending a hell of a lot of my time thinking and worrying about it.

Second, and much more important in the long run, I had achieved the goals I set when I decided to go to culinary school. I had built the confidence I needed to hold my own in a kitchen, and I'd gotten a good entry-level job in the field. I was learning so much at work – as a line cook in a busy restaurant with a wonderful chef who was also a committed and effective teacher – that I felt okay moving on.

For me, this was a tough decision that has worked out well. If I'd just made the decision based on money, I probably would've regretted it within months. But I had clear goals for what I wanted to get out of school, and I felt a strong sense of achievement from hitting those goals. I graduated myself, in a way, and felt good about doing so.

I guarantee you will run into decision points during your time in culinary school when you'll have to make the choice whether or not to continue. These might come from within – you're tired, you're stressed, you're achieving what you wanted – and from around you – you're broke, your scholarship or your support from a parent or spouse falls apart, your chef wants you to go full time, or says school isn't worth the money. So how do you make the decision? Should you stay or should you go?

Let's talk though some of the various situations I saw while in school.

If you're a dick, and you're two weeks into first quarter, and the instructor is already annoying and wrong, and you already know way more than your peers, and everyone seems to hate you – take comfort in the fact that there's one of you in almost every culinary school cohort. You're not alone. You should quit. Take some time, grow the fuck up, and come back when you're ready to learn.

If you have financial support, but you're thinking about quitting because you're struggling with your own performance, with classroom pressures, or in relationships with your peers or instructors, try to stick it out, for a few reasons:

- If you're questioning yourself, you're right on track. Change is hard. Learning a whole bunch of new skills in an entirely new field is going to be uncomfortable – if it's not, you're not throwing yourself in hard enough. Hang in there, camper.

- If you're frustrated with your performance, quitting is not going to improve things. It'll just give the shitty negative voices in your head more ammo to keep killing you with. Snuff them by asking for help and starting to plan and achieve small measurable improvements each week. A trusted and helpful instructor can help you make a plan like this.

- If the issue is between you and your peers, take a big step back and look for ways you can disengage and focus on just the school part of school for a while. Or use this as training for how you'll deal with the weirdos and fuck-ups you'll inevitably encounter in restaurant kitchens. A trusted and helpful instructor will see what's going on, too; without being a ratty narc, you can ask for help navigating these kinds of dynamics. That might require shelving your ego and hearing that there are things you could be doing a lot better, too – and if that's the case, what a gift they're giving you by telling you the truth. That's something you can act on (even if doing so is uncomfortable) that can change your entire work life for the better.

- And if the issue is with an instructor, talk to a program administrator or a school counselor. You've joined a school program, not a mafia family. There's no code of silence. If something genuinely shitty is going down, it's okay to talk to someone about it and get help.

Let's look at some other situations where staying in culinary school would be a good idea:

- If you're going for a degree that you do not already have, try to stick it out. Unless you're staying in school and switching into a more advanced degree program (for example, from a culinary AA to a BA in another field), get this degree done. Almost any degree will open up more choices to you in the long run, so it's worth gutting it out now.

- If the issue is solely about (realistic) funding, try getting more creative before you quit. Talk to every single adult in your goddamn school if you have to, and ask for help. Ask for grants, ask for loans, ask them if they know anyone else you could talk to about grants or loans. Ask if they know any organizations in town that fund students, and then follow up. Show the persistence and grit you'll need for kitchen work, and consider it practice in toughness. While you look for funding, cut expenses, too. Move in with classmates, or get a roommate. Sell a bunch of stuff; sell your car, if you don't need it to get to work and school. An important caveat, though: I think it's bugnuts crazy to pay $100k (or even $40k, for that matter) for a culinary education that qualifies you to enter a field where you might make $13 an hour for years. So when I say get creative about *realistic* funding, I don't mean hawk your future to pay some kookookachoo tuition now. In that case, getting creative might mean finding a competitive program that costs 1/4 or 1/8 of the price, and finishing there.
- If your legal ability to stay in the States depends on you being a student, don't take that lightly. The folks who deal with international student visas are not fucking around.

Then there are grey areas, when it's not as clear whether staying or moving on would be a better choice. For example, Michelle's experience is a pretty common one for culinary students to encounter:

Michelle Nguyen, Chef:
After my second quarter, I struggled with whether to continue in culinary school. I was working three different cooking jobs, and trying to go to school at the same time, and my chef said, "You don't need culinary school. It's all about experience in the kitchen – that's what makes you a good cook, not culinary school." I had a moment when I thought I wasn't going to come back to culinary school. But I enjoyed my classmates and my instructors were

really awesome, and I felt like if I did quit I'd be a disappointment to them. So I stuck with it. I'm very glad that I did.

My first chef never asked me to quit school, or gave any opinion about it one way or the other. He didn't attend culinary school, and if I had to guess, I'd wager that he doesn't consider it a necessary or even advisable path into the field. But I can't imagine him ever asking me to drop school. When I told him about my decision and said I could pick up more shifts in a month, he said "Oh, okay," and gave me two more days, and that was it. So I haven't encountered this pressure myself, but if your chef is pushing you to leave school, I'd advise you to take some time to do three things first:

1. Stop and consider motivations. Staffing is a continual fucking headache in restaurants, and if that chef knows you're a good and reliable worker, sticking you on the schedule more often solves an immediate problem. So if your chef is offering any resistance to school whatsoever, is he or she *also* offering an equal or greater investment in your learning? Has this chef demonstrated real mentorship, and is he or she taking the time to offer you hands-on instruction and show interest in the growth of your career over time? If so, move on to Step 2. If not, end the conversation by telling your chef "I always finish what I start," and he or she can wait another few months for your hot shit.

2. Think over the pros and cons carefully – for the next two years, but also imagine ten years out. Do you have clearly defined goals for two years out, and will this help you reach them? Do you have a plan that goes well beyond pleasing this one chef? Where do you want to work next, and will this move help you get there? How? Ten years out will be foggier for sure, but ask the Hail Mary questions, too. For example, most chefs won't care whether you finish, but if you want to own a restaurant down the line, bank officers might care about a degree when issuing bank loans. If you don't have goals, then you can't evaluate pros and cons. In that case, leaving school early might be an indication of impatience or wandering, neither of which advances a

cooking career. Persistence and grit do. If you're not persisting toward a goal, then persist in school until you have one.

3. Run it by a wise advisor. Is there someone in your life you can talk through tough decisions with, who knows you well? A culinary school instructor will probably tell you to continue, and it's unlikely your culinary school peers will be able to offer objective advice. But do you have a long-time friend who can take the long view? A mentor or teacher outside of culinary school you can meet for coffee? A spouse or parent who's good at bouncing around pros and cons without getting caught up in worries and projecting their ideas and goals on you? Talk things over with them, and show them your pros and cons. Be honest, and willing to hear their honesty in return. Do they say "It might be nice to finish something," or "Yeah, seems like an okay time to move on"? They're not making the decision for you. This is just to check your hunches and make sure you're not being hasty or shooting yourself in the foot in an old habitual way that you don't see in yourself.

What if it's genuinely quitting time, and you can gain more by moving on than you would by finishing school? When I thought I might be in this situation, I asked myself the following questions:

1. Am I giving up any future flexibility by leaving early? Specifically, am I walking on a degree that will give me a wider range of career options in the future, even outside the culinary field? In my case, I already had a BA and MFA, so walking away from a certificate wasn't a big deal to me. In contrast, walking away from a first AA or BA might be a bigger deal.

2. Have I achieved the things I wanted to in culinary school? I went to culinary school to build enough competence and confidence to work in a professional kitchen. Once I got there, "general competence" evolved into a very clear list of skills that I wanted to make sure I had. By being really clear about my objectives, I had a solid sense of achievement and no guilt or regret when I left culinary school. I got out of it everything I wanted to, and more.

3. What will I be missing in the coming quarter(s), and are those skills integral enough that I should consider continuing? The 3rd and 4th quarters in

my program were key for me. In 5th quarter, I would have solidified these skills, been exposed to new techniques, had more time to practice – it would've been great. The instructor is a kick-ass butcher and chef with tons to teach – that was the hardest part of my decision. Lots of the quarter focused on managing others, which I'd done a lot of in a previous career. And it included a molecular gastronomy unit which would have been really cool. I ultimately decided that all of these things would have been great, but not necessary. I'd hit all the things on my necessary list, and it was an okay time for me to move on.

4.   Am I evaluating an opportunity that will bring me leap and bounds forward in my specific career goals?

When I was making a decision about quitting culinary school, I knew that if I could be more available at work, I'd be in a good position to train for the baking position. My mom said, "Why don't you just transfer over to the Baking & Pastry program?" It wasn't an option financially, anyway, but I almost crawled out of my skin at the idea of five *more* quarters in school. I was really impatient. I also had confidence and a solid foundation now – I could learn these new skills on the job, in a structured training period with the baker. That was a next step in my cooking career worth jumping towards.

I briefly knew a guy named Alex who decided to leave school really early on, and many of us were surprised – he'd started so strong! But he'd become part of a four-man team that a very well-known chef in town started using as his opening crew. Every time he opened a new restaurant, which was fairly often, he'd send these four guys in first, to set up the kitchen, get systems in place, and get things rolling. That was work that fit well in Alex's grand plan, and an opportunity like that wouldn't wait around for him. He could come back to culinary school later if he wanted to, so he was comfortable with the decision to leave.

This was a long section because leaving a program early is a big decision, and never one to make lightly. It's not irreversible, but you also don't want to slow your momentum early in any career. Talk to friends, parents, mentors. Check your ego and be open to their suggestions. Ultimately, though, you're the one who plots your path and determines your future. As long as you're comfortable with your decisions, and making them from a place of strength and consideration – then *go do you*, whatever the fuck that means.

- A focus on traits is bullshit. Good habits and persistence bring success.
- "Follow your passion" is the worst advice ever. Fuck passion, and look instead for curiosity, interest, engagement – these + hard work lead to mastery, which brings satisfaction.
- Get involved in as many different ways as you can while you're in this intense learning period. You can't always predict which paths will become compelling.
- Do you need to finish culinary school? If you're grappling with this, look back over the scenarios in this section, because the answer is a decisive… it depends.

*   *   *

KEEP GETTING BETTER

One of the best things about working in food is that you will never know everything. That might not sound like a good thing – especially when you're just starting out and you're overwhelmed by all the shit you don't yet know – but it is. You will never know how to work with every ingredient, how to execute every technique. At any time, you can crack open a cookbook or an industry magazine and encounter something you've never seen before. You might be a hot shit chef someday and learn some new trick from a dishwasher or a newly-hired pantry cook that will blow your mind.

This means two things. First, if you're feeling a ton of pressure right now, you can let some of that go. If this is a field where you can never know everything, then you certainly don't need to know everything right now, just to get your foot in the door. This industry offers you a really long runway, so don't worry your way through all your fuel now, or you'll never get to takeoff.

Second, you have to be okay with always learning and growing, which sounds super nice in theory, but also requires that you set your ego aside and admit there are things you don't know. Not just admit it, but relish the chances to be a newbie again, to upend the hierarchy and learn from anyone in any position in your kitchen.

This means taking the long view. This is a tough industry, so you need a mindset that lets it feed you and not just grind you down. You need to find satisfaction and contentment in it – and after making your 57,000th salad, that satisfaction isn't going to come from the salad. So in this last section, let's chat about three things:

1. How to approach working with others in a way that brings the best out in all of you,
2. how to work on developing your palate so that you can begin to taste and understand and execute more interesting, complex, and nuanced food, and
3. how to lock in a mindset that will allow that learning and growing – even when you fuck up, even when you're kicking ass.

These mindsets and strategies will work for you in any corner of this huge and crazy food industry.

Your Better Self

It's time to get our OM on. That's right, we're going to delve into the big philosophical questions for a moment. If you're someone who smokes weed, feel free to toke and then pick back up here and continue.[19] [20] [21]

Throughout history, we've been arguing about what's most important in life. What purposes should drive our human existence? What questions should guide our short mortal journeys? If you're reading this very slim *No-Bullshit Guide* in order to answer the most fundamental questions of your earthly existence, you're in big fuckin' trouble, right? There are thicker books written by infinitely wiser people that I'd strongly recommend you consult instead.

---

19 If you are of legal age and residing in the states of Colorado or Washington, where this is a legal activity. Otherwise, do not do this. And furthermore, I never told you to do so; you must have misunderstood.

20 I pay my lawyer by the footnote. Can you tell?

21 He wants three more footnotes now on the dangers and liabilities of marijuana use. Fuck me, it was a joke, man.

But since I went ahead and opened the can of worms called MEANING OF LIFE, let's peek into it together for just a moment. If I had to come up with some of the essential questions of a well-lived life, my very secular and low-key list would include:

- How can I be my best self? Not *the* best, *my* best.
- How can I help others be their best selves?

Because my suspicion, or just my great hope, is that over time I'll be able to sort out lots of the other gnarly-big-weighty questions – What's my purpose in life? What am I here to do? What will I contribute, or leave behind? – if I can just spend lots more time being my best self than my worst self.

So why the existential field trip into this terrifyingly earnest terrain?

Well, we spend a lot of time at work in this country, and we assign it a lot of importance. It's a big-ass slice of the quality-of-life pie in American culture. So my point in bringing this up is that it makes sense to take a similar approach to identifying the most essential questions of any work:

- How can I do my best work today?
- And how can I help others do their best work?

One of my hopes in writing this book is that it helps you do your best work, each day. One way I hope to do this is by giving you a bunch of information about how culinary schools and kitchens work, so that you can make great decisions and develop solid habits that lessen the time you spend struggling with all the little shit. Why? So you can keep your focus on the big shit – like doing your best work, and helping others to do the same.

How you define "your best work" is personal.

For me, when I'm doing my best work, in the very broadest sense, I feel like I'm both expressing myself and also contributing to others.

I'm expressing something of myself in my work – maybe that means my ideas and creativity, or maybe it's just my sweat and effort. It depends on the task at hand. Otherwise, anybody could do that task, and I could be on some distant beach drinking mojitos instead.

But I also don't personally believe that expression alone is enough. Plenty of creative sorts will disagree with me here, but I feel like aiming solely for expression can be a bit narsy, and at its worst can just create more output-only noise in an already-very-noisy world. It might make me feel good for a while, but if it's not contributing anything to anyone else, what's ultimately the point? So as I express my creativity, my ideas, my work ethic, I'm also thinking – how am I serving others, and contributing to their lives? Maybe this is as simple as feeding them a meal, and maybe it's as complex as helping them achieve their best work.

There's a reason I'm getting all heavy right now. In professional cooking, you'll almost always be working with other people. And working with people can be really heavy. In fact, I can't think of a harder thing to do consistently well. You can master any cooking technique you'll ever need in a kitchen, given enough time, focus, and practice. But people are infinitely changeable and complex, often unpredictable and occasionally a total fucking mystery. In a kitchen, you'll be working with some of the weirdest and most wonderful of our species – and you'll be doing it in tight quarters, under tremendous pressure. So I think it's worth getting all existential for a minute, to consider: How can you consistently improve the way you work with others?

If you're already in school or working in a kitchen, stop for a moment and really visualize how a typical day would unfold if everyone operated with these two questions fully in mind: How can I do my best work today? And how can I help others do their best work? If you're like me, and afflicted with a chronic case of judgmentia, your first thought might be, "Wow, yeah, then X wouldn't be such an asshole all the time." Perhaps, like me, you also read self-help books and mostly just figure out all the shit that's wrong with your other family members? Quit dodging. Look inward, open up, and get a little more honest.

Imagine a day at school or at work in which *you* operate with these questions fully in mind. When *you* approach the day with the goal of doing your best work and helping others do theirs, are you more deliberate? More organized and well-prepared? Clearer in your communication? Kinder, nicer, and gentler? More direct? More patient? I am all those things, in my imaginary visualizations. Way more often than I can consistently pull off. So, great: That gap gives me a goal. Practically a to-do list.

There's a pithy, cheery statement that's been attributed to Gandhi: *Be the change you wish to see in the world.* There's not actually any solid evidence he said this, not to rain on your bumper sticker parade. He did say, "If we could change ourselves, the tendencies in the world would also change. As a man changes his own nature, so does the attitude of the world change towards him. ... We need not wait to see what others do."[22] But that won't fit on the ass-end of a Prius, so we've all taken some poetic license with the quotation.

It's a tall order, but how 'bout this version: Be the change you wish to see in your kitchen. Or even, *make one change* you wish to see in your kitchen. Do you get tired of working with dicks in the kitchen? Fantastic: Be less of a dick. Better yet, frame the same goal in a more measurable way: Can I catch myself before I snap at my peers this week? Say, five times? Or, even better still, frame the goal in a positive way: Can I communicate more clearly, just for today? Just for this week? Each time I hand over a task, can I take one extra minute to explain what I want? Or, each time I get handed a task, can I pause and ask a follow up question if I need to?

You won't have to work terribly hard to identify the ways you wish other people would do things differently at school or work. As you think about these annoyances and frustrations, though, imagine that you're filtering them through the goal of doing your best work, and helping others do theirs. Does that open any new possibilities? Do you come up with any ideas for how you can approach things differently? Or respond differently? What's the change that *you* can start to be?

Now, let me be super clear: Is it your job to improve everyone around you? Nope, it's sure not. And you won't get very popular by trying. But if you are genuinely trying to do your best work, and if you are genuinely looking for ways to help others, that intention will start to shift and inform how you work and how you work with others. Don't knock it 'til you try it.

Developing Your Palate

What tastes good to you? And how do you know that will taste good to your diners?

We could argue about these questions all day. They're questions we could take into sterile scientific-looking laboratories and analyze on a biochemical level while our colleagues are busy sawing BBQs in half behind us. They're questions you'll grapple with as you enter your cooking career.

---

22 Brian Morton, "False Words Were Never Spoken," *New York Times*, 29 August 2011, http://www.nytimes.com/2011/08/30/opinion/false-words-were-never-spoken.html

Answering the first question requires analysis; the second requires the kinds of educated guesses that come from experience. Since experience will follow analysis, let's focus on the first.

When folks in cooking talk about your palate, they mean your ability to detect tastes. Everyone can taste, but can you taste well? Can you pick out individual components of a dish, taste when something's missing, and use taste and smell to bring a dish into balance? In most corners of the professional cooking world, you'll cook from recipes – but this week's carrots may not be as sweet as last week's. This brand of seaweed might not be as salty as the one you usually use. This batch of vinegar could be totally different than the last one you made. So as you cook, the tasting spoons are piling up beside you. How is this coming together? Does this taste right? In each dish, am I getting to the same flavors and overall tastes that the chef showed me the first time he demoed the dish?

Like so many things in cooking, this comes from practice and repetition, but there are two ways to jumpstart your quest for a more discerning palate.

Become a Student of Good Taste(s)

Your Chef Instructors have developed incredible palates over the years. When they're designing the curriculum and the menus for the courses you're taking with them, they're drawing on flavor combinations that they've taken years to refine and perfect.

One of our instructors, who taught us fine dining and international cuisine, shared flavor combinations that were often surprising to me – that cauliflower goes well with cocoa pasta, for example. She introduced us to *The Flavor Bible* by Karen Page and Andrew Dornenburg, a book that lives up to its ambitious name, and which I've been using ever since. But it was her own understanding of flavors that she'd tested and refined throughout her career that blew my mind the whole quarter. If she said a dish was good, I tasted it immediately to try and understand what she thought was good, and why. If she said it was too X, I'd listen super closely to what she suggested to fix it, and taste again as the dish came into balance. You can't always do that in busy kitchens, so take full advantage of any time you get to taste alongside a more experienced palate, and bring all your attention to the moment.[23]

---

23 Chef Michael Jordan had the greatest way to describe this – he called it "chasing the palates you love." He went deep into how to do this, so I've saved that part of our conversation for the second *No-Bullshit Guide to Starting Your Cooking Career*, where you'll find it in the section called *Apprentice Your Palate*, since this is something we all continue to work on and develop once we're working in the field.

Because opportunities like these come along much more frequently in school than at work, culinary school became a fantastic chance to dive into decoding the flavors I was encountering. To figure out how each chef worked with flavor, and to pay close attention to what go-to combinations they consistently used and have worked incrementally over the years to develop and deepen.

Eat With Purpose

Start paying attention to what you're eating. It sounds simple, but the quality of attention you give good food will speed up how quickly your palate will develop. Imagine that your ability to navigate your way through a dish – creating, tasting, adjusting, perfecting – is like speaking a foreign language. In both cases, a larger vocabulary is better. It gives you more options, more chances to connect and get your point across. Think of every individual and distinct flavor as a word, and go after them. Go in search of them, take them in, think about them, learn them.

And then talk about them. Like foreign languages, sensory skills like taste and smell can actually be strengthened by talking about them, creating associations and locking them into your memory in multiple ways.

Kären Jurgensen, Chef Instructor:

There are some studies around language – when you talk about food, you start growing brain cells in that language area and making more connections. A great book is *Elements of Taste* by Gray Kunz – he talks about developing that language around flavor.

Sitting down for a meal with a flavor wheel beside you can be interesting. Playing games with a colleague or a friend – What do you smell? What do you taste? – and having a conversation, giving that language the chance to click in.

You smell it, but if you don't verbalize it, you don't necessarily connect what the smell and the flavor are. The more you talk about it, the more you'll recognize the thing you're smelling. Supposedly the more you say it over and over matters – you say, "It's cumin," and then the next time you taste it you've said "It's cumin" out loud, and in that way you can really train yourself.

Evaluating food is not necessarily enjoying food. You can sit down to meal and really evaluate it, as well. Think about going to a wine tasting and really concentrating on the flavors – it's fun and interesting, but it doesn't necessarily make you swoon over the wine. Versus sitting down to a meal, talking about something else, and just enjoying the wine.

Do you ever have trouble turning that off?
Yes. I do. I find myself to be an irritating dinner companion sometimes.

Talking about tastes and flavors as you consciously develop your palate also has a secondary benefit – it lets you bring value to your SWAT team of peeps. Few of us in culinary school or at the start of a cooking career have the money to go out to eat that often – especially at the places that are doing the exciting and innovative food that we newbies all crave more information about. So if you have the lucky chance to hit a good restaurant, dine for all your peeps.

That doesn't mean sit with your iPhone like Douchey McDoucherson "I'm a foodie" Yelp-Elite Documentarian #1, snapping pics of every piece of cutlery at the expense of a great meal. No photos needed. Just take mental notes. What are you tasting? What flavor combinations are interesting? What "secret ingredients" can you taste that aren't making it into the menu description but are making a big difference to the flavor and balance of the dish? What techniques are being used to create each of these components? Can you visualize the steps? What are you learning about the creative mind at work in this kitchen, and what – if any of it – can inform your work? Not in theory, but this week, in school, making student lunch, even?

Becky Selengut, Private Chef:
What's the best advice you were given early on in your career?
I was told, not by a chef but by a food writer, to pay very close attention to every single recipe I learned from another chef, and that at this point in my career I was in the absorption phase. That I should absorb all the styles,

recipes, personalities – and then eventually, I'd be able to sift through it all and come up with my own way, my own roadmap. She didn't say this, but between the lines I also heard: Now is not your time to show what you know. It's your time to shut the fuck up, be humble, and learn from all of these great people you're around. She said, "Start paying attention to the recipes that inspire you and move you, and write those down and start collecting all of these things. And soon you'll realize that there's a thread that connects all of them. And then you'll find out what your part in this big world is." It was good advice. I took that very seriously.

There's no moment when you "get" to be creative – there's no position within the food industry or kitchen hierarchy when your opinion automatically starts to count. Those moments can come at any time. You're a pantry cook and you overhear the chef talking to the sous about a dish needing a little lift somehow, and you reach into your <u>lowboy</u> and say, "Chef, I've got yuzu if you want it," and that changes the dish for the better. Or you have a chef who's into quizzing you all the time, and you keep passing – and slowly it becomes less about quizzes and more about conversations. Or you work as a prep cook and your food is always well seasoned, and all of a sudden the spoon is being passed to you to taste new dishes and offer your thoughts. It's never a good idea to insert opinions far above your pay grade when no one has asked you. But well-timed and well-considered creative ideas and solutions are welcome in lots and lots of kitchens.

An important caveat: Execute your dishes in the way the chef has instructed you, whether or not you think you could improve upon them. I'm not saying go and get all creative on your station any time you want.

A story about this: I went back to a restaurant I used to work at, and while my chef and I were catching up, he said, "I maybe hired the worst line cook ever."

Oh? I asked, perking up, all interested in the gossip.

We had a classic baked eggs dish – butter in a boat dish was the first step. Super French. "I look over and he's using garlic oil instead. So I say," and even in telling the story he got the very still and quieted-down manner that he has when he's pissed (which was always WAY more terrifying than ranting), "'Buddy, what are you doing there?' and he says 'I'm using garlic oil! No one thawed out any butter for me, so I'm improvising.'"

Long story short, my chef turned to the baker, who had started his shift hours ago, and said, "Can you stay a little longer today?" and the baker immediately said "Yeah, totally." So he told the terrible line cook to beat it, fired him on the spot, the baker worked until the dinner guy came in, and the garlic oil went back where it belonged.

Dream big dreams, kid, but please do remember: It's not your job to improvise yet. While you're in school, you're following the menus and recipes of your Chef Instructors, learning and using their techniques, and aiming to please their palates. Once you get out of school and step into a prep or line cook role in a restaurant, your job doesn't change much. You'll continue to try to execute your chef's vision, just right, every time.

But you can start to earn a place in the bigger conversation that's happening about food by thinking critically about what's happening in your kitchen, your city, and the general food scene unfolding around you, and being ready with solid and creative ideas *if you're asked*. So pillage and plunder all the good ideas you come across. Work them into what you're doing at school whenever you're given room to freestyle a bit; give 'em a test drive and see where they take you.

Right now (today!) you're developing your palate, your understanding of flavor combinations, your openness to possibility, your risk tolerance, and your own personal voice in food – even in school, even as a prep cook or a line cook, even if you might not have an outlet or platform for all this budding awesomeness for years.

Kaizen

In my culinary program, we spent second quarter bumbling around in a commercial kitchen for the first time, just trying to put up enough student lunch to feed our peers every day. Moving into third quarter was the biggest leap within the program – that's when we stated cooking for customers for the first time, in a casual bistro setting with an *à la carte* menu.

If you're a brand new line cook, like I was, you know that _à la carte_ means "to kick one's ass" in French. I look back now and I smile to see how hard we worked to put out so very few plates of food, but that's exactly why we were there – to take those very first, slow baby steps into line cooking while in school, so that we didn't get our ass handed to us rolling into a restaurant position untrained and unprepared.

The chef for this quarter was awesome – an Obi-Wan Kenobi who would see everything, correct things fast and decisively, and cook so much faster than it seemed like he was moving. He could come down on you like a ton of bricks when you were fucking around or doing something wrong, and he could occasionally seem impatient – but he had to be so patient to manage a whole line of total noobs like we were. It blows my mind to consider in retrospect how patient he was with us.

The mindset he kept bringing us back to again and again (probably, also in retrospect, to keep himself from going bonkers as well) was kaizen. At the end of every day, we'd clean the kitchen and then have a quick huddle. He'd talk about what went right and what went wrong. And at the end, when we'd break, everyone would shout in unison: *Kaizen!*

Even on the days it felt like we should be shouting in unison: *Seppuku!*

Especially on those days.

The Japanese word kaizen literally means "good change," and it refers to continual improvement. Any actions, or even mindsets, that eliminate waste and create large or even small improvement are kaizen.

Kaizen is a brilliant technique for accessing the right mindset again and again because it's not judgy (especially since it's not in English and it's also fun to say), and it's always relevant. There's no history involved – you can always, in this present moment, decide to aim for continuous improvement from right now onward – *Kaizen!*

It applies every day, however that day might be going.

You have a shitty day of service? Instead of just whining about it and then getting drunk, analyze what went wrong and work to fix those things, and have a better day the next day – *Kaizen!*

You have a brilliant day of service? Instead of just patting yourself on the back about it and then getting drunk, analyze what went right and work to push those things further, and have an even better day the next day – *Kaizen!*

You'll have lots of ups and down in culinary school and in the work you eventually do in this industry, and it's really important to develop habits that help you stay motivated. And I don't know of any habits that are better over the long run than continuous improvement. Who among us *doesn't* want to continually learn and grow and improve?

Jen Covert Mosinski, Food Writer:

The grades you get on quizzes and tests are personal, but when you're in the kitchen, your shit's on display. You can see when someone's a hot mess on their station. There was this really young kid who was in our class, and I remember they told us to peel onions, and we had our bowls for waste, and this kid had like a whole onion in his trash. I was thinking: What are you doing, man? He couldn't even get it together to peel an onion and chop it up.

But you build a lot of muscle memory in knife skills – and he got better! Sometimes it just takes a while to get your shit together. Very few people can cook well at the start of school. And maybe at the beginning you might think you won't make it, but you can get it together. Your chefs will be tough, but if you just keep going, you can do well. It was neat to see that kid turn into a cook when he had started out such a disaster.

Michael Jordan, Chef Instructor:

I have the joy of hindsight, but I can tell you: There's always a lot of work upfront. Whenever you do new and challenging things, it will always be hard at first, but then it will even out. You have to keep your focus, and really plough through in the beginning, and then all of a sudden you're cruising down the highway.

You get better at things the more you do them. Repetition is what leads to improvement. If it's the first time you've ever done something, it won't be the best you'll ever do. If you try it again, it will get better, just naturally. That's how you improve. You'll analyze and find the little tweaks – instead of starting from scratch, you're just adjusting this little part and that little part, and you see real progress.

I see this at school all the time. We get people who've never cooked before, and they think they'll just do a two-year program and it'll be this miracle. And when they're not getting instant revelations, they get frustrated – they say "I can't do that," and then they quit. You have to realize that the first time you do anything, you're going to suck. But don't quit. Come on back, try it again. If you keep at it, you will improve. With cooking, as with any craft, keep plugging away and cooking will absolutely give you back everything you give. But it's a wretched little bitch in the beginning. It doesn't want to give you *nothing*. It's just standing there like, "I've been burnt too many times. I've been hurt so often by terrible cooks."

On the Rail:

- Don't lose sight of the *biggest* picture – doing your best work, and helping others do the same.
- Apprentice your palate to the chefs and instructors you respect.
- Each taste is like one word of a new language. Build your vocabulary. And talk about what you're tasting to create associations and stronger taste memories.
- *Kaizen!* Focus on continual improvement, from wherever you are at this moment.

* * *

Part 4
The Bad News

A DOZEN WAYS THAT CULINARY SCHOOL ISN'T PREPARING YOU FOR RESTAURANT WORK

We've been focusing this whole time on how culinary school will prepare you for work in the food industry, and how to get the most out of this intensive preparation. Here's the bad news: There are lots of ways that culinary school *isn't* preparing you for restaurant work. Let's look at a dozen. And by that I mean 12 – none of that "baker's dozen" bullshit. That's just food theft.

1. At school, you have acres and acres of room to work in.

All that elbow room you have? Don't get used to it.

Walk through any school, and you'll always find a culinary or pastry student with a ten-foot-long table all to themselves, every inch covered with shit in disarray. They're usually standing still, all flustered, complaining they don't have enough space.

Every square inch of a restaurant that can possibly hold the rear end, footprint, or pegleg of a paying customer will be pressed into just that service, and the kitchen will be crammed into the smallest, least desirable leftover space possible. Which means that when you leave school, you will never see a long line of metal tables stretching off into the distance. Not ever again. Yes, I know: You have to share those tables, and sharing is hard. Especially when your classmates are messier and clumsier and generally less amazing than you are, in such very annoying ways. But right now – big school or small, big class or small – you're currently the real estate baron of Cutting-Board-Landia, and that's about to change.

In my first restaurant, my cutting board was 16 inches wide. I had two inches along its right side to slip my knives under the edge of the meat slicer. My left elbow hung over the dishwashing station, which was so close that servers routinely dropped food down my back as they ditched dirty plates there. If I had *ever* farted – and I'm speaking hypothetically here, people – it would've gone *inside* the dish machine, which was that close. I used my 7-inch santoku[24] because my 10-inch chef's knife was too big to use on my station. Let me repeat that: My *knife* was too big for the kitchen.

---

24 In case you just flipped here directly – this here guide has a glossary. Any terms that are randomly underlined like this will be defined in Part 5, at the end. If you haven't encountered industry terms like *kaizen*, lowboys, or metric fuckton before, flip back to see what they mean. If there are terms you wish I'd defined, or ones you feel I've left out, just email me through the website at www.NoBSguides. com and let me know. Or share your favorite kitchen language and swear words. I'd love to hear those, too.

So the space you complain about having to use in school? Divide it by four, stuff it chock-ass full of <u>mise</u> if you want to make it through service, share it with three or more coworkers who may enjoy gleefully fucking with you, and then roll out 40 servings of pasta on that station – while you're peeling 12 quarts of red beets (that can't bleed any color on your precious pappardelle).

Start working neater and tighter now. Right now, while you're in school. If you have a whole table, leave half of it clean and empty. Your teachers will notice, and that pants-for-brains classmate who keeps pulling sheet trays from the oven with a wet towel will appreciate being able to drop them on the vacant half of your table as soon as the steam burns start to register.

2. At school, you can take sick days.

On my paycheck, there's a little printed section that shows how much sick time I'm accruing.

I know! Thank you, thank you, I'll be here all week! And if *that* joke made you bend over laughing, just wait – I haven't even started my hygiene highjinx set!

Labor is a huge cost, so restaurants want to squeak by with just enough staff, which means there might not be someone available to cover your shift, however crap you may feel. This varies *a lot* from restaurant to restaurant. Is it a large chain that's really corporate, or a small independent business? Is it run well, or by seat-of-the-pants management? If you're deathly ill, you might have to call around and get your own shift covered. You might not see that sick time kick in to cover those lost hours in your next paycheck. Talk to your boss, and please do prove me wrong, but it's not easy being green (with the flu) when your ass is on the schedule.

Sure, sick days are legally-mandated in restaurants, but think of them as fables we tell – to teach a valuable lesson (*No one should work with food when they're sick!*), or to make ourselves feel better (*If I ever get really sick, surely I'll still have a job!*). Come, sit down here beside me. Once there was a line cook boy who said he had sick days, and all the animals hung from trees and laughed at him. But he did not ever make use of these magical promises, and so he kept his job and there was peace in the land.

3. At school, you ate sitting down.

If you ate sitting down, you were at school, and not working in a restaurant.

"But I only had 15 minutes," you say. In one line cooking job, I worked ten hour shifts, and if I really insisted – okay, badgered – my <u>sous</u>, I could usually get a ten-minute break. Friends who didn't work in restaurants invariably said, "Isn't that illegal?" and friends who worked in restaurants said, "Wow, howdja get a ten?" Another line cook at that restaurant who'd been crazy-anti-smoking all his life started up – just so he could get a smoke break.

It's hotter than shit in damn near any restaurant kitchen, so you're pounding water from quart containers, buckets, clown shoes, whatever. And no breaks means that when you get any moment of slowdown, you're eating in bites or spoonfuls between trying to restock for the next rush. And no, not bites and spoonfuls from a salad plate or an entrée bowl – how unbearably bougie *that* would be. You're chomping family meal out of a <u>ninth pan,</u> a butter insert – something that fits in one hand, doesn't spill, and is ridiculous to dine from.

4. At school, everyone's religious about glove wearing.

It's like a mantra in school: *No <u>BHC</u> with <u>RTE</u> food. Om.*

In fact, one of the nastier ways you can impugn someone's very character is to gossip about seeing them *touch food with their bare hands*. Those mangy pox-ridden unclefuckers!

Guess what? There are loads of restaurants where employees almost never use gloves. Working through a mountain of animal protein, or peeling a case of red beets? Great, go find that box of gloves behind the dishwasher and slip on a pair so that you don't look and smell like a serial killer after your shift's over. But in many restaurants, sauté is testing the meats with a finger, <u>pantry</u> is hand-tossing and plating up salads with bare hands, and everyone is washing up often and well, and keeping a sanitary ship.

5. At school, you don't see activities every day that should only happen at the start of OSHA videos.

OSHA is the Occupational Safety and Health Administration, and they're presumably the ones who are supposed to guarantee that you're not climbing rickety ladders perched precariously on sheets of ice in order to jam metal spoons into slightly-out-of-reach electrical sockets, and other such workplace safety hazards.

I don't think they've ever been inside of most restaurants.

At one point, I worked in a restaurant that was so tiny that everything went up – shelves 20 feet up the wall held bins of baking dishes that we used every week. Even reaching the 8- and 10-quart containers required ladders. Well, for me. The tall and lanky guys I worked with could take one giant step from the floor to the edge of the dish pit, and then climb the shelves from there. One kid did this with a broken arm in a sling. For weeks. I never did climb the kitchen shelves, but I did have to routinely climb the shelves in the back storage rooms, half-a-dozen times a day at least.

At school, you may be pushing carts from the dish pit on occasionally slippery floors, or lifting heavy pans off of high shelves, or occasionally grabbing a step stool to get to the obscure spices on the top shelf. You'll be using dangerous equipment – fryers, slicers, steam jacket kettles, ranges, and open flames of all sorts. But it's likely that your feet will be solidly planted on non-skid mats and you won't be treated to any demos of climbing closed ladders propped in open doorways, cleaning the slicer by turning it on and pressing your sani towel to the blade, or putting lids away by throwing them overhead up into bins (and dodging fast when you miss).

A restaurant owner and chef need to do everything they can to ensure your safety in a dangerous workplace. After that, it's up to you. So don't be dumb about your safety, even if your more-experienced colleagues are.

6.   You just learned the "right" way to truss a chicken.

You're in school to learn a whole pile of foundational skills that restaurant chefs will expect you to know when you list culinary school on your resume. Your Chef Instructors bring a wealth of knowledge and industry experience to the table, and as you'll find out (if you don't already know it), folks in this industry have some strong-ass opinions. So they'll show you the best way to truss a chicken, tie a roast, fillet a round fish and then a flat fish, etc. And that's fantastic, and one of the key reasons you went to culinary school.

But you didn't actually learn the *best* way to truss a chicken, tie a roast, fillet a round fish and then a flat fish, etc. – you learned *one way* to do those things. If you went to a really good culinary school, you learned more than one way, because even your instructors from quarter to quarter had differing opinions and preferences on techniques and procedures, which taught you to be adaptable and accommodating.

Because when you start working in a kitchen, guess what the best way is to truss a chicken, tie a roast, fillet a round fish and then a flat fish, etc.? It's *that* chef's way.

You will never make the rookie mistake of saying, "But Chef, we learned it this way in school!" Fuck you and the school you rode in on. You do it this chef's way, or you hit the proverbial highway. The techniques you learned in school are valuable and you'll keep using some of them, in just that exact same way, throughout your cooking career. But learn to be adaptable, because as soon as we run out of the larger mammals and start eating cats, I guarantee you there'll be more than one way to skin 'em.

7. Your parents are telling their friends that you're learning to become a chef.

You're not learning to become a chef. You're learning foundational skills for a cooking career, and if you work hard and do well, you'll land a cooking job, and you'll start at the bottom and work your way up, just like everyone does. Just like the kids who didn't go to culinary school at all.

"Well, wait just one moment, sire," you may be inquiring, "Surely that's not just and fair, for I've just paid a king's ransom in tuition!"

First of all, stop speaking Fake Medieval English, you great twat, this is kitchen work, not scholarly scholarship.

Second, kitchen skills are rooted in speed, in stamina, in muscle memory and physical accuracy, in the finest precision work you can do, and in the gross motor skills necessary to keep you upright while you do them. It's based on sensory input, knowing by look and touch and smell and taste when food is properly cooked and properly seasoned. It's based on intuition and informed and experienced gut feelings. And for all these reasons, the most important kitchen skills are learned by practice and repetition, and there are no shortcuts.

Third, if some restaurant chefs do hate culinary grads, this is the single most common reason: The idea, based typically on an inflated sense of ego and entitlement, that culinary school should give you a shortcut to higher positions in kitchens. In a business with no shortcuts, super talented people occasionally end up on a fast track because they can just develop and demonstrate superior skills faster than most mere mortals. But for every one of these rare and truly gifted birds, there are others who get promoted ahead of their skill level because of a degree or a certificate, and they can't work every station in their restaurant like a boss. They can't innovate or execute at the level of a chef who worked his or her way up step by step. Sure, there are corners of the industry where real innovation and boss skills aren't actually totally necessary. But in most kitchens, you earn your way up based on skills alone – not certificates, not degrees. To expect otherwise is to shit upon the vast investment of time and energy and focus that the people around you have been making for years and decades. And that's just not polite.

8.   At school, someone's keeping an eye on the FIFO, and a seemingly-endless stream of gorgeous produce and proteins just appear for your use, as if by magic.

At my school, a woman named Cindy took care of ordering, receiving, restocking, inventory, and one million additional responsibilities – and she was ruthless, ferocious, and generally pissed off about the state of things in the kitchens, inside the walk-ins, and between our ears. She had the toughest job in the school, and if she ever goes postal or walks out or both, they'll have to hire three people to replace her. She was awesome.

Of course she was always pissed – she deals daily with hundreds of students unaccustomed to the routines and rules of kitchens, and we were all lazy-ass motherfuckers about FIFO and labeling and putting things back where they belong, and all of that created a huge amount of waste and a lot of extra work – not for us, for Cindy. She couldn't fire any of us, but I'm pretty sure she wanted to murder most of us.

If there's a Cindy in your restaurant, you're damn lucky. Every food establishment should have someone as meticulous and detailed and pissed off – it keeps everyone safer, especially the diners. The Cindy in a restaurant kitchen *can* fire you, though, or at least get you fired – and if you waste as much as students collectively do in culinary school, she will. If you're as bad at labeling and FIFO as students in school collectively are, she should fire you fast, before the health inspector turns up and the whole restaurant gets cited.

Well-run restaurants order just as much product as they need and will use, store it safely, and use strict first-in-first-out (FIFO) rotations to reduce waste.

If we hammered an ingredient at school (e.g. the dark day that I boiled a pot of perfectly-diced sunchokes into a paste), it seemed like there was always a shitton more on hand, and another batch could be whipped up. Often that's not the case in restaurants. You will need to go immediately to your chef or your Cindy, confess your sins, and make sure that whatever product you hammered is accounted for and incoming orders adjusted accordingly.

If you step into a role that includes any receiving, it's not like school, where a pushcart of pristine produce just rolls into your classroom. In a restaurant, you need to open every box, inspect the produce, smell the seafood, check that there are tags on the shellfish, verify quickly that everything's quality and not crap, check the guy's list against your order sheets to make sure that nothing's missing, and pass along any verbal or written notes about shit they shorted you on and why. This sounds pretty clear, but the dudes who deliver to restaurants have this demonic sixth sense that compels them to show up at the precise minute you're cooking caramel, you're juggling three tasks, or you just got a fistful of tickets from a server who's been storing them up for you.

9. Your school day's over in six, seven, maybe eight hours?

Nope, not in most restaurants. Many line cooks routinely work 10 hour shifts, and in some restaurants that can regularly creep upwards during busy times into 12+ hour shifts. In my experience, the only time restaurants give one fuck about how long you work is when they're paying you too much overtime.

But it gets better once you work your way up the ladder, right? Wrong-o. In many restaurants the sous is that harried indentured servant guy who just took a birdbath in the sink in the ladies' loo. And those salaried chefs? They probably do rent places that they could sleep in, though no one's ever seen that happen.

10. Your classmates can't shank you.

Okay, I'm stretching on this one. Your coworkers in a restaurant really shouldn't be shanking you either. You're heading into the food industry, not prison. But things that can fester as inconveniences in school often have quicker and more serious consequences in restaurants.

In school, you might see a classmate lose the support of his peers – usually by being a slobby, corner-cutting, mediocre dickwhistle of some sort. And guess what? It doesn't matter much. He may linger on and on, and someone still has to partner with him on stations or for group assignments, and everyone complains but nothing ever happens because the lazy fuck keeps paying his tuition and doing the minimum needed to squeak by.

Restaurants want to do as much business as possible with as few employees as possible, and that basic food industry economics will never change. So someone who isn't pulling his or her weight *can't* last long, or the restaurant won't. In consistently difficult working conditions, people notice when someone doesn't set up and mise out the station well for the next person, uses the last of something without restocking it, always carries the lightest box, works differently when the chef's not around, throws away product to avoid dealing with it, etc. Some people are flat-out narcs about these things, but even a friendly, low-key colleague who sees someone take enough short-cuts will find a way to pass that along to the chef when a casual "So how's [insert Butthole's name here] working out?"conversation happens to come up. And believe me, those conversations come up in kitchens.

You can slide by in school, but that's a bad damn habit to develop. Work hard, so that even the people who think you're a total prick have to grudgingly admit that they'd rather be paired up with you than that friendly lazy dude with the Flock of Seagulls hair.

11.   At school, you think you're working fast, but you're not. Yet.

The culinary schools that tend to best prepare their graduates for real industry work are the ones that incorporate some practical and hands-on service to the public into their curriculum.

At our school, you spent first quarter learning knife skills, assisting, and doing the grunt work of the school. Second quarter, you cooked student lunch for everyone else. Third quarter, you cooked for the public at an *á la carte* casual bistro. Fourth quarter, you cooked for the public in a fine dining restaurant. But even in these "cooking real food for real customers" settings, the pace doesn't even begin to approach restaurant work. You wouldn't want it to – you're paying tuition for the personalized instruction that can happen *because* the pace is much slower than you'd face at any restaurant.

So don't kick yourself that the pace is slower. But don't fool yourself into thinking that you're working at restaurant speed, either. In our school bistro, we'd do 100 cov-ers at lunch – with 18 students. I was working at a restaurant at the same time that did 150 daytime covers on a busy breakfast and lunch – with two of us in the kitchen.

So if you're fast enough that you're doing just fine in school, get a lot fucking faster. If you're so fast you already have down time, work on your accuracy. Keep pushing yourself, as much as you can – speed, then accuracy, then get even faster, then more consistently accurate. You'll set yourself up way better than someone who's content to be good in school, which is kind of like being the smartest guy still in Ohio, or the world's tallest dim sum cook.

12.   At school, you didn't get fired for that dumb shit you just did.

We already talked about how being a FIFO felon and a lazy receiver can get you in trouble, but more than half the dumb shit you can get away with as a tuition-paying student will get your ass kicked to the curb in a restaurant.

Overslept your alarm and showed up at school 90 minutes late, or not at all? Revel in writing that next tuition check, because it's why you're still welcome in the building.[25] At a restaurant, you'd be out of a job. Hammer a bunch of expensive product, or let it go to waste? Restaurants can't afford to keep you around. Act like a selfish dildo and earn the spite of your coworkers? It may not be immediate, but you'll eventually get benched in favor of better team players.

Relax, though. There's a flip side to this.

Culinary school is a luxury – a chance to ask a million questions, to take the time to learn complicated processes, to ask for another demo when you're really working hard on a technique and still can't quite get it.

You get to make mistakes in culinary school – to work out the kinks, and get the dumb stuff out of your system. You get to learn by feel, and if your dough is lumpy or too dry or too wet, you get to try again, so that by the time you leave school you can make a sexy dough by feel. If the grill marks on your first three or four or five steaks don't look like a glistening Outback Steakhouse ad, you get to keep working at it, and with practice they'll start to look more like evenly-spaced diamonds and less like the charcoal imprint of a drunk bird's nest.

---

25   Notice I said *in the building*. That's because I interviewed a friend who said, "At CIA, if we were five minutes late, we were sent back to the next cohort. I started drinking coffee."

This time in school is your time, and it's your privilege and your responsibility to make the most of it. Culinary school may not prepare you perfectly for every aspect of restaurant work, but if you throw yourself into it and work your ass off, it will help you lay a solid foundation for a culinary career. Prove yourself to your instructors, and they'll be some of the best champions you'll have in your new career. Prove yourself to your classmates and you'll form badass friendships and build a strong professional network that will make the rest of your cooking career more interesting and fun.

Go on, get cooking.

Kaizen!

Part 5
The Glossary

86 – To deny service, in one of two ways. If a kitchen runs out of key components for a certain dish, it will get 86'ed from the menu and customers can no longer order it (and if that's a cook's fault, he or she is in deep shit, so avoid this like the plague on your station). Also, if a customer is a serious <u>dickwhistle</u>, he or she can be 86'ed from the restaurant, and told never to come back. In an industry that boasts sub-5% profit margins, you can imagine how poorly a customer would have to act to be 86'ed, but it does happen. Oh, and if *you're* the one 86'ed, you've just been fired.

Á *la carte* – French for "to kick one's ass." What? Are you back here checking up on me?

All day – The total number of current orders of a specific item. Table Four ordered two trout, Table 17 ordered three trout. "That's five trout all day."

Anglaise – Short for crème anglaise, a classic French custard that can serve as an ice-cream base or a super-rich and dreamy sauce for desserts.

Anthony Bourdain – He's been called a "bad boy chef" and a "maverick food porn poet." He graduated from the CIA in 1978 and worked his way up in restaurants to executive cheffing at Brasserie Les Halles in New York City. The reason we know this is because in 2000, he wrote the book *Kitchen Confidential: Adventures in the Culinary Underbelly*. This wasn't the first gritty portrayal of what it's really like to work in kitchens (Bourdain himself credits Michael Pierre White, who wrote an earlier tell-all kitchen memoir, as the original bad boy chef), but has definitely been the most influential and popular one in this country. He's all over TV now – don't miss *Mind of a Chef*, and if you're into travel, check out *No Reservations* and *Parts Unknown*, all on Netflix at the time of writing. Not that culinary students should be tempted with Netflix streaming accounts.

Aspen Food & Wine – Technically called the Food & Wine™ Classic in Aspen, this is the mother of all culinary schmooze-fests. Entry tickets are well over $1,000 (which doesn't cover any of the $1,000- and $2,000-per-head dinners thrown around town that week or include any blowjobs), but it's always sold out anyway, which is why the chance to attend is usually part of the winner's package on shows like *Top Chef*.

Back of House (BOH) – Chefs, cooks, prep cooks, dishwashers, and anyone who has traditionally (before the trend of exhibition kitchens) worked out of view of the customers.

Bain marie – Either a metal container (similar to a hotel pan, but round and usually taller), or a fancy name for a water bath used when you're cooking custards or terrines that need gentler heat.

Beurre blanc – A luscious sauce made by reducing vinegar, shallots, and white wine (use red and it's called a *beurre rouge*), and then emulsifying this with butter by stirring in small cubes of cold butter, one at a time. Once you learn the classic technique, you can pimp out the flavor all different ways.

BHC – Acronym for bare-hand contact. No BHC with RTE food = no bare-hand contact with ready-to-eat food, which will be on your ServSafe exam about seven times.

BOH – See Back of House.

Brigade system – The kitchen hierarchy, still used in many restaurants today, that Escoffier nabbed from the military to systematize kitchen roles and duties. Don't fuck with it.

Brunoise – A perfect 1/8th inch dice, made by cutting a nice, squared-off julienne first, and then dicing up all your little matchsticks into tiny perfect cubes.

Chef de Cuisine – This is the top dude in the kitchen. In large or super-corporate kitchens, there might be higher-ranking executive chefs, who still wear the coat but exclusively push paperwork all day. But this is the boss who might also be saddled with a shitton of paperwork, but still runs the kitchen and touches food – if not day to day, then at least pretty often. See "Kitchen Rules" in Part 2 for a breakdown of the brigade system.

Chez Panisse – Food activist Alice Waters opened this café in Berkeley, California in 1971 with this crazy idea that we should eat organic food that's grown locally, we should know our farmers and respect the foods they grow, we should cook in humane work environments, and use the best ingredients possible and prepare them without a lot of fuss. The fact that today many cooks will read that and think, "Um, yeah: No duh," is a testament to her success. Other than the bit about humane work environments, her revolutionary ideas caught on so well they're (high-end) mainstream these days.

Chiffonade – Cutting herbs or vegetables into long, thin strips. On the unfussy end, think coleslaw cut. On the fussy end, you're rolling sage leaves and making tiny slivers of them.

Chinois – A very fine mesh strainer with an odd shape that looks like a cone fused to a handle. A two-ounce ladle is just the right size to push liquids and purees through a standard-sized chinois, and moving it up and down in the liquid inside of the chinois in a jerk-off motion speeds the whole process up significantly. A strainer with the same conical shape but larger holes is called a China cap. Why yes, that terms does have racist (or at least pitifully Orientalist) origins.

Conversions – Going from cups to grams to milliliters to tablespoons to ounces to teaspoons to gallons. Mind-bending math. Do yourself a solid and memorize the basic ones in school, and then memorize the multiples and formulas, and then practice until you can do these in your sleep and/or while you're on fire, which could both happen during a shift on the line.

Coulis – A sauce made from pureed and strained fruits or vegetables. Made poorly, mucky baby food.

Cover – One customer. If you do 150 covers at lunch, you've fed 150 customers, however many individual plates or courses they've ordered.

Culinary Institute of America – When a chef says she trained at the CIA, she wasn't assassinating bureaucrats overseas. That's the other CIA. She meant she went to one of the top-ranked culinary schools in the US (alongside with the Institute of Culinary

Education, and the original Johnson & Wales program in Providence). Now, are these programs worth their astronomical price tags, in an industry where you won't make much money for years? That's the subject of huge debate.

David Chang – The Momofuku / Lucky Peach / Mind of a Chef chef who must inspire the hatred of every health inspector in New York City with his long fermentation, aging, and rotten foods experiments alone. Also does crazy shit with ramen noodles. Also does crazy shit with mayonnaise. Also does crazy shit with etc.

Dickwhistle – A total turdburgler. See also, douchekazoo.

Douchekazoo – A total dickwhistle. See also, turdburgler.

Douchenozzle – Obviously totally different than douchekazoo, above, this is someone who thinks they're God's gift to kitchens, but is well liked and respected by none. See also, Shoemaker.

Drop – Signal to start cooking a side item, as in, "drop the fries." Into the fryer oil, btw. This doesn't mean drop them on the floor.

Egronomic – Designed not to fuck up your body (as fast, or as completely, at least).

Eric Ripert – The gracious and well-mannered chef (does he ever lose his shit in the kitchen, I wonder?) who owns Le Bernardin in New York City. He started working at the 400-year-old Paris institution La Tour d'Argent at age 17, trained with legendary chefs, and is now a legendary chef. See how that works?

Escoffier – The Dude, who came along in the late 1800s with revolutionary ideas like, "Hey, shouldn't food taste good?" and "What if we served food hot that should be eaten hot?" bringing an end to centuries of elaborate banquets that looked amazing and tasted like shit. To pull off his ideas, he snapped kitchens into shape, borrowing a military pecking order that many kitchens still use today. He also nailed down recipes for the mother sauces (learn these please!), the culinary equivalent of cruising down off a mountain with stone tablets carved with suggestions. And by suggestions, I mean commandments.

Executive chef – Whether or not his or her name's on the door, this is the chef who's worked his or her way up the ladder – and usually all the way out of the kitchen. A phantom, a mere rumor to line cooks. One of the small and petty joys of cooking competitions is watching big-name ECs who've gotten out of practice get schooled by peers who've actually held a knife in the past three years.

Expo / Expeditor – The person calling orders to the line. Manages the timing when firing multiple components of a plate, or multiple plates going to same table, and for that reason should be a very experienced cook with a solid handle on fire times. Often a job given to new cooks, sadly.

FIFO – An acronym for "first in, first out," which refers to strictly dating and rotating food so that you're always using what needs to be used up first, and decreasing (or ideally eliminating) food waste. I said to my girlfriend once, "If we ever get a dog, let's name him FIFO," thinking that was hilarious. Like Fido, right? But for food people? She looked at me like she was seeing me for the first time and said, "That's appalling. Absolutely not."

Finger condoms – According to any health departments I've encountered, you need to double-wrap cuts, first in a Band-Aid, and then in a barrier like a glove. So in theory, if you have a cut on your finger and don't want to glove up, you could slip one of these little latex finger condoms over just that finger. In practice, you're more likely to end up serving a finger-condom salad and getting canned. And, in any case, you will never find these in the first aid kit, ever. If the first aid kit ever included them, they were removed upon arrival, and immediately used to mock the dishwasher.

Fire – To start cooking, as in "Fire Table 17's trout, five trout all day." See prep, and see hold, and while you're at it, see drop, too.

FOH – See Front of House.

Fond – You take a great piece of meat and roast or sear it, and it leaves fat and browned bits behind in the pan – little flavor bombs, that you hit with liquid so that you can scrape them up (called deglazing) and create a basic pan sauce or gravy. US cooks call the browned bits fond; French cooks call the sauce that results fond. Either way, it's deliciousness that's criminal to send to the dish pit.

Food cost(ing) – The cost of all the food used in a specific menu item (or, as a verb, the process of finding that number). In school, you typically learn the restaurant rule of thumb that food costs should average out to about 32% of menu prices.

French top – A cooktop that, instead of having separate burners, has heavy metal plates that heat from below, so that you can use the whole surface, moving pots around from the hottest areas to cooler spots on the side. Slow to heat up, but these sombitches get monsterfucking hot once they do.

Front of House (FOH) – The restaurant staff that interacts directly with customers – i.e. servers, bartenders, general managers, etc. Should be outgoing and personable, and also, apparently, great at texting and shameless about making way more money than the BOH.

Galantines – First, debone a whole chicken, but leave all its skin intact. Then, stuff it with ground meat or other ingredients. Then roll it up and tie it, and either roast it or poach it in stock. In my program, this was one of the products everyone had to complete in a second-quarter butchery rotation. It was time consuming and fairly detail-oriented work. When I was a first-quarter commis, the chick I was paired up with was intimidated, I guess, and completely delegated the task to me. Please don't ever do this. It was a weenie move that deprived her of the chance to better her knife skills, even if she never made this again. I pulled it off decently well, and was so pumped to have the chance to tackle something so far above my pay grade. I immediately went home and made one for my roommate, who thought I'd been reincarnated as Julia Child. By the time it was on my To Do list in second quarter, I was comfortable and confident with the process.

Garde Manger – See Pantry. Also, see "Kitchen Rules" in Part 2 for a breakdown of the brigade system.

Genoise – A sponge cake that uses air suspended in the batter through mixing to give it volume. Invented by the Italians, stolen by the French. I did not master this; my first genoise in school had all the airy lift of a Birkenstock sole.

Hammered – See Slammed. Hammering can also mean totally overcooking product. If you hammered or nailed a steak, you cooked it well past medium rare. If a customer requests a well-done steak, they're an idiot, and Expo will call for a hammered steak, dead steak, *steako muerto*, or whatever version of this they think is super funny at the time.

Hold – Every restaurant will have its own series of calls, but sometimes these will include both fire and hold. A hold is just a heads up. If the expo calls, "Table 17, fire two soups, hold one salmon one chop," and you're on sauté, it means that Table 17 is going to be eating soup now, but in about 15-20 minutes, you're going to get a call to fire their salmon and pork chop entrees. This is the time when you check and make sure you have the <u>mise</u> for those dishes; gods forbid you don't, but at least this gives you ten minutes to solve the problem somehow. See fire, and see prep.

Hotel pan – Square pans used in every kitchen, not just in hotels. They're typically made of stainless steel, and their rectangular shape is standardized to fit into steam tables, chafing dishes, onto lines, etc. You'll use a lot of hotel pans, and the way they're named is systematic, and good to know:

- A full hotel pan is a 12 x 20 inch standard rectangle.
- A half pan is – you guessed it – half that size.
- If six smaller pans would fit into the same space as a full sized pan, they're 1/6th the size. What do you think we call them? That's right – sixth pans.
- Ninth pans are 1/9th the size.

After a week or two in a kitchen, you'll be able to spot which is which in a ninth of a second.

In the weeds – Fucked, way behind, running out of mise, generally getting buried. See also, Slammed.

James Beard – The über-mentor of dozens of influential chefs in his time, he was a super-sized food personality (cookbook author, columnist, early TV guy) whose foundation now grants the well-regarded James Beard Awards each year.

Joie de vivre – French for "joy of living." I was almost going to write something super snarky, like "in restaurants, as rare as sick days," but there's actually loads of both *joie* and *vivre* in restaurants; you just have to take the time to keep them fed and nurtured.

Julia Child – Okay, listen. I've introduced you in this glossary to Anthony Bourdain and David Chang, Eric Ripert and James Beard. This is where I draw the line. If you have not seen her quirky and hilarious cooking shows, head directly to YouTube (do not pass go, do not collect $200).

Julienne – Making matchsticks that are 1/8-inch x 1/8-inch x 2-2.5 inches long. Slightly fatter (think thin fast-food French fry), and it's called a battonet.

Kaizen – Continual improvement. There's a whole section about *Kaizen* in the "Keep Getting Better" chapter in Part 3.

Kitchen Stadium – Ever seen the TV show *Iron Chef*? This is the massive two-kitchen "stadium" where chefs face off with chosen "Iron Chefs" and do battle over who can make the best five-course meal in 60 minutes. The "secret ingredient" isn't really a secret to either chef, they have 45 minutes of prep time we never see, and the judging is usually ridiculous – but the cooking is fun to watch, and if you catch the dubbed Japanese originals, they're even better than the new *Iron Chef America*.

Lowboys – Short refrigerators that fit beneath your line / station.

Metric fuckton – Much larger than a metric shitton. Learn your metric system, okay? And not just so you don't keep having to flip back here.

Michelin-starred – Most of us know of Michelin as a tire company first. In 1900 the Brothers Michelin put out a guidebook of restaurants good enough to warrant a journey – by car, so that they'd spur the demand for tires. The Michelin Guide is now one of the most highly-regarded international rating systems for high-end restaurants. Getting one star is a big deal. Getting (or losing) the max of three stars is a matter of life or death for some chefs.

Mise en place – French for "having all your shit together before your ass gets handed to you in service," or something close to that. Made into a verb (which every noun in a kitchen eventually is), miseing yourself out means preparing all the components of any menu item you may need to cook during service, and having close at hand any equipment or tools you'll need as well.

Modernist cuisine – This is the experimental style of cooking that has emerged from plundering the knowledge and tools of food science and industrial production and using them to achieve visually stunning, playful, and more flavorful outcomes at higher price points. If you're spherifying mango juice or powdering olive oil, you're cooking in this style. I'd be dead curious to see a reliable breakdown on the percentage of chefs who love it or aspire in some way to get involved vs. chefs who hate and disdain it. See molecular gastronomy, next.

Molecular gastronomy – Another term for modernist cuisine, above. This term was coined in 1988 by a physicist and a chemist (Hervé This, who wrote the book *Molecular Gastronomy: Exploring the Science of Flavor*), who identified three aspects of cooking – social, artistic, and technical – and really pushed on innovating on the technical side. This term seems to have a bit more traction in the general public. Chefs seem to use the term modernist cuisine slightly more often, or they'll try to seem like mavericks and make up a new term for the same thing. In another century and a half, we'll either be calling this peasant food or peak oil food, depending on how things shake out.

Morels – Pricey mushrooms with a gorgeous dark and earthy flavor that's made downright sultry sexy with the addition of a fuckton of cream and butter. Called dog peckers in Ohio, for their looks (no beauty queens, these).

Ninth pan – See hotel pan.

Old Overholt – The best cheap rye whiskey. Sometimes it's important to evaluate things carefully and develop an educated opinion about why one thing is better than another. Other times, just get on the fucking bus. My first restaurant chef ever drank Old Overholt, and that just makes it the best whiskey.

On the rail – An order that immediately becomes top priority and is needed yesterday. Usually (but not always) the result of a server fuckup – they forgot an order, fucked up the order, dropped the steak on the dining room floor, etc. and the item is needed 5-10 minutes in the past, and it's now your emergency. Similar to crying wolf, should be used sparingly.

Pantry – Also called Garde Manger, cold station, salad station. This is your first stop in most restaurant kitchens. It's the entry-level spot, but that doesn't mean it's easy. There's high turnover in most restaurants, but this station in particular can seem like a revolving door. See "Kitchen Rules" in Part 2 for a breakdown of the brigade system.

Par – The minimum quantity of any ingredient that you should have on hand at the start of service. Depending on context, this could mean the prepared components of any dish you need to have mised out in advance and ready to go. Or it could just mean minimum quantities of un-prepped ingredients or dry goods that should be held in your stockroom or walk-in at any given time.

Please Use shelf – Most culinary schools (and some restaurants) will have a please use shelf inside a reach-in or walk-in refrigerator, that's just assorted bits and pieces, ends and scraps – anything too good to throw away, but of no use at the moment. It's my happy place; my own personal episode of that show *Chopped*, where you get a mystery basket of random ingredients and have to create brilliance, often for student lunch or family meal. It's a quirky flea market of free-to-use ingredients – right up until they rot there. Then it stops being my happy place.

Prep – If you don't look around and see a prep cook, you're probably the prep cook. In most culinary schools and restaurants, if you work a station, you'll have a prep list (of shit you need to mise out) and you'll also be responsible for firing a certain number of these dishes. The overlap might not be 100% – you may need to prep things that others fire, and vice versa. Ask questions and clarify early. See also, fire.

Prep sheets – In every culinary school program, you'll be expected to come in well-prepared to make the most of your kitchen time, which will often involve writing up a plan in advance. Whether it's called a prep sheet, mise sheet, plan of action (PoA), or yer mum's list, it's the guide to battle that you put into writing ahead of time, and must sometimes submit for grades or points.

RTE – Acronym for ready-to-eat food. See also, BHC.

Sancho – I apologize. This is going to seem like a dick move, but I'm not going tell you about Sancho until the second book. You will never learn this one in culinary school, so don't worry that you're missing out on something now. You'll learn it as soon as you start working the line at a restaurant. So check the glossary next time around. I promise it'll be there.

Sani buckets – The red ones. Part of setting up any kitchen is to fill sanitary buckets with water and the correct percentage of sanitizer or bleach, and then distribute them throughout the kitchen – ideally, one at each station, so that every cook is using them religiously and frequently.

Santoku – An all-purpose knife shape from Japan. From *Santoku bōchō*, which literally means "three uses," referring to slicing, dicing, and mincing.

Saucier – In a big fancy kitchen, with the staff to run a whole brigade system, this is the dude who makes sauces. Usually the most senior line cook. Touch this guy's chinois, or take his 2-ounce ladle, and prepare to die.

Scaling – On the culinary side, doing the maths involved in doubling, halving, or in any other way fucking with the quantities of a recipe. On the Baking & Pastry side, measuring anything on a scale.

.

Seam butchery – Here in the US, we have a bunch of standard meat cuts, and many of them depend on using big-ass band saws to cut directly through muscles and bone. It's fast and efficient, and part of our assembly-line, industrial approach to butchery. In Europe, older butchery methods are still prevalent. Butchers use their knives for the whole process, and cut through connective tissues (and not muscles or bones) by following the seams between muscles – hence the name.

Shoe / Shoemaker – A totally shitty, lazy cook.

Sixth pan – See hotel pan.

Shift drink / Shifty – In most restaurants, you get one free drink (and sometimes, but not always, food) at the end of each shift you work.

Slammed – Busy, but specifically, Busy < Slammed < Hammered < In the weeds. See also, In the weeds.

Sodium alginate – A chemical used (typically along with calcium chloride) in the spherification process. See modernist cuisine.

Sous chef – The chef's deputy; literally "under-chief" – the boss when the chef's not present. In a big kitchen, the sous will probably be your direct supervisor, and you'll see a lot more of him / her than you will of your chef. You know the whole good cop / bad cop gig? Your chef wants to be the benign Word of God in the kitchen, admired and respected. Which means that the sous's job is to be his wrathful, avenging angel. Hell hath no fury like a sous chef wronged, slighted, disappointed, or hungover. If you think your sous is the biggest dickhead on the planet, he might be. Or he might just be doing his job. See "Kitchen Rules" in Part 2 for a breakdown of the brigade system.

Stage (do a *stage*, be a *stage*, *staging*) – This is a stolen French word, so it's pronounced "stAHHjzh" and not the way we'd say theater stage. Refers (as a noun) to an apprentice who works in a restaurant, usually for free and for an agreed-upon length of time, in order to learn from the chef and cooks there. Or (as a verb), to doing that kind of apprenticeship. Or (as a different noun), the apprenticeship itself. Basically, use the word however the fuck you want, just don't expect a paycheck with it.

Subprimals – An animal carcass is first cut into primal cuts (huge pieces), and then broken down into subprimals (still big chunks of funk), which are in turn broken down into common fabricated cuts.

Tapioca maltodextrin – A cheap additive that used to bulk up industrially-processed foods, now it's mostly used in molecular gastronomy to do things like powder fats. See also, Modernist cuisine.

Thomas Keller – The French Laundry dude, and the reason most of you will have to learn to make cornets in school. Was he the first man on earth to perfectly behead an egg and use it as its own serving vessel for some dainty bite of food? Probably not, but he owns that move now. Was he the first chef on earth to play with the "oysters and pearls" idea? Probably not, but those other guys have to footnote *him* now.

Tournet / Tourneting – Pronounced "tour-nay" on account of it's French. A classic (read, frustrating and time-consuming) method of making humble potatoes into fancy things by carving them into seven-sided footballs.

Turdburgler – A total douchekazoo. See also, dickwhistle.

Acknowledgements

Holy shit, it really does take a village to get a book done. So many of you have helped in amazing ways.

I am so grateful for those of you who spoke with me and agreed to add your voices to this project: Becky, Mr. D, Chef Gregg, Jen, Josh, Julie, Chef Kären, Karen, Kristina, Michelle, Chef Mike, Rachel, and Rebecca. I can't thank you enough. You rock, and I had so much fun hearing and including your wisdom.

You know those big chef crushes early on in your cooking career, when you're just in awe of your chef's skill? The warmest and crushiest thanks to the first chefs who trained and mentored me, whose palates I've chased, and who've taught me so much of what I know about food, flavor, and hard work: Jack, Becky, Mike and Kären. And to the best culinary school pardners a girl could ever want: Oğuz, Camiller, and Morgan.

So many thanks to the people who helped with the nuts and bolts of getting this damn thing up to snuff. This book wouldn't exist at all without the heroic help of Julie DuRose – I'm endlessly grateful. Becky Selengut and Matthew Amster-Burton, you've gone so far above and beyond. And huge thanks to Ivan Popov (Chupavi on 99designs. com), who designed the book and ebook covers and was fantastic to work with, and to the Createspace designers who took care of the book's interior layout.

So many loving thanks to Jenny, Mom & Dad, Jack & Claudia, always.

And a big thank you to all of you I haven't even met yet, who will buy a book, leave a review, pass this on to a friend, help get the word out. Each of you are helping me build a quirky and creative cooking life, one step at a time.

Did you dig this book?
Was it helpful to you and worth the read?

Please share the love!

Cruise back to wherever you bought this book and leave an honest review. These matter a lot, and you'll have my greatest thanks and endless appreciation.

Please stay in touch!

If you're interested in more resources like this, check out www.NoBSguides.com. You can also sign up there to get a heads up when a new book comes out.

Please share your feedback!

Any suggestions for how to improve this book? Any burning questions that I didn't address? Any anecdotes from your own experience that I should include when I update this? Would you like to introduce me to someone in the field who I should absolutely talk to and interview? I'd love to hear what you think. Please do get in touch with any constructive feedback, unanswered questions, or introductions. I'm at Kim (dot) NBCG (at) gmail (dot) com.

An Excerpt from Book #2

The No-Bullshit Guide to Starting Your Cooking Career

Book #2 is for you if you're looking to get your first (or second) cooking job, find a valuable mentor (or two), and make the right strategic moves now to start your cooking career right. Work ethic and desire? Required. Culinary school experience? Not required, but certainly beneficial.

This book is for cooks starting out – if you've been in the industry for dogs years, or you're looking for sous chef positions and above, this guide's not for you. You should know this rodeo by now, pardner.

The Tasting Menu:

1. What's a *stage*, and who the hell works for free? Finding your Obi-Wan, and the importance of mentorship.
2. The nuts and bolts of finding a restaurant job, getting the boring shit like letters and resumes in good working order, and making first contact.
3. The specific tactical steps for killing it in a *stage* or working interview.
4. Succeeding in the job you just got, and strategically looking ahead at where you want to go.

Below is an excerpt from early in Part 4, wherein I get my ass handed to me, and learn a valuable lesson. Like a classic fuckin' fairy tale, but with more sweat stains and swearing. *Please ahnjoy.*

The No-Bullshit Guide to Starting Your Cooking Career
Part 4: Stepping Into the Role
Learning to Make the Time

Really successful professional cooking is 40% about the cooking itself, and 60% about all the time management that allows you to be successful at that cooking. That's an ASS statistic (as in, I pulled it out of my ass), but it's so important to take the time to do all the various things that will set you up to cook successfully.

Time just fucking flies by when you're cooking – and that's mostly a wonderful thing. You get to be in the zone, cooking your ass off, getting things done, food out, people fed, onto the next, and it's fast paced and the hours just go go go. When it's going well. When you're in the shit, time rolls over your puny ass like a lawnmower and feels just about as good.

Whether you're cranking or getting spanked, there are four things that are really, really hard to consistently make time for, but it's so important that you do:

1. Taking Care of Yourself

During the first two weeks of my very first restaurant job, I had a sous chef I'll call "Lil G."

I say first two weeks because he either left or got fired about two weeks after I started – and I was both relieved not to have to work with him for longer than two weeks, and also so immensely thankful to have had those two weeks with him at all – because he taught me one of the best and hardest lessons of a busy kitchen. You have to make the fucking time to take care of yourself, because it's not anyone else's job to do that.

In just two weeks, I half loved him and half hated him. He was on his way out, and like anyone who over time has fallen completely out of love with their job, I was probably seeing him at his worst. He was hilarious and magnetic and high energy and high drama in a hot mess of a way. He'd get his paycheck and head immediately to a casino and try to double it. Guys I worked with said he'd get arrested for being in brawls, and turn up on time for work looking like hell and say, "Seriously, I was in a fucking jail cell like 90 fucking minutes ago, motherfuckers!" Shit like that.

I was so green, and so slow. A year later, one of the dishwashers I worked with went off one day and was like "Girl, you were so fucking slooooow, aye que slooooow,

Holeee!" mimicking the slowest ever gestures of using a tiny knife right up by his eye-ball. It was fucking hilarious, and I chose to take it as a compliment – I must be faster now if he's ragging on me in the past tense. Right?

I'd had my two days of training, and was on the line by myself. This was maybe Day Four or Five of my entire restaurant experience, so I was just barely starting to get the hang of my pantry station. After the lunch rush, though, I'd have to run back and forth and do both the pantry and sauté stations, and I was still lost on how to pull that off. I was dreading 2 PM when Lil G would step off the line. I wasn't dreading it for long, though, because it was before 1 PM when he said "I'm fucked on orders – you're on your own, call if you need help," and left. The tickets were still rolling in – not fast, but steadily. I was sacred (and slow: Did I mention I was slow?) and I busted my ass, and worked to my very best ability – and at that point, my best wasn't good enough. I was almost keeping up, but not quite. I was working so hard and I didn't want to fail, I didn't want to ask for help, and anyway, it seemed like I was hanging on, except that in reality my fire times were inching up up up, and I was falling behind. I wasn't drinking water, and I was sweating buckets. Then two servers came back and dropped a bunch of tickets, and that's when Lil G came back in.

"What the fuck are you doing?" he yelled at me. "Get the fuck back there," he gestured me off of sauté and back onto pantry, "and give me three fucking vertes, two trout plates, one petite going foie-saucy-pate, one tartine going duck, three Sammies – Jesus, what the fuck were you doing in here?"

I was crushed. I was the student who wanted the A, the kid who wanted a pat on the head from Dad for doing a good job while he was gone. I hadn't done a good job, I'd fallen behind, but I'd worked my ass off not to fall behind *more* – and can't he see that, and don't I get an A for effort? And fuck if my face didn't go red and I started tearing up. Worse, though, my head started spinning. I reached for my bucket of water, still full, and as I gulped a mouthful of water my stomach flipped and I started sweating all along my brow line. I felt lightheaded.

"What the fuck are you doing?" he barked, suddenly right beside me.

"I feel lightheaded."

"Get off my fucking line," he said, with very clear disgust.

"I can catch up."

"Get out of here. Now." He pointed at the back door.

I wasn't sure if I was taking a break or getting fired, and at that moment, I didn't totally care. I went outside, I sat, I drank water slowly, in little sips, but a lot of it, I had my little cry, and then I went back in nine minutes later. He was a little calmer, and he'd blazed through so many tickets during that short time that he was on the very last one already.

As soon as he saw me, he got mad again, and got really in my face, and I'm paraphrasing hugely, but he ended up giving me some of the most valuable advice anyone's ever given me in a kitchen before or since. He said: It's not my fucking job to take care of you.

I'm going to repeat it, because it hit me like a lead brick of epiphany to the head. He said: It's not my fucking job to take care of you. I need to know that you're going to either do the fucking job or ask for fucking help, and I need to be able to count on you to do one or the fucking other. Because it's not my goddamn job to read your fucking mind, or to hold your fucking hand and make you drink water, or wipe your fucking ass, or whatever the fuck it is you can't seem to do for yourself.

And I hated how he was saying it – all pissed off and up in my face like a bully – and I also understood he was totally right. I had to take care of myself. By not taking care of myself, I was fucking the team, actually.

And I had to know when to ask for help for the same reason. Trying to gut through when I wasn't good enough was ultimately giving the customer a worse experience – they were waiting longer for less-good food. Which reflected worse on my restaurant, and perhaps made them grumpy and tip less, which made the servers' day a little worse, which was an energy they carried to other tables and then back into the kitchen – I saw all those tiny outward ripples, that day. I wasn't honest with myself about needing help, and had too much ego to ask for help, and I fucked us, and Lil G was good enough to unfuck us, but it should never have come to that.

We had a 52-year-old dishwasher named Leo who wore a belt buckle the size of Texas, and gave no fucks, and watched us cooks come and go, and said little, and took his eggs over hard (*huevos muertos*), and knew more about making the charcuterie than most of us in the kitchen, and only ever listened to the owner, and I really miss that guy.

After that day, the guys would tell me, "Don't be macho. Leo is macho enough for all of us. No one else needs to be macho, because we have Leo."

You have Leo now, too. He's macho enough for everyone in every kitchen everywhere – that's how fucking macho this guy is.

So you don't need to be macho, either. It's not helpful, ultimately. Yes, work your hardest and do your very best and don't be a wimpster. But don't be a macho, either – ask for help, and do what you need to do to take care of yourself.

Taking care of yourself is your job. No one else in a kitchen has the time or the desire to take care of you, so *you* have to take care of yourself. You have to make the ten seconds when you're busy to drink that fucking water and stay hydrated. You have to eat that breakfast or eat that lunch before you come in to work. You have to eat that staff meal, even if you're leaning against your cutting board wolfing it down (okay, you'll always be doing that). You have to wash your hands more than humanly possible, and drink more water than humanly possible, and do all the things you need to do to maintain your focus and your energy over hours of intensely physical work – because no one else will do that for you.

You must.